André Aciman is the *New York Times* bestselling author of *Call Me by Your Name*, *Out of Egypt*, *Enigma Variations*, *Find Me* and the essay collection *Homo Irrealis*. He's the editor of *The Proust Project* and teaches comparative literature at the Graduate Center of the City University of New York. He lives with his wife in Manhattan.

Further praise for *My Roman Year*:

'The book is a cornucopia of wonderful impressions and emotions . . . a superb portrait of a complex city through the eyes of a complex teenager, on an exciting journey through this unpredictable life.' *Irish Times*

'It's [Aciman's] slow appreciation of the city that shapes this transporting coming-of-age memoir in which beauty and the anguish of exile and displacement are rendered with the same sensuous, questing intensity that characterises his fiction.' *Observer*

'Aciman's characteristic roman d'analyse style of writing allows the memoir to read like a novel . . . just below the surface lies generational trauma and displacement, which has been masterfully woven into the narrative. *My Roman Year* gives a touching insight into the influences of André Aciman's well-loved literary world.' *New Statesman*

'An absorbing exploration of the challenges and slivers of beauty that formed life as a refugee in Rome.' *Kirkus Reviews*, starred review

'There is a warmth and a humanity in Aciman's prose that enraptures with its slow, easy embrace.' *Financial Times*

'[Aciman] writes with typically hypnotic elegance.' *i*

T0381955

ANDRÉ ACIMAN

MY ROMAN YEAR

faber

First published in the UK in 2024
by Faber & Faber Ltd
The Bindery, 51 Hatton Garden
London EC1N 8HN

First published in the United States by Farrar, Straus and Giroux
a division of Macmillan Publishers, 120 Broadway, New York, NY 10271

Book design by Gretchen Achilles

This paperback edition first published in 2025

Typeset by Faber & Faber Ltd
Printed in the UK by CPI Group (UK) Ltd, Croydon CRO 4YY

A CIP record for this book
is available from the British Library

ISBN 978-0-571-38519-5

2 4 6 8 10 9 7 5 3 1

To my all-time friends David Ostwald,
Lloyd Lynford, Pasquale Tatò, Paul LeClerc,
James O'Higgins, and Mark Gerald

Contents

CONTENTS

Acknowledgments

With all my thanks to my wife, Susan, without whose advice and constant support I'd simply be lost; to my agent, Lynn Nesbit, who reminds me to come down to earth when I'm soaring elsewhere; and to my editor, Jonathan Galassi, who always tells me to cut some sections, and maybe cut some more. My deepest and sincerest gratitude to all.

MY ROMAN YEAR

— 1 —

Please, Don't Hate Me

A nd please, don't hate me. I'm no ogre," said my great-uncle Claude as he was about to walk out of our new apartment in Rome and head toward the stairway.

Standing at our door, Uncle Claude, or Claudio as he was known in Italy now, was quoting the very word his sister had used months earlier in Egypt when trying to gloss over ugly family rumors about him. "He has a very good heart, so stop thinking of him as an ogre," she'd say, looking straight at my brother and me and using a word drawn mostly from fairy tales. "Yes, he does have a bad temper, but think of him as impulsive—we're all a bit impulsive in our family, aren't we?" she'd add about the man we were to meet as soon as our ship reached Naples. "Impulsive" was a far more tactful way of describing a man whose bouts of seething rage were forever impressed in the memory of those who knew him. Aunt Elsa must have written to him from Egypt telling him that we were thoroughly terrified of meeting him.

By using her very word, *ogre*, at our door that day, he had found a sly, mean-spirited way of showing that, thanks to Aunt Elsa's tireless letters, he was fully aware of what was being said about him in our household in Egypt. Aunt Elsa had a big mouth. She couldn't help it, and was the first to admit that she talked too much. "*Je suis gaffeuse*," I'm a blunderer. She must have told him countless things about us: how my parents always quarreled, how she could hear my brother and me tussling in our bedroom, and of course how we were mean to her and showed no respect for an older woman in her late eighties about to lose her eyesight. How could he not want to show that he was all too well aware of the goings-on in the family?

In his letters to us about Rome, Uncle Claude's description of the three-bedroom apartment he offered to lease us had been candid and accurate enough. Nearby, he wrote, were a small public park, a super-market, a department store, all manner of groceries, and four movie theaters that, unfortunately, played dubbed films only, but one easily got used to this. We were going to love Rome; he was sure of it. My grandmother, his sister who was older than Aunt Elsa, their other sis-ter, had written to tell him that I was interested in history. He wrote back promising to show me the famous and not-so-famous Roman sites, some unknown to tourists and locals alike. As with so many things, he added, one needed more than one lifetime here, even two weren't enough—nothing like that cloaca of ours, Alexandria.

The little I knew about Rome I'd gleaned from a small map I'd obtained from the Italian consulate in Alexandria. Our neighboring streets in Rome would bear dignified names drawn from Virgil's *Aeneid*: Via Enea (Aeneas), Via Turno (Turnus), Via Camilla (ditto), while Via Niso (Nisus) led directly into Via Eurialo (Euryalus), as if the city planners knew that, as in Virgil's epic, the love of Nisus for Euryalus could never have borne their separation. I did not expect to run into Camilla or Turnus girding for battle as they buckled their cuirasses, but I knew that the weight of legend and history permeated every facet of Rome. By contrast, in his view, our city was a cloaca. I had to look up the word.

I liked Uncle Claude's impish sense of humor. You could even de-tect it on his envelopes, which always arrived in Alexandria marked with two capitalized and underlined words beneath our address

4

stating "French Language." He was, in effect, making it easier for the Egyptian censors, who read all mail from abroad, to pass his letter to those responsible for reading the mail in French. It was also his way of announcing to the censor that there would be nothing compromising or incriminating in the letter, since, by declaring its language, he was already showing he was fully aware it would be read. In fact, the censor always opened Claude's letters, read them, and then sealed the side of the envelope where it was opened with a label to inform the recipient it had been scrutinized. I liked his "purloined letter" approach, concealing evidence in plain sight. He had managed to keep the Egyptian authorities in the dark about my father's bank account in Switzerland by writing that he had found Aunt Berta's spirit quite uplifted on seeing her granddaughter safe and sound following her short vacation in Greece. Aunt Berta was none other than my father's banker in Geneva, and the granddaughter a trusted Greek courier in charge of funneling funds abroad. Eventually, the Greek turned out not to be so trustworthy; he gobbled most of the funds in the Swiss account and then decamped with his family to Brooklyn. Uncle Claude, who was an experienced lawyer with contacts in Switzerland, heard of the theft and communicated the fact by telegram to my father in Egypt: *grave sickness of our beloved Berta stop granddaughter so broken-hearted not responding stop.*

Uncle Claude had wisdom, smarts, and a rakish sense for subterfuge and double-dealing. He recovered some of the money via Interpol, but most of it had disappeared, or so Claude claimed. My father instructed us to show him our enduring gratitude, but never to trust him. Meanwhile, he had asked his uncle to give us a set sum every month.

From aboard the deck of our ship the fateful morning of our arrival in Italy, my mother and I looked out, hoping that Uncle Claude might pick us up in Naples. But I wasn't certain that the man I'd spotted from afar on the pier was indeed Claude. Our ship had not yet docked, and the sunlight was in my eyes. I could only make out scattered groups of people crowding the wharf, baggage porters, shipping

5

and customs personnel, but also friends and relatives who must have traveled from all over Italy to welcome people they hadn't seen in years. All I could remember of Uncle Claude dated back to my earliest childhood when he sat me on his lap facing the steering wheel and allowed me to pretend I was driving his antiquated car, which everyone in the family had nicknamed the *hearse-mobile* and continued to call by that name long after his sudden flight from Egypt. I remembered his wavy black hair, his hat, his special sunglasses with dark cloth blinkers around each lens, and the clicking sounds he made with his teeth to mimic the tiny rotary crank that he kept turning left then right to open and shut the windshield while putting on a mystified expression meant to amuse children. I must have been scarcely three. I hadn't seen him since the day he'd driven my grandmother and me back from the beach to the usual daily lunch at the large apartment still run by his mother, my great-grandmother. His car with the sunken, flaky, ridged, old leather seats had intrigued me, as I had never seen, much less sat in, a car so thoroughly antiquated. I knew its nickname but was warned never to call it that in front of him.

Hearse-mobile stuck like a moniker meant to deride Uncle Claude's inveterate stinginess, a quality he shared with all his eight siblings, my grandmother and Aunt Elsa included. All preferred to consider their stinginess a form of acquired thrift wrought by years of hardship that went back generations but that everyone who knew the family, from my mother down to their youngest servant, called by its real name after extending a forearm at the end of which was a clenched fist signifying nothing short of avarice—sheer ugly, obstinate, incurable, entrenched, tightfisted avarice. That branch of the family gave nothing away and hoarded everything as a keepsake long after it had served its purpose, justifying their reluctance to part with it by using the oft-repeated French motto *on ne sait jamais*, one never knows, meaning one never knows when a throwaway might prove handy or when a discarded friend might turn out useful after all.

As for the ageless square-box car, it went down to the junkyard along with Claude's hat, his blinkered eyeglasses, and the tiny crank for the mobile windshield whose gears made raspy, clicking sounds. He would have waited to sell each to the highest bidder, but the Egyptian police were onto him for siphoning funds to Switzerland. A distant acquaintance tipped him off just in time. Uncle Claude narrowly escaped through the kitchen door and was never seen in Egypt again.

My mother looked out at the wharf once more and was now persuaded that the man we first spotted couldn't be Uncle Claude. "Too well dressed," she said. He'd never spend money on fine clothes. Instead, she spotted another man who looked, she thought, emphatically *juif*. But then she changed her mind about him too. Then a man standing far away on the dock seemed to recognize her and was eagerly waving at her. That didn't make sense to her, she said. "He never liked me, and I couldn't stand him." As it turned out, the man was waving at someone leaning against the railing next to us and was desperately screaming her name, "Rina, Rinaaaaa." "Not him," my mother finally said. "Besides," she added, "it would be unlike the old miser to come to meet us here. The cost of gas from Rome alone would prohibit it." Plus, we weren't important enough for him to undertake the drive. My mother, my brother, and I were, but for my father and Aunt Elsa, the last family members leaving Egypt, and he had repeatedly reminded us in his letters that he'd already made the trip to Naples countless times for his many relatives—in-laws, nephews, nieces, as well as siblings, including my grandmother. He couldn't be expected to show up on the wharf each and every time. As we concluded that he would not come to Naples for us, my mother reminded us that the people from the refugee service would be taking us to a transit camp after all. I was to translate for her, she added, turning to me with a minatory smirk whose meaning was not lost on me. All those private lessons with Italian tutors over the past few years in Egypt had better pay off now. "Focus on what they say, not what you think they're saying. And try not to let them know I'm deaf. They'll rob us." Then, realizing I was growing nervous, she added, "We've survived worse, we'll survive this too." Now that we were about to set foot in Europe, Egypt could sink

7

in filth, for all she cared, and stay mired in its *ziballah*—the Arabic word we continued to use, meaning "garbage." Her only worry was my father, who had stayed behind in Egypt and was still vulnerable to the whims of the Egyptian police, who were known to be ruthless, especially with Jews.

What eventually told me that the man standing on the dock could only be Uncle Claude was not his dark, wavy hair or the leering, sinuous smile fluttering across his face in old family albums. These traits had completely disappeared. Instead, it was his sudden and unexpected resemblance to his far older brother Nessim, who had died in Egypt at the age of ninety-two a couple of years earlier. The black, wavy hair of old pictures was totally gone in 1966, and when I watched Uncle Claude repeatedly doffing his hat to salute us from afar, I was immediately reminded that, like his brother, he was completely bald and made the same ugly pout when he wasn't trying to smile, showing an identical protruding nose so curved that he looked like a cross between a bald eagle and an unfledged parrot. Sigmund Freud, minus the beard.

One more thing told me that the man in the trim tweed jacket, felt hat, and maroon cravat standing at the dock surely belonged to my family. When our ship had finally docked and we could see him clearly, we watched him remove a white handkerchief the width of an oversized pennant and start waving it to us in a gesture so uncompromisingly obsolete that it could only have been lifted from vintage Hollywood films: he, too, like my grandmother and her sister, was permanently sealed in a pre–World War I universe where people waved handkerchiefs. It was a subtle and delicate motion, able to communicate hope, welcome, and mirth, yet adaptable to sorrow, subdued despair, and funerals. The Cohène family (with the de rigueur accented *è* proclaiming their fictitious French descent) always had their way of doing things. No reason for them to comply with what momentarily passed for current chic. The world would have to bend to their terms; it always had.

Their terms, however, were not just dated, they were extinct. They refused to accept this and continued to favor courtesy but seldom

8

candor, good taste but not good morals, always judging people less by what they said or did than by how they held a knife and a fork. All of it decidedly old-world.

When later that morning I told him I'd recently been enrolled in an American school in Egypt, he thought the idea preposterous. I should have gone to Italian schools instead. When I explained that there was a possibility we might move to the United States, Uncle Claude burst out laughing as if I'd uttered the most far-fetched nonsense.

"What? Become Americans! You're in Italy, my little man, you're going to behave and become an Italian like everyone else. None of your savage American claptrap here. America is an unborn country, or didn't you know?"

I had better judgment than to argue or talk back. My brother also kept quiet, though of the two of us he was by far the more enamored with American culture, American films, American songs—anything American. In Egypt, he had managed to buy a pair of used Levi's from an American classmate, loved roasted marshmallows, which he'd discovered as a Cub Scout, and had even managed to obtain a regular supply of Juicy Fruit gum. "What a farce!" my uncle added. "The boys have no character but want to become GIs," he mumbled to himself as we headed to a registry building, though I am sure we were meant to hear each syllable. I stayed quiet, little realizing that silence in Claude's world did not forestall abuse but invited more of it.

～

Uncle Claude was, as his sister had warned, *impulsive*, but it was difficult to see how anyone might prove cruel to blood relatives who'd been expelled and arrived needy, lost, and totally vulnerable, especially a deaf mother with two sons who'd never traveled before. My father's opinion of his uncle was more guarded, in good part because he was reluctant to influence our view of him, which already implied we should expect the worst. Eventually, my father broke down: "Regardless of what Elsa thinks, he can be unequivocally bestial." But my mother was not going to be intimidated. "There is no need to keep scaring us about him," she said. "Not scaring you, just reminding you to beware of him," he argued. My mother was quick with her reply: "If your uncle is so horrible, you should be leaving Egypt with us to protect us, not staying behind." "I'm staying behind because there are loads of things I need to salvage here," he retorted, about ready to lose his own temper. All his property and assets had been nationalized, so, yes, he probably thought he had lots to salvage in the space of his remaining two months in Egypt. But my mother was onto him and couldn't resist complaining to my grandmother: "Salvage, my eye! I know exactly why and for whom he's staying behind," she said, "and everyone knows who she is and where she lives." This was hardly the first time she'd lamented my father's infidelities, to which my grandmother offered the listless, languid answer I'd heard her sigh so many times before. "It's a family curse," she'd say, adding that it ran in all five of her brothers, in her husband, and in every man she'd known, including her own father. My mother hardly found solace in these words. She didn't need to read tea leaves to know what awaited us in Europe: "We'll arrive like paupers in a city we know nothing of while he's going to live it up in Egypt."

We were prepared for the horrors of life in a refugee camp once we landed in Naples, and had been warned repeatedly by people who had been in a camp that you had to wash your own dishes before returning them to the canteen, eat what you were served and not complain, and use a Turkish-style toilet. And if there were lice, added Aunt Elsa, who always liked to expect the worst, so as to be pleasantly surprised if it failed to occur—well, lice and nits there'd be. Who hadn't survived lice once or twice in a lifetime? Both she and her sister had lived through two world wars, witnessed massacres of Armenians, and suffered through forcible displacements, the most perilous being her escape from Lourdes on her way to Marseille during the war in circumstances so befouled that running water was more precious than bread and soap itself. As for lice . . . *We've seen what we've seen*, another favorite locution, which meant *Don't make us relive what we're happy to forget*.

My mother didn't respond when she was told about lice and nits, though she confided that she did worry about dirty bedding and soiled towels. She didn't know Italian and in any case, being deaf, would need me to interpret everything anyone said to her. She had prepared two suitcases of real sharkskin into which she had put everything to tide us over for two weeks. We'd been told that a bus would take us to the refugee camp, so the three of us were prepared to ride with the suitcases spread across our laps. We'd all been told tales about Naples. We were never to let the bags out of our sight.

Uncle Claude was indeed waiting for us as we came down the gangplank. He had driven from Rome very early that morning and had sped down the highway in time to catch our arrival. "Not bad for a seventy-year-old man, don't you think?" he exclaimed. His accent in French was the same as his dead brother's, but the falsetto in his voice was altogether surprising. My mother barely understood a word he uttered. But she smiled graciously, which he was happy to infer was an intimidated woman's way of cowering before the proclaimed virility of his manner.

With a chuckle, he explained to us that we were going to go through customs but that customs in Italy was not the barbaric rite of passage it was in Egypt. In an effort to say something warm and grateful, my mother asked me to convey that she loved the weather in Italy. She loved the sea air of Naples; she had grown up next to the sea, and it brought her back to her childhood in Egypt.

He heard my words, but said that Egypt was out of our lives. "The sea air here is Italian. No nostalgia, please. If you have any regrets," he added, "it's that you should have left Egypt years sooner."

Someone from customs came to us holding a manifest and asked if we were the occupants of third-class cabin number 6. We were, I replied. Customs officials, he said, had counted the number of suitcases: thirty-one in all. I explained to my mother what he'd said, adding, "Plus these two." I was holding one, my brother the other.

On hearing the number of suitcases, Uncle Claude slapped his thigh and, within a few seconds, turned red and uttered an enraged and ferocious yelp. "Where do you expect to put these suitcases? In my car?" The official, who had given my uncle a scrawny, dented pencil to sign the manifest, immediately tried to calm him by saying that the suitcases were going to be stored, then shipped in three to four weeks once he provided an address. "Did you just say thirty-one?" Claude asked, raising his voice a decibel higher. "Please, *Dottore*," said the official, "do not be offended. I simply meant three to four weeks." "Thirty-one!" I thought my uncle was going to strike him. With an apologetic tone, the official repeated, "Three to four weeks, *Dottore*." Again, Uncle Claude gave out an apoplectic shriek, but this time even louder. There was no mistaking it: he was not yelling at the customs official but at my mother, who hardly understood anything he was shouting, while I was so dumbfounded by his screaming that I froze on the spot. Uncle Claude, at the top of his lungs, asked what in God's good name were we thinking, bringing thirty-one suitcases to Italy? What could possibly be in them? A grand piano? An automobile? A tank? What? My mother, realizing what had brought on his conniption, said only, "Clothing. And maybe some silverware?" "Silverware?! Are you mad? You could have been arrested in Egypt for smuggling." The customs guards in Egypt had been bribed to let us pass, my mother explained. "Bribed? And did you think bribing them would have stopped them from arresting you? Ten days ago they were mere street vendors and ruffians, and you—or was it your husband or my foolish sister—were going to bribe them?" And then came the coup de grâce. "Why on earth did I have to get myself involved with this band of idiots," he said. "*Oray Kapa. Basta!*" he blurted out in Turkish, then in Italian. And with that he threw to the ground the pencil that the customs official had just handed him and then, in a still more violent fit, using the hard heel of his shoe, ground it several times.

A part of me wished my mother had screamed back at him to let him hear what a deaf woman can produce once she's been pushed to the limit. No one I'd ever met had rivaled my mother's scream.

But had my mother yelled back, he would have abandoned us there and then and never spoken to us again. She knew it, and we knew it, which is why neither my brother nor I attempted to translate what he was shouting.

~

The official asked my uncle to accompany him to an office where he'd have to sign release forms. But instead, Uncle Claude handed my mother his Bic ballpoint pen to sign the forms herself. The two of them headed to the office while my brother and I stood watch over the suitcases, which were lined up in a row that ran half the length of a long, begrimed hangar filled with timeworn, decrepit bric-a-brac. Each suitcase now seemed smaller than in the large, formal living room that had once been my great-grandmother's *salon* when she received guests.

In the stuffed hangar in Naples, I kept staring at our suitcases and, for the briefest moment, thought that some were even happy to see me again while others turned away, determined to ignore me, perhaps because after spending so much time in our old living room, they were upset at being abandoned to handymen who spoke a language that no suitcase could fathom: Neapolitan—a language it would take me years to understand and ultimately to adore. I looked at the suit-cases, as though prodding them to acknowledge me, but the swollen leather boxes were determined not to respond.

I remembered when they had first been brought into our family, a gaping litter lying about shamelessly open-mouthed in the large living room. They were made of thick, industrial leather and held tight together by two thick belts that were fitted through two wide leather-strap tabs stitched into the suitcase itself to keep the belts in place. Egyptian customs regulations prohibited locking anything, as customs officials wished to examine the contents of each suitcase. But at customs, no one had required us to open any of our cases, as they were satisfied by the future prospect of receiving one bribe when my father left and another upon Aunt Elsa's departure.

We all felt sorry for Aunt Elsa. Her eyesight was deteriorating, but she did not ask the servants to help her pack; nor was she willing to ask the help of her few remaining Greek and Italian friends in Alexandria. She didn't want anyone nosing around. *Je suis indépendante*, she used to say whenever questioned about her congenital parsimony and her lifelong status as a widow. She had never wanted to marry anyone except for the shiftless Victor, who had barged into her life, married her, and then died, because, as my grandmother used to say with a wry expression on her face, *he preferred to die*. My grandmother's husband had also preferred to die before his allotted time. Indeed, everyone who married into the Cohène family found in death the perfect exit to a marriage where what passed for love had consented to spend a couple of token evenings but not a second more.

When Mother asked Aunt Elsa how many suitcases she might need, Elsa replied that five would do. My mother didn't believe her, but complied. She purchased suitcases from a merchant on Place Mohamed Ali, ordering thirty in all. Ten for us, ten for my father, five for my grandmother, and five for Aunt Elsa. Little did we know that within weeks we would more than double the order, and indeed watch the owner of the shop admit that he had no more to sell, but that for the time being, he had a few sharkskin suitcases that were more supple and could easily fit under a bed. My mother had begged him to have more of the larger ones made as the date of our expulsion from Egypt was drawing near. The merchant promised. This, after all, was the selfsame man who had purchased all our furniture, both in the city and at our beach house, paying a pittance for everything we owned. There was no discussion, no haggling, and as soon as he had named his price and my mother accepted it, he reached into his breast pocket and, pulling out a large leather wallet, hastily counted a wad of bills, placing the agreed-upon cash in my mother's hand. Within days, our furniture and almost everything that the government hadn't already seized was whisked away. I didn't watch the removal of our furniture. But when I stepped into our old apartment, I was startled to see bare rooms and no rugs on the floors, just the white trace of missing paintings on our yellowed walls. The dining room furniture was gone, and the kitchen as bare as a newborn. I still expected to see our cook, Abdou, there, but one of the service doors was locked shut, and there were piles of dirt behind where the refrigerator and the oven once stood together, like close cousins who'd been forced to separate. My mother wanted me to see this, she said. Why? I asked. "*Comme ça*," because. That explanation stayed with me for life. Her two words spoke everything in her heart.

Her one regret was that she should not have settled for his price. She should have asked for more. He had the money with him, she saw it. And he would have paid. Instead, he fleeced us. My mother, who was known for being a defiant haggler in the marketplace, had taken what he offered and even thanked him. When you've lost everything and time has run out, you settle for the first offer.

It made perfect sense somehow that the man who purchased our furniture should also be selling us suitcases. He was in the business of plundering foreigners and then seeing them off with suitcases sold in his store. The money he paid for the furniture he got back by selling suitcases. The summary expulsion of foreigners and Jews was an added measure meant to close the deal and make it impossible for people to renege on their sale or turn back the clock.

No wonder the suitcases avoided my glance each time I attempted to extract some recognition from them. All they did was sit bilious and sullen, as if I were guilty of a sinister misdeed whose brunt was now theirs to bear. "Why have you brought us here?" they seemed to say, "and what's to happen to us now?" They were asking me questions that I could just as easily have asked myself. *What am I doing here? What's to happen to me now?* We were, like the suitcases, marooned and landless, and I saw this for the first time by staring at their strapped leather shapes standing gawkily lined up in the hangar, fattened, lumpish, and scared, like doleful cows waiting their turn, mistrusting everything, down to the feral cat who'd seen too many suitcases and wasn't about to offer a sympathetic glance.

~

After signing the papers, my mother left the office with Uncle Claude and informed me that we needed to go to the refugee camp to sign more papers to declare that we had a residence in Rome and would not need to stay in Naples.

The three of us got into Uncle Claude's car. It was not the *hearse-mobile* but a late-model Alfa Romeo, not totally ostentatious, but clearly upscale. Our uncle exuded comfort, perhaps even wealth, and his aftershave was noticeably pleasant. I could tell he might have been thrifty once, but he was no longer the miser everyone claimed. He had become patrician, and the way he carried himself was meant to declare it.

We followed the refugee bus through numberless streets and narrow lanes, up a hill, and farther up until, twenty minutes later, we reached the camp. The sight of it must have horrified my mother, and once out of the car, she began to cry. She tried her best to conceal her tears, but one of the camp attendants walked up to her and in Italian said, "Don't be upset, *signora*, we are not Jews here." He must have meant bandits, criminals, lawbreakers, assassins.

I didn't have it in me to translate for my mother, but the well-meaning look on the man's face communicated empathy and compassion, maybe even pity. Humbly, she nodded several times to thank him. My uncle, having lived through the Second World War, especially with a surname that could only have been Jewish, did not react. He either failed to hear what the guard had said or feigned that he hadn't. We were the first in line at the registry. All my uncle said was, "There are a lot of people behind us, so please hurry. I am in charge of these three and have already offered them living quarters in Rome." His words were polite and deferential but his tone was so authoritative, if not imperious, that the young woman at the desk figured that perhaps she, too, should address him as *Dottore*. As my father had told me in Egypt, Uncle Claude had mastered the art of posturing with numberless masks but didn't own a conscience among them. The young lady kept addressing him in the third person. *Does the dottore this, would the dottore that?*

In the camp, I spotted what looked like a very poor woman washing her naked toddler under a tilting long-necked garden faucet. She was wearing a bonnet and a bedraggled housedress. She looked at me, then let a bashful, self-conscious smile travel over her features, ashamed that this was the only way to wash her child.

I recognized several of the passengers from our ship. I had never spoken to them, and had no idea that they'd turn up as refugees in the camp. Among them was a woman I had avoided speaking to. Now she approached us, and there was nowhere to duck. Madame Marie had been our nanny for about two years before being replaced by another Madame Marie. She was Italo-Maltese and was awaiting passage on a ship that was to take her to Malta, where she was hoping to be hired as an interpreter. Like so many born-and-bred Alexandrians, she knew French, English, Greek, and Italian. She had also worked as a beautician in Alexandria, including for my grandmother, which is how she came to be hired in our home. She was hoping to make a living as a private beautician in Malta to supplement her income as an interpreter. I had never liked her and had always considered her a source of backbiting and mischief in our household, pitting the cook against the servant and ultimately my father against my mother. I was finally happy that my mother had given her two months' salary and told her never to set foot in our home again. Unlike my father, who would have dismissed her in private, my mother had shown her to the door right before my brother and me.

We said hello to her respectfully, while she greeted us with diffident cordiality, and as we waited for my mother and my uncle to finish signing release forms, she walked up to me, put her hand in the right pocket of her wide skirt, and as had always been her custom when we'd get back from school, gave each of us a candy wrapped in transparent paper over which was inscribed in both English and Arabic the name of the confectioner, Nadler.

My brother, who did not know how to thank Madame Marie,

embraced her with the unwrapped candy still in his hand, while I said thank you, then, embarrassed and not knowing what else to do, pretended to be looking for my mother. Madame Marie withdrew without saying a word and rejoined the people she'd met on board the ship. I never saw her again.

What surprised me as I stared at the round yellow candy whose papaya flavor I loved was that I could still read Arabic. I was under the impression that as soon as I landed in Italy everything about me would be erased. I'd forget who I was or what I'd learned in Egypt. Instead, to my amazement, I saw that nothing had changed when I moved from one shore of the Mediterranean to the other. I was still me and the person I'd been a few days earlier hadn't vanished. I wanted to forget who I was, turn a new leaf, be someone new. But I was the same and I wasn't pleased.

My mother and Uncle Claude finally stepped out of the office. My uncle put back on his hat and smiled. "Now we're headed for Rome."

Little did I know that the worst hour of my life was about to start.

It happened quite suddenly with Uncle Claude's attempt to leave Naples and head north onto the Autostrada del Sole, the relatively new highway connecting Naples to Rome. The problem, however, was how to find the entrance to the autostrada.

At first my uncle stopped the car and, addressing a traffic conductor, stuck his head out of the window and with his high-pitched voice shouted, "*Scusi, vigile*," and proceeded to ask directions to the highway. The tall, elegant *vigile*, dressed in white with a white tapered helmet, pivoted with the agile grace of a ballerina, politely lowered his head to the driver's window, and briefly explained the way to my uncle, who thanked him and drove on. But on reaching an uphill crossroads, he felt lost again and determined to ask another traffic cop, "*Scusi, vigile . . .* ," but once again, not finding the directions in any way fathomable, banged both palms on the steering wheel and began shouting, first at the car, then at Naples, which he called a befouled hole filled with urchins and criminals, and then let out his fury on the three of us. I was a complete imbecile, he said, with a fourth-grade knowledge of Italian, my brother a simpering toad who might as well be deaf like his mother, and finally my mother, who should have tried a bit harder to help him with directions but naturally couldn't understand a word because her illiterate parents had put her in the care of witch doctors who made sure to keep her a deaf-and-dumb mutant condemned to deaf-dumbness for the rest of her deplorable, meaningless life. My mother had no idea what he was saying but could tell from his ruddy complexion and protruding mandible that he was beyond furious. At the next crossroad, "*Scusi, vigile . . .*": high-pitched voice, affected deference, and seething incomprehension. By then my brother and I were almost ready to guffaw when, hearing my brother whispering something to me, he turned around and, raising his voice again with a stare filled with undiluted venom, said, "As for the two of you, eat your puny candies and shut your little mouths." Any excuse for humor instantly ebbed from the back seat. But to this day those two words, *Scusi, vigile*, have remained a source of humor and horror between us.

At some point one of the *vigili* had suggested taking a *sinistra*, a left turn, but my uncle was turning right. So, thinking I was being helpful, I reminded him that the traffic conductor had said left, not right. What ensued was a battery of insults. "Keep that tongue of yours in your silly mouth and don't dare open it again in my car. You're unable to understand anything, least of all the instructions of a *vigile*." Then, under his breath, "Failures and imbeciles, the three of them, the mother, the son, and that holy idiot"—me.

Never in my life, before or after, had I known such abuse. The trouble with abuse when it is dealt so implacably is that it leaves a mark, and you end up believing it. And for a long time I did believe everything he'd said to me that day. If I struggled not to let myself be swayed by his bullying, I always had the feeling that he had seen through me and assayed every shortcoming, every failure, real, imagined, or yet to come, and from these there was no hiding. I was a prattler, I didn't know my left from my right, I was an imbecile and, above all, a failure, something I'd been fearing since writing my first poem at the age of ten. I'd written about an escaped slave who knows he doesn't stand a chance and, sooner or later, will be caught, because the Roman family who owned him was bound to track his whereabouts. Facing the Mediterranean, he doesn't know whether to run left or right; he stares at the beach and is thinking of his wife and children and is tempted to turn himself in, but something holds him back. He is hungry, he needs to eat, and though he knows he is doomed, he cannot turn back. They'll find him and, for the sheer fun of it, put him to death. So he keeps fleeing, never knowing what awaits him.

This was my welcome to Italy.

Eventually we did emerge from the city and started driving on the highway. "These idiot *vigili* don't know their own city! They need a man born elsewhere to teach them their own streets, their history and their own language too." As he drove, my uncle decided to test my logic and math and gave me a puzzle to solve, which, I vaguely recall, went something like this: if a car drives at eighty kilometers per hour and bypasses another running at forty kilometers per hour, how much faster will the slower car have to accelerate if it wants to reach destination X at the same time as the faster car?

I couldn't understand the question, let alone figure out an answer. I said I knew the formula but didn't recall it just then. "You don't need a formula, you simply don't know. Why not say *I don't know, Uncle Claude*." Then, pricked by some evil insect, he asked my brother to decline any Latin noun he pleased. My brother told him he didn't know Latin but had just started studying it on his own. "So you know nothing, my good man. He doesn't know math, you don't know Latin, and clearly neither of you knows Italian, since you couldn't understand what the *vigile* was saying."

I was almost tempted to tell him that he couldn't understand the *vigili* either, but stayed quiet. Still, he wasn't giving up, and turning to my brother, he asked: "What's the plural of *house* in English?" "*Houses?*" the rise in my brother's voice almost asked rather than answered, no longer certain of being right. "No, it's pronounced *houzez.*" "What about the plural of this?" he asked me, pointing to his forehead. "*Foreheads?*" Like my brother, I hesitated. "Almost right, except you don't pronounce the *h*. So English isn't really one of your strengths either. Now tell me this," he said, turning to me again, "what book have you read recently?" I told him that I was reading *The Greeks* by H. D. F. Kitto. "*E chi è 'shto Kitto?*" Who might this Kitto be? A kitten? he asked in mock-Roman dialect. "An author of detective novels?" And before hearing my explanation, he began poking fun at the name with all kinds of rhymes in Italian, howling with intensified laughter each time he came up with yet another rhyme: "*Vitto fritto, zitto zitto, fritto misto, letto sfitto.*" My mother, seeing him laughing, and not realizing that her sons were being systematically demolished with derision and scorn, affected a muted smile to harmonize with his beaming joy, which made him think that she agreed with him, and he threw a look of winking complicity at her. "Even your mother thinks you're a fool, even your mother!"

At some point on the highway he decided we needed to stop at a snack bar. My uncle parked the car and, staring at my mother, brought the bunched fingers of his left hand in front of his mouth to signal the word *food*. As he locked the car and we began heading toward the restaurant, he put a tentative arm around my shoulder, and I would have accepted and been pleased with the conciliatory *let there be no bad blood between us* gesture had he not shoved me through the revolving door with a renewed surge of contempt, meaning, *Don't just stand there like a child, be a man and move in. Haven't you ever seen a revolving door before?* Quietly I entered the restaurant. I did not look back, but I was sure that the thought had crossed his mind to slap me on the nape.

From that moment on I swore I would one day come to spit on his grave.

Claude ordered a dish with his favorite wine, Rosatello il Ruffino. My mother ordered a ham sandwich. We ordered spaghetti with tomato sauce because we couldn't tell what the other sauces on the menu were. And for a quick dessert, my brother and I ordered a strawberry ice cream. Claude ordered a bowl of raspberries. He encouraged my mother to order the same. Knowing he was a miser and that another bowl of raspberries would cause an added expense, she declined the offer. I knew that my mother adored raspberries. But I also knew what was running through her mind. She was still hungry. Watching my mother fold her cloth napkin and put it away, I felt for her. He told me to tell my mother that when eating ham, one should always remove the fat, which is something he'd always done. I took my time passing along his message. "Tell her!" he said. I told her. But she was quick to sense the enmity in the air and simply nodded and whispered that I should tell him to go hang himself. She, too, by then, had determined to spit on his grave.

Several years later, he died in his sleep in a glamorous hotel in Monte Carlo.

I never made it to his grave.

～

It was late in the day when we arrived at Via Clelia. The neighborhood, it took me no time to realize, was thoroughly working-class—many buses crowding the main thoroughfare of Via Appia Nuova, drab, ill-lit stores everywhere, and so much soot on buildings that time had discolored them. The grandeur of imperial Rome had no place here. Via Clelia itself was ugly, dirty, and at the approach of dusk seemed sad. This, I thought, was a neighborhood for poor folk, not a refugee camp, but not much better. I said nothing, my mother said nothing, my brother sat totally stunned in the car. When we parked and opened the door, we saw a group of screaming boys playing *calcio* on the sidewalk.

Uncle Claude walked upstairs with us, while my brother and I lugged our two suitcases. He opened the door to the furnished apartment he was subletting to us, and a whiff of something between incense and old wood shavings hit me, as though the place hadn't been aired in weeks. The apartment was very warm. Uncle Claude opened one window, and all I heard was the sound of the same boys playing downstairs. He then gave my mother the keys, saying that we should make copies at the *ferramenta*, the hardware store, down the street. He said he hadn't had time to ask Grazia, the *portinaia*, our concierge, to purchase some staples for us, but if we hurried we still had time to go to the supermarket on Via Appia Nuova two blocks down. We'd find everything there. Grazia was under instructions to bring up pots and pans and a tiny refrigerator, all of which for some reason she'd been keeping in her basement. One of her brothers had promised to carry it up as soon as he was back from work that evening. "These people are so lazy," Uncle Claude said. He told us he would come by in three to four days; he was a member of a golf club on Via Appia Antica nearby and had many obligations there. "They made me an important member of the club because I am Jewish. We are in a completely different world here. And you want to go to America!!!"

Another put-down.

He said he would send a telegram to my father that very evening to tell him of our safe arrival.

As he was about to go, he remembered to give my mother some bills for buying food. On leaving Egypt, we'd been allowed only the equivalent of five dollars and had spent what we had for extra food in the snack shop on board. Once again, he reminded us to hurry, as the supermarket might be closed; otherwise we'd have to buy what we could at the corner grocery or see what the caffè-bar nearby had for snacks. He explained that every month he would give us a certain sum drawn from my father's small account in Switzerland, which was under his care. "Not a gold mine by any means, let's be clear," he added. Then, before shutting the door, he took a good look at us and said something totally startling: "And please, don't hate me. I'm no ogre."

I smiled politely, as if to say, *What could possibly have put such a notion in your head?* But he didn't pay me any heed. He nodded three times as though he'd been granted a pardon. Atonement, in his view, however perfunctory, always expiated the crime.

Once he was out the door, my mother, who had a gift for mimicry, imitated his features when he'd tried to charm the girl at the refugee camp. It made the two of us burst out laughing. My brother imitated her imitation, which made me laugh even harder. But we were crushed.

This was our first late afternoon in Rome, and not only had my uncle's attitude already made me hate Rome, but the thought of living in this small apartment stirred a wave of gloom that none of us was able to tame. We sat facing one another in what appeared to be a living room and didn't say a word. I don't know how long this lasted, but when I looked outside again, the streetlights on Via Clelia were already glowing. So this was evening, I thought. I felt the evening's full weight and couldn't shake it off. I wished it hadn't come so soon. I wasn't ready for evening yet. Maybe it was much later than I thought. Maybe we needed time before facing our first night in Rome. Eventually, Mother found a light switch, and the light helped, but the oppressive, mournful feeling wasn't lifting away and was heavier the darker it grew outside. When we stood up and walked over to the narrow kitchen whose back window already faced the night, concealing everything that lay beyond, we realized we didn't even want to know, much less see, what darkness hid from view outside.

What I felt at that moment was not sorrow, not even anger at my uncle. What I felt was the persistent, undefinable numbness that eventually overtakes you and won't let go. You feel nothing because there's nothing to feel, the pain is still working itself out, has yet to come, will come, just never when you expect. I tried to feel grief instead; grief was easier because it was factual and thinkable—grief for what was lost, for who we'd been and had left behind, grief for old habits that were meant to die but hadn't yet, grief for my father, who was still in Egypt and might be arrested on who knows what trumped-up charges before even being allowed to rejoin us, grief for my deaf mother, who knew not a word of Italian and was as broken

24

and rudderless as my brother and I. I felt like a child who had strayed from his mother's grip and was now stranded and helpless in a huge department store that was about to close for the day, except that I knew Italian and my mother did not, and I was the grown-up and she the child.

That night we did go to the supermarket. We'd never been in a supermarket before, nor pushed a shopping cart, nor could we tell one coin from the next. We liked the supermarket. The only ones we'd seen were in American films. But none of us was hungry. All we wanted was to sleep and put the day away. The apartment had three rooms and a tiny alcove, but that night the three of us slept in the same bed.

— 2 —

They're in My Pocket

Aunt Flora, who had moved to Rome after being expelled from Alexandria two years earlier, lived with relatives who had long resided in Rome. Theirs was a large house, where she and her niece and nephew lived on a separate floor. Flora's was the first telephone call we ever received in Rome, and hearing her voice after two years was an instant source of comfort. She said we should meet on Largo di Villa Peretti. "Impossible to miss," she said, "it's the very last stop on any bus line going from Via Appia Nuova to Stazione Termini." There was a tiny caffè where she said she'd wait for us. But how were we to take a bus? my mother asked. "Very simple: you step in the back of the bus, you pay fifty lire each." Did we have money? Yes, we had money. Did we know where Via Appia Nuova was? Yes, we did. "Simple, then," added Aunt Flora. Cast into the role of perpetual interpreter for my mother, I kept hoping I hadn't misunderstood my aunt's instructions. But my mother was not nervous at all. We had breakfast—Rice Krispies, using the few pieces of stainless-steel cutlery we found in one of the drawers. No one, it seemed, had used these spoons in ages. But we rushed through breakfast, washed, put on clean clothes, and were about to leave the apartment when my mother remembered to take our garbage pail and leave it outside our main door as Uncle Claude had reminded us to do. Outside our door I found a pair of bottles of mineral water that had been delivered. We'd been warned about bad tap water. Grazia had told me that we'd have to return the bottles every few days. Or we could cancel delivery of bottles and buy our own water as needed, the cheaper option. I'd forgotten to tell her to cancel the deliveries.

Downstairs, we greeted her as she sat on a stool by the main entrance clipping green bean pods and placing the pods in a neat row on a newspaper spread open on an adjacent bench. What awaited her after the beans was the rice she was going to sort, one grain at a time, to avoid cooking either hardened clay or grit or brittle chips of stone, she said. She asked if we'd slept well. I replied that we had, using a tone so deferential as to suggest that she herself might have had something to do with the general silence we'd been experiencing every night since our arrival. Had the noise really not upset us? I hadn't heard any noise, I lied. "Did your mother hear anything?" No, I said, my mother was deaf. Yes, the *dottore* had told her as much. "But doesn't she hear even a tiny bit?" I shook my head. As so frequently happened, my mother had intuited exactly what we were discussing, and, pointing hastily to both her ears with an index finger, shook that same finger to mean *Ears don't work*. Grazia uttered a few words of sympathy and commiseration in pure Roman and, in an attempt to establish some kind of parity between my mother's ailment and hers, with her paring knife in one hand and her cigarette in the other, she pointed to her swollen ankles and to her bean pods with an expression that seemed to say, *Look what I've been reduced to myself*. She would remain a loyal friend to my mother, as would Grazia's mother and both her brothers. My mother's smile and her humility would have won over a famished beast ready to pounce on the first human it ran into.

What I didn't tell Grazia was that no one had warned us about the marketplace set up on Via Enea every weekday at dawn. By five in the morning, the owners of a long line of market stalls came in small loud trucks or in equally loud three-wheeled mini truck-scooters bearing all manner of wares: shoes, shirts, kitchen utensils, vegetables, fruits, cheeses, pizzas, breads, and countless kinds of meat and fish. Some of these merchants brought wooden pallets while others brought long planks that needed to be nailed to hold up their stalls and keep awnings in place. By day's end, though, everything had to be taken down and brought back to their depot. The racket of engines, people yelling, and the relentless nailing of the planks would become my alarm clock until, eventually, as happens with the blare of fire engines in large cities, one simply slept through them. In the evening, as I soon found out, not a sprig of parsley or a wedge of garlic or a rotten tomato was left on the street. This happened every day of the week except on Sundays and holidays.

I told Grazia that we were headed to meet my aunt near Termini. It was to be our first trip away from Via Clelia and I wanted to know where to find the nearest bus stop. "*Di fronte al Diana*," in front of the Diana, she replied. "It's a cinema," she said. So Uncle Claude hadn't lied. I was so grateful to Grazia that, by way of showing some enthusiasm for her city, I told her I couldn't wait to see the Colosseum and the Vatican. "They say they're beautiful," she said. Then she confessed. She had never seen either. "And I was born here," she added upon seeing the stunned look on my face.

It was as if someone raised in Alexandria claimed never to have seen the sea, or a Parisian not to know the Eiffel Tower. Foreigners often know a city far better than its denizens, the way they know an acquired language better than its native speakers; they just speak with an accent, which will always mark them as outsiders regardless of their efforts to brush off those dead-giveaway inflections that disclose the beat of their hearts.

I was under the impression that my knowledge of Italian was passable but I didn't want to be spotted immediately as a foreigner, though I was no less Italian than any Roman. My ancestors, Jews displaced from Spain in the early sixteenth century, had indeed resided in Italy for centuries, and my home was Livorno, though that was a bit of a stretch, since some of them, after moving from Italy to Turkey, hadn't lived there for at least two centuries. When my father had given up his Turkish nationality in Egypt, the easiest and most natural option was to reacquire our lapsed Italian nationality, but the only city that we could claim as our home was Livorno, not just because many Jews had settled there when the Medici opened the city to them following their expulsion from Spain, but for the simple reason that the records office in Livorno had burned down and anyone could allege having roots there. To prepare for what seemed our fated move to Italy, my father had hired an Italian tutor, an elegant and kindly gentleman who had escaped Mussolini's regime and settled in Egypt partly because it was a British colony and he had always liked Britain and had learned English with great zeal, though he spoke it with a very thick Italian accent. Signor Dall'Abaco was originally from Siena, which he claimed was the one city where perfect Italian was spoken.

Grazia's Roman dialect, however, especially when spoken very quickly, was unfathomable. Hers was a spare, almost infantile Italian though cluttered with idioms, expressions, and figures of speech totally beyond my comprehension. I learned to nod, something I had picked up from my mother, who did so just when a nod was called for and never before. She had an instinct for where to use her nods for punctuation, all based on nothing more than mere guesswork and facial observation. As a child I was not aware of her gift for penetrating the minds and motives of others, but as I grew I was always surprised at how right she was when she said that so-and-so was to be trusted, but never such-and-such. Thus, within a few months of the start of our life in Rome, she told some of the people in our immediate neighborhood that she was good at giving injections, which she'd learned as a nurse during the Second World War. When our sixteen-year-old neighbor across the street, Amina, kept coming for injections because, her parents said, she was far too skinny and needed to put on more weight and had seen a doctor who recommended injections to that effect, my mother's guess was not entirely wrong: "She is coming for my injections, but she is here for you, and if she sits with me at the kitchen table and watches me cook or asks me to wash her hair in the sink, it's all for you." I was not attracted to Amina, so the more I avoided her in our apartment, the more she found a reason to knock at our door and sit with my mother in the kitchen, eventually teaching my mother how to cook typically Roman dishes. Her parents knew a great deal about food, as they owned one of the stalls in the marketplace on Via Enea, a block away.

~

After waiting for what seemed like an hour for the bus that was to take us to meet Aunt Flora, we finally saw one approach in the distance. We paid for the tickets as if we knew what we were doing, and my mother pocketed them with the self-assurance of someone who'd been living in Rome her whole life. My brother spotted an empty seat, looked at my mother, read her lips, and right away walked over and sat down. After all, we came from a place where you grabbed an empty seat as soon as you saw one.

But my brother was mistaken. About two stops later an older woman came on board and asked him to give up his seat, as she was *stanca morta*, dead tired. He relinquished his seat, not sure whether he was doing so as a young man who felt sorry for an old lady or as a well-behaved boy who'd been asked to give up his seat. To make light of the incident, he pointed to the old woman and, whispering in Arabic, said she had a massive ass.

As soon as the bus swooped to its final stop on Largo di Villa Peretti, we immediately caught sight of Aunt Flora. She was seated at the caffè she'd indicated by phone, had ordered and finished an espresso, and must have been reading a newspaper, which lay folded over sloppily in her failed attempt to recompose its original folds, which meant she'd been reading it for quite a while. She was well-dressed, more attractive than I recalled, and her pronounced wide forehead, now that her hair was pulled back, allowed her aquiline nose and full lips to acquire an almost bold and emphatic look that did not agree with the Flora I'd known, whose mild, attenuated, frequently submissive mood made her the person I loved most after my parents. Were we late? I asked as we embraced her. She said no. Meeting us, she explained, allowed her to escape her relatives, who were simply suffocating. How did we like Rome? she asked, avoiding further talk of her family. The bus ride, our first in Italy, had taken twenty minutes through a city that felt emptied of people. Sunday, said Flora. Sitting next to her, I made out the scent of suntan oil, which she'd always used, and told her that I'd have recognized that scent in the most crowded spot on earth. "What we need is our beach, especially on a day like today," she said, with her usual brevity that voiced her ageless, self-deriding tilt to nostalgia. Once we could walk to the beach, she added, but here in Rome you needed public transportation to the train station, then the train ride itself, and then the long walk from the station, all of which eventually snuffed out the very desire to dip a toe in water.

She missed the beach. She missed so much, she said. She hadn't changed. My mother liked the beach, but as something she'd enjoyed, not something lost. In this, the two women were completely different. With Flora, even in Egypt, the essence of the life she'd been robbed of when fleeing Germany was grafted onto her bones and choked her ability to give herself over to so many things, and ultimately, I suspect, to love. My father, thinking of his brief crush on Flora, told me years later that for her to know she loved someone, she needed to distrust her love, then deny it, rehearse its loss, and eventually bring about that very loss before realizing she truly loved the person she'd lost. My mother was not like that.

I grew to understand Flora.

But I knew one thing more about her: the loss of Germany was probably incidental. Flora had already lost herself well before losing Germany during the war when she joined her brother in Egypt. This was what everyone said about her. Some people are born lost and may never find themselves. Others are born without love and struggle to find it however they can.

Coffee was good, but never as good, she said, but stopped, realizing that she was about to repeat herself. And as for the juices here, they added water to them, something unheard of in Egypt. I ordered a chinotto, a drink I'd started to tolerate in Egypt when it had temporarily replaced Coca-Cola, but I'd grown to prefer to Coca-Cola. My mother ordered a coffee, my brother a cheese sandwich, which I realized I should have ordered instead but I didn't want Flora to buy me one, now that it was clear she was the one treating. The waiter, wearing a contemptuous frown that was to become the habitual look of all self-respecting waiters in Italy, tossed the receipt on our table. As always happened at the *jus de fruits*, their old fruit juice spot in Alexandria, the two women squabbled over who was to pay, but my mother still hadn't learned to distinguish Italian coins and had to yield to Aunt Flora. The two lifelong friends decided right away that they would meet here and, to simplify things, rechristened the caffè the *jus de fruits*, which gave Rome a sudden Alexandrian tilt. Flora said she didn't want to leave the waiter a tip. My mother, who knew nothing of Italian customs, said something had to be left.

All the shops on Via Nazionale were closed on Sunday and looked so neat, not like the shops in Alexandria, whose old names were yellowed or whose windows were sometimes covered up by large cardboard panels sitting inside glass cases with ill-shaped letters and frequently misspelled French words. Alexandria, or at least *our* Alexandria, was dying, everyone knew.

We walked the length of the avenue until we reached one movie theater and then another, then we turned to our right and headed toward Via del Corso. This street also looked emptied, its shops mostly clothing stores. Aunt Flora said we were going to need to buy winter clothes and maybe the large department store off Piazza San Silvestro would suit our means better. More than an hour later, we approached Via Frattina, then found an ice cream shop that offered all manner of flavors, many of which I'd never heard of before; in Egypt we had lemon, mango, strawberry, chocolate, and vanilla and sometimes pistachio. Flora suggested I try *nocciola*, hazelnut, which I'd never tried before. I preferred to stick to strawberry, but in the end relented and ordered *nocciola*. My brother liked pistachio. My mother borrowed a flat spoon and had a taste of both. Much, much better than strawberry, she said.

Did we want to sit down? Flora asked. My mother said we liked walking. It was clear that, though they were repeating old habits and taking the same long walks together, the two were also avoiding spending anything, which may have been why neither my mother nor Flora bought ice cream. Flora explained that she was on a perpetual diet now. What surprised me about the two friends, who for two decades couldn't have been any closer and had witnessed the sordid turns life had taken for each, was that both hid from the other what each would easily have called poverty.

Both had seen the other's heartbreak. Flora had once witnessed my father's mistress buying clothes at the most expensive store in Alexandria and billing them loudly for all to hear to my father's account, while my mother had seen how Flora's brother had thrown himself from a window when news of his parents' death in Germany finally reached him long after the end of the war. Each woman understood that the other lived off a pitiful allowance doled out by relatives who'd settled in Italy decades earlier. But neither would admit it to the other.

As we walked on Via Frattina, Flora announced that she might have found a position with a cruise company as a multilingual secretary. Then, to dampen the news, perhaps not to hurt my mother, who had never held a job in her life other than as a volunteer nurse and who feared she'd have to start looking for a position as well, Flora asked me if someday soon I might look over her English translation of her shipping company's brochure, which was meant for American tourists.

On our way down Via dei Condotti, I suddenly understood that Rome was indeed a wealthy city; I'd never seen such lovely, well-kept shops in my life. These were all small boutiques, but from the exclusive jewelers to the antiquarians, one could easily spot luxury even if their stores were closed that day and their windows mostly but not alto-gether emptied of merchandise. In a store window I suddenly caught sight of the very brand of tie that my grandmother had bought me several months earlier in Alexandria but which I hadn't had a chance to wear. My grandmother had bought them on the black market in a tiny shop so dingy and soiled that, regardless of her admiration for the ties or for how she had rubbed their silk approvingly between her thumb and forefinger to determine their quality, I was persuaded that they were worthless and bound to fray within months. Now, see-ing their prices on tiny labels in the window, I realized they could eas-ily be the most expensive ties I'd own for years to come, maybe forever. Meanwhile, Aunt Flora and my mother were staring at this year's new collection of scarves, which they said they admired so much.

A part of me knew that onto these very ties was inscribed the larger tragedy of our lives. I knew huge changes had occurred but I couldn't quantify them, much less fathom their reach.

~

From Via dei Condotti we walked toward the Piazza di Spagna and from there headed on Via del Babuino toward Piazza del Popolo. Then we wandered down Via del Corso again, without real purpose or any sense of leisure. The city was vacant on Sunday, as it would always be on Sundays, dull, sluggish, and bleak, where the scattered groups of buoyant young tourists making so much noise and wearing identical colored hats could do nothing to lift the mood that had settled over us. I couldn't wait for the evening. All of us must have felt the same way; it was time to head home. I wanted the Rome of movies, of grand monuments, of beautiful women turning their heads to smile at young men my age. But that Rome was nowhere in sight, maybe never existed. Instead, this was black-and-white Rome, like the films shot in Rome in the mid-fifties and early sixties.

Aunt Flora looked at her watch and realized that we had been walking for three hours. Walking, she remarked, was the poor man's tourism. There was no need to say it. My brother and I knew it; my mother knew it too.

Flora walked us to Piazza San Silvestro, where she said we would need to take a different bus to get home. This one would go down Via Tuscolana, not the Appia Nuova. All I needed to do was ask the conductor to let us know when we neared Via Clelia. It's two stops after you pass the bridge, she explained. I had no idea which bridge she meant but I yessed her and nodded. As soon as we stepped onto the bus, Aunt Flora had a second thought and went to the back for a moment to ask the conductor to please remember to indicate our stop to us. He nodded. Then we said goodbye.

Inside the bus we bought our tickets, stood, and because it was hot, my mother lowered one of the windows. The three of us enjoyed the platform in the back of the bus, from where we could watch the city unroll behind us. Flora had told us that on this bus we'd be passing by a lovely surprise and that I should make a wish when we reached it. An older lady who was standing in front of us complained that there was a draft coming from the window we had opened. When I cautiously told my mother that the old lady had complained, my mother, unfazed, shrugged her shoulders, turned to the old lady, and fanned her palm across her face to show it was boiling hot in the bus. I was always embarrassed when witnessing her blustering indifference to those trying to scare her or shame her into bending to their will; but I also envied her courage, her cheek. She had always shielded us, and often made fun of my easy acquiescence before those who intimidated me.

As our bus sped its way down Via del Corso, I recognized some of the shops we'd seen two hours earlier. The bus passed the Victor Emmanuel monument and Via dei Fori Imperiali, flanking the Roman Forum. Then suddenly we saw what Flora had called a surprise. I'll never forget the first time I set eyes on the Colosseum. The three of us were facing the window with the wind fanning our hair and couldn't believe that the monument we'd seen so many times before in picture books, magazines, and films stood before us, impossible to observe in its entirety because of its size and because of our speeding bus, but more because of our sheer incredulity that what stood before our startled eyes was almost in reach and so present to our gaze. It was early evening and the arches of the Colosseum were all aglow with muted orange floodlights sweeping its walls and leading the way within. Nothing I'd ever seen could rival this. I wanted the bus to spin around the Colosseum another time, just to make me happy, and to spin yet once more, because I knew that I could easily have overlooked aspects of the monument I'd never forgive myself for failing to spot the first or second time. Then, as I watched the Colosseum drift from sight, I caught myself trying to grow indifferent to the large monument. Something made me say I'd finally seen the Colosseum and that it was now time to move on.

The conductor, who sat at the back of the bus, forgot to warn us that we were nearing Via Clelia, but my brother noticed that we had just passed under a bridge. To confirm that we were indeed almost there, I nervously asked the conductor whether perhaps we might be close to our destination. I knew he had forgotten but I didn't want to offend him, so my tone verged on the apologetic. The conductor, rather than admit he had forgotten, turned to me and, with a loutish tone, said, "If you knew where the stop was, why did you ask me to point it out?" A woman who'd been chatting with the conductor, and was resting her whole body on the pole closest to him, gave me an arch look that emphasized his point. *Yes, why did you ask, then?* I apologized, almost persuaded that he was right. My mother sensed that something had gone wrong by the snarky expression on the man's face and flung the dirtiest look she could muster. It said, *I know all about you, you scoundrel.* As we were about to get off the bus, I could tell what my mother was doing. She'd noticed that the bus driver had been speeding along the avenues and was probably rushing to reach the last station and finish his shift. She took her time getting down the stairs and then, just before touching the ground with one foot, hesitated as though she were uncertain that this was indeed her stop and might within seconds change her mind and step back on.

My mother did not know a word of Italian, but she had mastered the unmistakable eloquence of the dirty look.

That night she boiled water for pasta and for the first time in our lives, rather than have Abdou stew fresh tomatoes to prepare the sauce, she opened a can of precooked tomatoes we had bought and double-boiled them, her way of heating anything that came in a can. We had only three pots in the house, but those would have to do, she said, until our suitcases were brought to us, if indeed they were ever coming back. The good thing, she said, was that her jewelry and the silverware were in one of the two sharkskin suitcases that we'd brought with us in Uncle Claude's car.

She wanted to have a proper dinner that evening. So she took out a tablecloth and placed it over the bridge table in the tiny living room and on it placed three matching napkins whose pattern I recognized right away. The tablecloth had to be folded four times, as the bridge table was much smaller than our old dining table in Alexandria. We'd been using the old marble-top table in the kitchen for our meals since our arrival. But tonight, maybe because we'd seen Aunt Flora and were reminded of better times, the sight of the old tablecloth brought back warm home habits—maybe it was its smell, or the welcoming feel of its old cloth, or a few stains that hadn't quite washed out in Egypt and that I'd never really paid attention to but was grateful to find again, which is what happens on playing an old record and finding ourselves comforted to hear a scratch we'd disliked but grown used to. Maybe this is why we keep certain objects and relics, why they become amulets over time, to remind us not just of places or of people we may never see again, but of things about us that must endure outside of us because, without them, we can no longer be trusted to vouch for ourselves.

The tablecloth was a frail bulwark against the invasive, unfamiliar, and alien world we'd found ourselves dropped into. We didn't know how to begin hating a city that wouldn't welcome us and couldn't even tempt us with monuments I kept trying to overlook for fear they wouldn't confide in me or let me into their secrets. The tablecloth took us back; it might keep us unharmed, untouched, unchanged.

In setting the table, Mother thought of adding a fourth napkin, then she changed her mind. She was superstitious.

She hated the flat stainless-steel silverware in the kitchen drawers, along with three corkscrews and a lightly rusted, beaten-up cheese grater with dented and flattened spikes that hadn't been used in years. The knives had colored plastic handles, and the forks kept bending if you so much as used them to cut a piece of meat. As for the spoons, they were so flat and shallow that it was impossible to use them for anything except to stir sugar in one's cup.

"We're not going to eat like this," she finally said, then went back into the room adjacent to the kitchen and brought in a very thickly padded rolled cloth with stitched slots in each of which lay paired a silver knife and a silver fork, tucked together like prisoners lying face to feet in a tight bunkbed. I recognized our favorite knives and forks. At least these had stayed with us.

～

Supper that night was joyous. We had pasta, several slices of ham on the side, and a lettuce salad as well as a separate tomato salad. Then we had three popsicles that my mother had bought the previous evening. They felt like sugared water, with a tinge of strawberry something that melted away, leaving a stick in our mouths that yielded nothing of what the picture on the package had promised.

I offered to wash the dishes, hoping my mother would refuse my help, which she did. But she said I should watch how she washed them and maybe tomorrow it would be my turn, and the next day my brother's. My father had implored us to help in every way we could in Rome. Hearing him, Aunt Elsa repeated his advice. Gone was *le luxe*, she said, reminding us that in Lourdes she had lived the life of a pauper and learned to sew, cook, iron, wash, and mend her clothes and her husband's. *You don't eat if you don't work. It's that simple.* She was a good saleswoman who had learned to sell statuettes and artifacts to the Christian pilgrims who flocked to the sanctuary's gift shops. Every penny mattered. Her husband used to smoke his pipe while she scoured the floor and the walls of the shop and then dusted the wares before clients entered. "This is where I learned to waste nothing." "So, you were not born a miser?" my father would ask, pulling her leg. "Not at all," she'd reply, unaware of the joke, and would follow with her tireless saw, *Je suis née indépendante.*

After supper, the noise began, as it did every evening. At first I thought it must have come from the Diana or, as Grazia told us that evening, from another movie theater called Il Trianon, which she explained had a roof that opened up at night so that spectators could watch a film al fresco. I assumed that the sound of voices booming in the large courtyard surrounding our building must come from that theater. But then I heard what sounded more like a news program. Soon I realized it was the sound of every television set on Via Clelia, tuned to the same program. There were only two television channels at the time, but most people watched the same one, which meant that every time a singer sang or an actor yelled or wept, one could hear everything. Several months later, during the San Remo song festival, I heard every song without having to turn on my radio. We had never owned a television in Egypt; my father was against it. In Rome I envied people their televisions. I asked my mother if we could buy one. "Too expensive," she said.

It occurs to me in retrospect that she would have been the true beneficiary of the television. She read books and magazines instead. *Point de vue*, which she had been reading for several years in Alexandria, was a magazine that kept her abreast of news, fashion, society, blue bloods, while *Jours de France* was her infallible source regarding films, movie stars, gossip, culture, and books.

She had brought with her recent issues that she had been unable to read during the tumultuous last weeks in Egypt, and would always read a few pages at night. In the months that followed, she would occasionally purchase issues that she devoured and then passed on to Aunt Flora, and later, when Flora returned them, to Grazia, who didn't know French but liked the pictures, and finally to Madame Renato, whom we'd known in Egypt and who now lived, as my mother found out two months after arriving in Rome, a few blocks away on Via Turno. Like Grazia, she too was a *portinaia*.

Madame Renato, as we called her, using her husband's Christian name, could read just enough French to understand what the photos tried to capture about the French aristocracy but spoke the weirdest French I'd ever heard, totally ungrammatical but with words sprinkled without compunction from Italian, Greek, sometimes Arabic. This was also how she spoke Italian, with words and expressions borrowed from every other language, though she knew none well enough to claim it as hers. Her mother tongue was no language but a hodgepodge of at least four that borrowed the imperfect from one language and grafted it to the conditional of another with an ease that verged on syntactic *sprezzatura*. It was all the same to her, or, to use her favorite expression, it was all *fifty-fifty*. When I heard her pour out her doleful tale of her husband's compulsive gambling debts and of how he tried to hide them from her, it was nearly impossible to hold one's laughter. She would complain that he *played the papers*, he was always *playing the papers*, and always losing, and when he did win, he would hide his winnings to go spend them on who knows what filthy *man things*. Although it was not difficult to infer what she might mean by *man things*, none of us had any idea what *playing the papers* meant, but my mother, who colluded to get her to unburden herself, would ask her if her husband had *played the papers* that week—"But he always *plays the papers*," she'd lament. Eventually my brother figured out what *playing the papers* meant. Monsieur Renato was playing cards all the time, but the word for "card" in Italian is *carta*, which also means "paper."

Madame Renato held Grazia's custodian and janitor job in her own building on Via Turno and would every day take a pail with liquid cleanser and water, head up to the top floor, and mop the stairs all the way down to the basement. Of all the people I have met in my life, no person was ever able to better hold my attention, with her tales of endless spite, misery, complaints, laughter, all spiraling around her sheer love of gab. Her enigmatic language, which required continuous reconstruction, was a joy to fathom.

Occasionally, Madame Renato, like my brother, would drift into Romanaccio, the dialect spoken in Rome. Neither, it turns out, knew the Italian for words they'd heard in Romanaccio only. I knew my turn would come soon enough, but I resisted. There are songs that can be sung only in Romanaccio and were taught to me by Amina, when she came for her injections and afterward would knock at my bedroom door and, before stepping inside my room, always ask, *Posso?* meaning, May I? Then she'd leave my door barely ajar behind her. My mother knew not to disturb.

~

One morning soon after our arrival in Rome, my brother and I were awakened not only by the continuous roar coming from the marketplace, but by another hooting sound that froze me to the spot. Someone must have opened the apartment door and was cooing a teasing, high-pitched "Yoo-hoo" from the tiny corridor leading to our rooms. When I did not answer, not believing that the voice actually came from within our apartment, it came again, "Yoo-hoo," more insistent this time, reminding me of what I imagined a crooning castrato must have sounded like. Then I heard the main door close and made out the sound of footsteps almost hesitating outside my mother's bedroom, the closest to the entrance. My brother, barefoot, rushed into my room to tell me that Uncle Claude was inside. "But you are all still sleeping!" said Uncle Claude.

He could tell that we were baffled and not very pleased to see him suddenly inside the apartment so early in the morning. My mother would be furious, I thought. She must have sensed something—she always did—as she opened her door and appeared in her nightgown in the corridor. It was not even eight. I didn't need to tell my mother what was happening; he stood right there before us, in another tweed jacket, an ascot, and his usual felt hat. She tried her best to gather her thoughts and put on a robe and told me to ask him to please wait in the tiny room where we'd decided to move the bridge table. My mother shook her head in disapproval, and to lift our spirits, when he wasn't looking, imitated his expression, down to the hat, which he wore in Bogie fashion. I don't know how she managed to convey his hat by tilting her head and aping his pout and what I'd never noticed was the beginnings of a goiter, which with her talent for mimicry she was able to suggest as well—all in the space of two seconds. Today I am no longer able to remember his face at all except by recalling her mimicry of it.

But she was polite and as always deferential to a man who made it clear that he owned the apartment he had allowed us to sublet. He made a habit for the next few days of walking into the apartment uninvited and without warning. "Well, it's still his apartment," said Aunt Flora, who loathed him. My mother thought it was inappropriate, especially if he walked in when she was there alone and wasn't able to hear him enter. As a result, she would lock the door with a chain that had always been there but that we didn't dare use at first because it would have been an affront to him. On the fourth time that he used his key and was unable to get in, he must have understood how grotesquely inconsiderate his free entries had seemed to us, especially to a deaf woman. Eventually, he finally got in the habit of ringing our doorbell. By then my mother had asked Grazia's brother to install red bulbs throughout the apartment that lit up whenever someone rang. I would ring four times and the light would flash four times. My brother rang three times.

As Uncle Claude waited in the little room, I spied him crossing his legs and scribbling something on a blank piece of paper. Then he said he had a few errands to run regarding the hotel he owned at the other end of Rome, but that he would be back early that afternoon. He needed to discuss a few matters with us. He handed my mother the piece of paper on which he had been writing and said that this was not for her to read but that she should pass it on to my father when he finally joined us in Rome.

But that was two months away and my mother couldn't resist taking a quick peek at his note the moment he walked out the door. She unfolded the sheet of paper, read it, then showed it to us, unable to believe her eyes. On it he had added the cost of gas to and from Naples, the cost of our monthly rent, the lunch on the highway to Rome, an accounting of various expenses and tips needed for the people on the wharf, at customs, and in the refugee camp. Plus the money he had given my mother to buy food. We didn't expect charity, but this niggling accounting was something she'd never seen before.

My mother was so outraged that when he came back a few hours later, she gave him the cold shoulder. "Is she in a bad mood or what?" he finally asked me. I did not know how to answer him and said that sometimes she got that way. I was, without meaning to, siding against my own mother. I was ashamed of myself. My brother said I should have told him that she was upset with him. Why hadn't he told him, then? I asked. "I'll tell him if he asks again." Claude told us to sit down and each take out a sheet of paper. I had a notebook that I'd purchased in Egypt and was planning to use as a sort of Roman journal, but then and there it lost two sheets, one on each side of the staple. I gave up on the idea of a journal.

He dictated a few sentences in Italian. He took a look at my Italian spelling and then at my brother's. He didn't seem pleased, but he didn't say anything. He asked my mother to brew him a cup of coffee. My mother couldn't make coffee because the only coffee maker she had was in one of the suitcases still in Naples and it was a Turkish coffee maker. But there must be a moka—as he called it—somewhere in the kitchen. Indeed, there was, but the very tiny espresso maker was so old and begrimed that we didn't dare use it. Besides, we hadn't bought coffee. "In Italy we drink coffee," he muttered.

Then came Uncle Claude's pièce de résistance.

He asked us to write something about our voyage on the ship. All he wanted was a few sentences. While he would have been drinking his cup of coffee that never came, I scribbled in Italian something as best I could. When I handed him my short composition, he read it through, caught several mistakes, and said that I had a fourth-grade knowledge of Italian. My brother's Italian was a third grader's. This would mean that, unless I took private lessons, we'd be enrolled in grade school. I'd been a junior in an American high school in Alexandria, and my brother a freshman. Now we would be placed with students seven to eight years younger. Uncle Claude said that we would have to be registered immediately in an intensive summer course at an Italian institute that specialized in pupils who had failed exams and didn't want to repeat their school year. We would have to work very hard to perfect our Italian to be admitted to a higher class than the one he feared we were destined for.

This was something I hadn't been prepared to face, though I had no idea what schools I should be contemplating, having no idea yet of which were available in Rome. I had heard in Alexandria that Italian high schools usually offered two paths of study, the *classico* or the *scientifico*. In the first, one studied Latin and Greek, languages, literature, history; in the second, math and sciences. Uncle Claude was pleased to hear that I knew the difference but right away dismissed *liceo classico*. "What can anyone do with classics after you've left school? Nothing." He wanted me to become an engineer. "In today's world . . . ," he went on, lauding today's world, where only facts, not fantasies, were trusted. But I wasn't good at math, I said. "Yes, I'm aware," he said, recalling our conversation in the car from Naples.

He left. Both my brother and I were totally shattered. I could just see us surrounded by ten-year-olds.

My mother thought he was bluffing and was just trying to scare us.

But Uncle Claude was not bluffing. The next morning, he returned with an old duffel bag filled with clothing he thought we might need come wintertime. There were many thick beige wool shirts that smelled of having been stored in mothballs for decades.

"Thank you so much," said my mother with a grand smile.

45

"Do these date from World War Two or from World War One?" asked my brother, not aware of the impertinence of his question. As always, whenever he managed to throw a pointed dart, he did it un-intentionally, because he liked humor and didn't think that people might take offense at a small joke, even at their expense.

Claude understood the joke. His quick comeback was a veiled rebuke.

"Winters are cold here, and I doubt you have enough wool clothing."

I wanted to say *Thirty-one suitcases, remember?* but decided not to.

What I hadn't noticed was that these custom-made shirts, which one could wear with a tie even, came accompanied by underpants of the same coarse wool. Just looking at these antiquities made me itch. My mother whispered, "Say thank you."

Uncle Claude did not hear her. I thanked him; my brother thanked him too.

The unspoken question between us was how to dispose of them the moment he'd turned his back. To my mother, he said, "I'm taking your sons to a summer school on Via Furio Camillo, an institute for students who need to brush up on their Italian."

He asked my mother for the sheet that he'd handed her the day before, and to the figures he had jotted down added one month of tuition, which he was paying out of pocket. The next month we'd have to pay for ourselves, he said.

We walked two blocks over to the school, and were greeted by the director, who obviously knew everything about us. My uncle had clearly gone to the trouble of finding an institute close by and had even spoken to the director. He took these matters seriously, it seemed, which surprised me, as I thought he couldn't wait to be done with us the moment he'd driven us to Rome.

Once again I was asked to write down a few sentences on a subject I knew something about. I decided to write about the destruction of Ancient Athens during the Persian invasion, my brother about our great-grandmother who had died about three years earlier. He had never allowed her to kiss him because her flabby, wrinkled lips disgusted him. When the director read my brother's description of how he gave his great-grandmother his ear rather than his cheek for her to kiss, he burst out laughing. True, there were several mistakes, he said, but the boy had a certain *vis comica*. What my brother had not realized was that our great-grandmother was Uncle Claude's mother. As for the pages about Ancient Athens I'd written, "The less said the better," said the director. They were going to do their best, but of course it was doubtful that we'd be able to be put with peers our age.

Did I have a grammar or exercise book at home? asked the director. "Yes, I do," I said.

The book had been bound by a bookbinder a few weeks before our leaving. It was given to me by our tutor, Signor Dall'Abaco. We had not opened it once.

The next day, I brought the book to our new teacher for her approval. Signorina Longo did not seem interested in us. She looked at the book I'd been told to bring and started laughing. "This is an auspicious beginning," she said with irony inflecting her voice, using an adjective I did not understand. She right away showed it to another tutor who had stepped into the room. She opened the book and said that it looked exactly like the kind of grammar book her mother used to have. "Or your grandmother," added the other tutor. She giggled each time he said something. I could right away tell that there was something between them, and throughout my tutorials that summer, they flirted in sentences they believed we'd fail to understand. "Do you think they fuck?" I once asked my brother in Arabic in front of them. "I'm not sure, but they're too friendly," he replied. Then, on second thought: "Yes, they fuck," he said.

A few evenings later we wrote to my father. We tried to spare him the sordid details of our arrival, but it was impossible to avoid telling him about our uncle's outbursts in the car that lasted till we'd almost reached Rome. We told him about Uncle Claude's habit of letting himself in without ringing. And we told him about our probable enrollment in an elementary school. My brother always had a mischievous sense of humor and told him all about the old wool shirts and the sagging underpants that stank of mothballs. In short, Uncle Claude was someone whom everyone in the Roman family, according to Aunt Flora, called *un gran pezzo di merda*, a big piece of shit. When the envelope was sealed, I did what Uncle Claude used to do and wrote "French Language" in underlined capital letters a few spaces below my father's address.

~

We did not see Uncle Claude for an entire week, though his figure with his Bogie hat and squealing *Yoo-hoo* loomed large whenever we spoke of him. His presence gave us an image not of an eternal Rome, but of a dingy, ill-tempered, piddling town into which we'd been hurled like a hapless litter trying to call our old corrugated box a home.

But Claude's absence allowed us to explore the city as we wished. Aunt Flora's relatives told us about the French Institute on Piazza di Campitelli, where one could borrow French books and read magazines. A distant cousin of hers met us one evening on Piazza San Silvestro and together we walked down Via del Corso till we sighted the Capitol, which I already knew from a picture of the statue of Marcus Aurelius in Aunt Elsa's room in Egypt. In the distance, as always, the Colosseum. At the French Institute, my mother borrowed a French translation of *Doctor Zhivago*, I borrowed *Scènes de la vie de Bohème*, a novel by Henri Murger, and *Sapho* by Alphonse Daudet. I carried the three books as we ambled around the area, where Aunt Flora came to meet us in a different caffè. She had started her job at the maritime company and was told by the president of the firm that within a year she'd have to relocate to Venice. She loved the idea, and this was why she accepted the position. Venice, which she'd visited for an entire summer with her parents before the war, was surrounded by water, and of all things Alexandrian, water was the most stirring and the thing she missed most.

How could one really miss water? I asked her.

Impossible to define—or maybe I was just too young to understand, she said.

Eventually, it was she who taught me to love water—once water was no longer available, that is. But in Venice proper, you can smell seawater and you see it, and you hear it, but you could never touch the water. "Not our beach," she said. She wasn't thrilled.

I felt for her.

It didn't take much time for me to like Piazza di Campitelli. Maybe it was because of its secluded quietude on that warm early evening, or because no sooner had you stepped inside the French Institute than you heard at least two languages being spoken, or maybe because the piazza's unusual rectangular shape offered a stark contrast to a sixteenth- and seventeenth-century city that always favored curved and sinuous spaces. But its quietude my first time there matched nothing I'd known in our bustling area off Via Appia Nuova. The piazza was growing dark, though I could easily imagine how its upper floors and its roof gardens basked in undying sunlight during the day. I could see living there instead of on Via Clelia.

I was curious about a restaurant at the corner of this lovely square called Vecchia Roma. "Leave that alone," said Aunt Flora, "it's for tourists and the rich." We brushed past the restaurant's outer tables, looked at those having early *aperitivi al fresco*, only to be reminded yet again that this was not for us, that this, as she liked to say, looked back to another lifetime.

I didn't know it yet, nor perhaps did my mother or my brother, but Flora knew it and she'd repeat it to me in one way or another whenever I saw her. She'd already known loss back in Egypt, after the government had seized her bank accounts and looted her property, down to her expensive furniture. Unlike us, she had left Egypt with only one suitcase, less by far than she was allowed to take with her when fleeing Germany. In her last months before leaving Egypt, she'd spend hours at home perfecting her typing and shorthand, while next to her bedroom a university student from Cairo rented her older brother's room, while a young engineer from Libya rented another, the two helping her afford life in Egypt. Later in the afternoon during her last weeks in Alexandria, she'd come to visit us, and for a while we'd sit next to each other on a sunken, pillowed sofa, and there we'd read aloud either plays by Molière, because they were the last vestige of order, humor, and justice in the world, or the novels of Virginia Woolf, because hers spoke of a bygone, pre-war world not too different from what ours had once been in Egypt. In Italy, my aunt no longer wanted to read Molière. Molière, like Woolf, belonged to a lifetime that was as closed to her now as was the memory of the great wealth she'd once grown to expect was to remain hers.

Her definition of *another lifetime* was erratic and quixotic. She taught me to see that we didn't have one lifetime, or only one identity; and not only two, but three, four, five simultaneous ones, some you can't wait to jettison, others you're jettisoned from, some you can't make up your mind about, some growing obsolete, some that should have lasted far longer but never did, and the darkest of all, those you're still waiting for but already know won't come. We house all these lifetimes like Russian matryoshka dolls, each nested in the others. Flora understood this, as did my father. Both, after all, were born elsewhere and had fled their own birthplace but could still heed the echo of one lifetime resounding in those that followed. "So which is your lifetime these days?" I asked her after she explained how each folds into the others. "I don't know whether you're being cruel or just an idiot." "Let's face it, just an idiot, Flora," I replied, mortified by what I'd just asked.

I had always loved her as she loved me, but sometimes I overlooked the bounds of tact. I didn't know limits and needed others to remind me of borders most people spot without thinking. I was awkward and gauche, even with someone like Flora, whose sudden outburst that day chilled me and reminded me that, despite so much love and candor, we were not identical. What we did have in common was the reptile in us: we were born cold-blooded. Others, my mother or my brother, taught us what warm-blooded people said, did, and felt; on our own, we'd never have known. We learned to mimic them.

We didn't belong to this planet, its people, its time, its roughshod rhythms. We were, and this is what kept Flora and me so close, aliens among earthlings.

~

Somewhere along the way from Piazza di Campitelli that day, we stopped to have a quick bite at a small bar. Then we said goodbye and made our way to the bus terminal on Piazza San Silvestro. We wished her luck at her new job. She was going to call to let us know how it went. Meanwhile, she insisted, we had to call to let her know that we'd gotten home.

When we left the piazza with our books it was already nighttime, and by the time we reached Via Clelia, suddenly this was the Rome I always found so oppressive and disquieting, the real Rome, the Rome I didn't want to call a home.

A few evenings later, we found Uncle Claude sitting in our living room, looking over my homework. He was not pleased. Not pleased at all, he said. The work was sloppy, silly, *complètement bâclé*. He showed my mother his markings on my composition. This way I would definitely end up in grade school. To say nothing of my poor parents, who were paying for these private lessons in gold.

My mother tried to change the conversation by telling him she would be happy to brew him an espresso. She had bought the coffee expressly for him, she said.

"Thank you, but not so late in the day."

"Not late at all," she said. She was going to have one herself.

He shook his head impatiently with a dismissive, condescending gesture normally reserved for servants and beggars to whom even saying *Leave me in peace* takes effort.

At a loss for words, she asked if he wanted to taste her artichokes.

"But what artichokes?" he exclaimed, exploding with impatience.

"Artichokes, cooked with my mother-in-law's recipe."

After seeing his markings on my work, she thought that food

might tone down his criticism of my Italian. She said she'd be happy if he had a taste. She had cut off all the leaves and had cooked the hearts only, along with a good portion of their stems. She showed him her blackened hands, which lemon juice had not completely cleansed earlier that morning.

Hearing that the bracts had been eliminated, he said he hadn't had artichokes in a long time. His cook never made them, or didn't know how.

My mother showed him into the kitchen and lifted the glass lid of a square casserole she'd bought a couple of days earlier, into which she had fitted three rows of four artichokes sitting in a flour sauce, made with oil, not too much salt, and plenty of lemon juice.

He asked her for a small plate. She also gave him a fork and a knife.

How many did he want?

Just one, to taste. He was being polite.

What happened next took me by surprise. After cutting a wedge of the artichoke heart with his knife and fork, he tasted it and then put down the knife and fork and stared at the dish. I could already tell that he was considering how to tell my mother that her cooking was appalling, grotesque, and downright inedible. I was rehearsing the words he'd say so as not to be aghast when they spilled out. He stared at the artichoke heart and lowered his head a bit as if about to spit out what he'd just put in his mouth. Then, still as he was, he began to weep. A moment later, on realizing that he was indeed weeping and there was no hiding it, he started to bawl with a high-pitched little boy's voice, which explained where his bawling had originated and told us that he hurt somewhere deep in his memory that went back who knows how many decades. "This is my mother, my mother is here, this is my mother's cooking," he kept repeating in his own superannuated, mellifluous style.

I was already thinking of how my mother would mimic his crying the moment he stepped out of the apartment, which brought me to the brink of laughter. He must have interpreted my faint smile as a sign of compassion, and right away took out a huge handkerchief from his pocket and dried his eyes, most likely to hide them. He smiled at the two of us, even apologized for crying. But the crisis was by no means over, because even after blowing his nose, he began weeping again, then apologized again, then cried for a third time. "God gives us one mother only. I was not with her when she died." Moments later, "And I was not a good son. My brothers were. But not me. Not me."

When he recomposed himself, he went on eating the artichoke and wondered if he could have another.

My brother stared at my mother and, with his mouth but without using his voice, said that we should *send him a bill for the artichokes*. But she said nothing, and to make Claude feel at ease, she said she'd sit with him and have an artichoke herself. She even served him slices of bread we'd just purchased from a *forno* in the center where Flora said the bread was the best in the city. It also cost a fortune. With her eyes, my mother signaled for us to step out of the kitchen.

When they were finished, he said he wanted to come next week and would be happy to pay her one thousand lire if she baked him a dozen artichokes the same way. The sum was a paltry one. The artichokes hardly cost much, but the labor was intense and the soiled and cracked skin of her hands would take days to heal. She accepted the offer.

He said he was going to the baths at Montepulciano for a few days and would be back to discuss our schooling. My Italian had hardly progressed, he said, and he could see that improvements might take far longer, judging from the quality of my written work after almost three weeks of intensive tutoring.

A week later when we saw him again my mother noticed that he had more color in his face and hands, and sensing that his vanity was his weakest spot, she told him he looked much younger and no longer so pale. He also looked less irascible, she said, and more *détendu*, relaxed. "Irascible—who, me?" he asked, meaning to be humorous.

He put down his hat, removed his jacket, and looked over the mail that my mother had left on a little table but hadn't had time to open. One was a postcard from her sister in New York, who kept promising to visit us this summer with her husband. There was a letter from my grandmother, who was staying with one of her sisters in Paris before visiting her brother in England. The third letter was from my father.

He picked up my father's, whose handwriting he immediately recognized, and started to open the envelope. All three of us stared at him with incredulous and horrified expressions, because this was an act we'd never witnessed before, though none of us had the courage or the presence of mind to rip the letter out of his hands. My mother gently tried to remind him that he was mistaking my father's letter for one addressed to him. "I know," he said. He took off his hat, sat down, crossed his legs, and began reading the letter aloud. He was not reading it for my mother's benefit; he knew she could neither hear him nor be able to read his lips. He was reading it for himself. But also to shame and demean us by proclaiming his total domination. The man who had wept on eating the artichoke hearts had vanished.

In the letter my father was telling us that things were looking very sad in Egypt and that his departure date was set for late July. Almost all the tickets on the ship had already been sold to people in conditions similar to ours. He was traveling third class, which was, ironically enough, exactly how he and his mother and his younger brother had had to travel when they left their affluent life in Turkey under equally dire circumstances thirty years earlier. *Life repeats itself* was my father's favorite maxim, and he quoted it again this time as well. He had tried to help Aunt Elsa with the sale of furniture and with packing the suitcases, but she categorically refused his help and wouldn't even let him see what she was taking to France, nor what she was compelled to leave behind. "'We all know how she is, with her antiquated hair curlers and her totally frayed carpets, a sneaky little miser like all of them, brothers and sisters alike,'" Claude continued reading aloud.

Then, in his letter, my father tried his best to remind us that "'Uncle Claude is also who he is, tempestuous, ill-tempered, but a good soul who's had a difficult life but always manages to bounce back like a ping-pong ball, so no matter how life tries to sink him, he always bobs back up, light, agile, and of course altogether hollow. He is definitely a *grand blagueur* (a total fibber), but he is forever *serviable* (helpful), and as for the kindness we owe him, it is beyond repayment. Yes, his Borsalino hat makes him look like Popeye imitating Bogart, and yes, his voice is as high-pitched as a harlot's, and he should be more welcoming and a bit more patient, but don't forget that he came to pick you up in Naples, a city everyone says you should see before dying, but where dying is guaranteed if you stay longer than one day.'

"A witty man, your father," Claude noted. But he continued reading aloud. "'Yes, it is truly lamentable that he offered you old underwear and shirts that even beggars wouldn't touch. But he does mean well. As for schooling, we'll need to rethink everything before the school year starts. You've been studying English all your lives; it would seem pointless to change course now that you are both close to attending university either in England or the USA.'

"Again with this America?" Uncle Claude exclaimed. "Hasn't your father realized that you're in Italy now, and that in Italy you're staying?"

There was no point in arguing with him.

"'Besides,'" he went on reading, "'we don't want Claude to do to you what he did to his son who wanted to be a painter and a poet but was compelled to study engineering instead.'" Here the reader smirked.

"'Sometimes a parent is the last to know who his child really is. We all knew his son, and maybe the father knew that engineering was not his calling but that it would toughen him up. More to the point, do not react, do not talk back. He can be ten times crueler.'"

Uncle Claude must have always known what people said of him. All feared him, none loved him. As for his wife, she was probably the only one who screamed what she thought of him, and then banished him from her house, her children, her life. He'd attempted to rob every person in her family, which surprised no one, since he had robbed everyone in his.

Uncle Claude folded the letter back into its envelope and handed it to my mother. She must have guessed, from the shaken look on my face and my brother's, that Claude had read something highly compromising in the letter, and as a result, she looked more unsettled herself. She could tell that his light chuckle once he'd finished reading the letter was contrived; she was expecting yet another flare-up of anger and hostility. What threw me off and embarrassed me the most was not that my father had said things he'd never have written down had he known who'd be reading them but that I had lacked the presence of mind, the courage, the gumption, to tear the letter from Claude's hand and tell him that what he was doing was downright shameful. But he knew it was wrong, and his haughtiness, which he carried wherever he went, may have been a huge bluff that had aged well with him, and which he deployed with demonic speed and unflinching nerve. He dealt his blow before you even knew you had come to blows. He shot before you'd loaded your pistol.

If he was in the habit of striking first, he had also mastered the art of having the last word. By the time you'd decided how to frame your darting little comeback, which was going to put him in his place once and for all, he had already turned his back and was out the door and down the stairs. What disarmed me was his skill and dexterity. He was an old man, whose handshake was not just unsteady but whose bony fingers seemed to rattle in yours. But he was still the fastest gun.

He put on his jacket, donned his hat, and lowering his lips to Mother's hand, reminded her not to forget the artichokes.

~

A few days later, I received a call from a man who spoke with a very distinguished Italian accent. His one or two past-tense subjunctives were especially noticeable. He said he didn't mean to disturb but was wondering if he could speak to the *dottore*. I replied that the *dottore* was not at home but I would be happy to pass on the message. The gentleman said he was trying to find a secretary and was wondering if the *dottore* would be kind enough to recommend someone competent, serious, and trustworthy. As we chatted very briefly and maybe because my voice hadn't quite yet broken at sixteen, he kept calling me signorina and said he liked my French accent. I did not disabuse him but, after a few pleasantries, found a way to convey Aunt Flora's phone number, hoping he might offer her a position to allow her to remain in Rome and not be taken away to Venice. He was, he said, very, but very, grateful.

Things happened fast, and two days later, Flora went to see him. The interview, which she assumed was taking place in his home to avoid her meeting his current secretary, lasted about ten minutes. He led her into the living room, and after offering her a glass of wine, he asked her to write down her full name on a sheet of paper, as he didn't quite know how to pronounce her German surname. She wrote it down, and while she was still writing in capital letters, he placed a tentative hand around her shoulders, spoke very softly, which is when she suddenly realized the nature of my well-intentioned but totally misguided referral. The man in question was not really looking for a "secretary"; *secretary* was a code word for an entirely different position. With the same pen, Flora quickly scribbled over every letter of her surname and said she was sorry, but "*C'è stato un malinteso,*" there had been a misunderstanding. He looked at her speechless and then added, "*Forse,*" maybe, and attempted to persuade her to at least finish her glass of wine. "Wine doesn't really agree with me," she replied. He very courteously walked her out of the living room, offered to help her put on her linen coat, and, leaving his front door open, pressed the elevator button for her. He was, she called to tell me, a true gentleman, but it seemed clear to the two of us that I would be receiving more calls in the days and weeks to come requesting "secretarial" help.

Indeed further calls did come, which is when I resolved to tell the callers as curtly as I could that we were the new tenants of the apartment and that no one in our family sought secretarial employment. This, along with the laughter it would occasion whenever Aunt Flora came to visit, eventually led us to suspect that perhaps these calls were no accident. Grazia, the *portinaia*, had inadvertently let slip one day that many people visited the apartment, but never as regular lodgers. There was a maid who came late in the morning and went home at night after the last guest had left.

Suddenly a light flashed and things couldn't have been clearer to either Flora or my mother. Our apartment didn't have an outfitted ordinary kitchen before our arrival, nor could we understand why it had two large bedrooms and two tiny rooms but no dining room. Flora and my mother put two and two together and figured out that our apartment had been nothing more than a brothel and that, by extension, my great-uncle was hardly better than a pimp who serviced his affluent and distinguished friends looking for a discreet, lower-middle-class corner of the city where they could come and go without running into anyone they knew. The living room was where clients waited behind closed French doors so as not to run into each other, while the maid must have served coffee as clients waited. I knew about the coffee because there had been several espresso cups and saucers and the small, beaten-up moka coffee maker in the kitchen but hardly any coffee left in a tiny, abandoned glass jar snuggling behind the oil and vinegar bottles by the stove.

It took months for me to suspect that everyone in our complex of five separate buildings knew that our apartment had been a home for prostitutes. But everyone had kept quiet about it to avoid offending us.

The idea, however, stirred me no end. The thought that at night I slept in a large bed on which prostitutes had lain naked aroused me with the most indecent, raunchy thoughts. One such woman might ring our bell, say she had dropped an earring under my bed, and finding me alone at home, and seeing my bed undone, decide to remove her clothes and lie next to me, her flesh against my flesh. That night, in my bed, I tried to make out her perfume on my sheets, or on my pillow, but was unable to draw out anything remotely evocative. Eventually, by dint of sniffing deep into the pillow, I made out the distant and fugitive scent of chamomile soap, Italian and alien enough to arouse in me the figure of the naked woman lying under me with her legs parted and her knees snug against my waist. Eventually, I realized that hers was the scent of the chamomile soap my mother had bought at the supermarket on our very first night in Rome. She smelled of us, was almost one of us, which suddenly humanized her and made her as ordinary as a close neighbor who, before stepping into my bedroom, would be sitting at our kitchen table, sampling my mother's cooking and offering to rinse some of the dishes. I wanted her familiar but I wanted her exotic too: maybe unreachable, difficult, dirty, and taunting, but always eagerly acquiescent once she'd knock at my door and ask, *Posso?*

A few weeks later the smell on my pillow had entirely disappeared. Then I realized why. My mother had bought a new laundry soap: lavender. I'd have to conjure a new person now. I didn't mind. I knew I'd gotten tired of the chamomile girl and was ready for someone new. Perhaps I was born not just cold-blooded but disloyal and fickle too.

~

Near the end of June, Uncle Claude asked many of Aunt Flora's extended family to an evening reunion at the home of Marsilio Ancona, the head of the extended family to which both Uncle Claude and Aunt Flora belonged. The purpose of the meeting at the large Ancona apartment was to address our schooling. Aside from Flora, we knew none of those in attendance and figured that the die was already cast: we were going to be condemned to an Italian grade school, and Flora would be powerless to speak her mind.

For the meeting, Claude had asked us to wear a jacket and tie. Did we own ties? Yes, we owned ties. My mother decided to borrow an iron from Grazia as our old iron was in our suitcases still stuck in transit from Naples. We'd never worn our "good clothes" in Italy, and though they'd been hanging in a closet, they still bore creases from being tightly packed in our two suitcases. My mother said she'd take care of them. Our clothes were terribly crumpled, I added; we felt rumpled and creased ourselves. "You and your symbols—you romanticize everything!" said my brother, taking his cap to join the new friends he'd made downstairs.

Claude came to pick us up at six in the evening and said that, before heading to the home of the Anconas, we were going to have dinner at his home on the Aventine Hill. This was the first time we were to see him in a formal setting, which made things potentially easier for us, as the mildly official air of the evening might compel him to behave. My mother, unable to afford a hairdresser, had combed and brushed her hair herself and looked very elegant. I had decided to wear the new shoes that my father had had his shoemaker in Alexandria make for us: black pointed shoes with a golden buckle on each side, fashionable among rock stars.

Mother knew that tonight's meeting was going to be more like a tribunal with its attendant verdict, so there was no need to irritate everyone by appearing too dapper. Had she known that the tie I was wearing was priced beyond our means, she would have dissuaded me from wearing it. It was Uncle Claude who recognized the tie right away. "Where did you get such a tie?" he asked. "Even I don't own one of these." "A gift," I said, affecting total nonchalance, because I knew it would rile his jittery ego. I told him I had another one at home. I was about to promise it to him after the night's meeting if he would procure me some secretarial help. He would have been, I was almost sure, happy to oblige.

On the Aventine Hill, where he lived, he stopped the car, asked us to get out, and made us peep through a keyhole from which one could see the dome of the Vatican. "I wanted you to see this because I've heard from a mysterious source that one of your passions is old architecture and antiquity." Why was he being coy all of a sudden? Did I know what SPQR meant? I did know, and I told him. He chuckled. It meant *Sono pazzi questi Romani*, these Romans are crazy, or, if I preferred, *Sono porci questi Romani*, these Romans are pigs. He tried to explain to my mother the alternative meanings of the ancient Roman initialism for Senatus Populusque Romanus, the Senate and People of Rome, but she was unable to read his lips, nor would she have been able to infer the play on words. But the way she smiled and seemed to stifle a laugh was vintage Mother. "I think she finally understands me," he said, clearly pleased with himself. I wasn't about to disabuse him. Why he was taking his time to be so kind to us all of a sudden baffled me. Surely he had better things to do, especially with the *baronessa*, his lover, whose name he had dropped a few times already.

He parked his car nearby and showed us to his home on Via Sant'Anselmo. I could not help saying, "So this is the famed Via Sant'Anselmo," referring to all the envelopes we'd received from him in Egypt and to which my father always wrote back. I told him that we seldom said that we'd received a letter from Uncle Claude; instead we said that a letter arrived from Sant'Anselmo. "Why?" he asked as we were going up the stairs to his apartment. I didn't know why, but that was how everyone referred to his letters, maybe to retain an air of anonymity regarding the provenance of his correspondence. Via Sant'Anselmo, that beguiling and seemingly unreachable, mysterious, quiet, and lofty street, was finally unveiled to me on this muggy summer evening. It was more than just a street name. It stood for another Rome, a Rome I suspected existed but had never visited, much less seen except in films, and might never find on my own.

His home was decorated with dark wood furniture, some bearing rococo trimmings but for the most part similar to the furniture in my great-grandmother's home: old, defunctive, and oppressive, as were the three arrases decorating the walls of the dining room. He didn't let us step into another room in the apartment.

Dinner at Uncle Claude's didn't last long and was a relatively ordinary meal served by his maid, Rosalina, whose name I never forgot. Rosalina was meek and driven to petrified submission by the man who employed her. She was old and fat and a good cook. She knew how to serve well, serving on your left a large bowl of pasta with an exquisite tomato sauce as a first course, followed by a beef dish with fried and lightly sautéed potatoes, accompanied by peas, and a short while later a salad. Wine for him and my mother, water for my brother and me. The best was the dessert, a large bowl of wild strawberries with sugar and lemon juice. He could tell we were happy and he seemed happy for us. "Of course, none of this compares with your artichokes," he said, trying to throw my mother a *charmeur*'s compliment. Then, turning to me, he reminded me to please behave tonight and not to speak my mind unless asked, not before. "I have found in life that it is best always to speak less and to listen to what others say. Sometimes silence makes people uncomfortable, so stare at them but keep saying nothing, wait for them to squirm and fidget, and if there is silence between you, never, never be the first to break that silence. Once they say one word you've got them in your pocket."

That was to be his favorite expression: putting someone in your pocket. I had never heard it before. It must have entailed having easy dominion over people, shaking and thrashing them about, then owning them. I finally understood why people said of him, even in Egypt and later in Italy, that he was a *pistacchio chiuso*, a closed pistachio, sealed, impregnable, impossible to pry open—i.e., constipated.

He was, he later told us, an ace bridge player, and even as a twenty-year-old during the First World War had used bridge to play with the officers to avoid serving in the trenches.

Claude that evening was wearing a maroon vest with an ascot. When my mother asked him why he always wore an ascot, his reply could not have been more honest: "Because an ascot conceals the dewlap on my throat, whereas a tie does not." He added, "Age, my dear." My mother stared at him for a moment, pulled down his vest a tiny bit so that it looked snug, and then did something that probably no woman had done before in his life: she unbuttoned the last button of his vest. "Why?" he asked. "You forgot to leave it unbuttoned," she said. He hadn't forgotten; he didn't know, he said. Who had taught her that? he asked. A wealthy British officer whom she had met and loved during the war and who died at El Alamein, she explained. I had never heard about this British officer. Uncle Claude looked at her with startled, admiring eyes. "You're a real lady," he finally said, still marveling at her, "and your husband is the last to know it." She did not reply. But I am sure she understood because he had made a point of facing her directly and speaking very slowly.

He was, I was sure, trying to seduce my mother.

Romanticizing as always, said my brother.

We were never invited to Sant'Anselmo again.

I passed his building only once, half a century later.

~

The evening at the Ancona home was not just a reception but a *convegno*, a gathering, almost like a council of the gods on Mount Olympus. There were tiny cakes and juices just about everywhere when we walked in. My mother's one glance at my brother was sufficient to prohibit him from touching any cake. Her silent lips said that he should wait a while. He shrugged his shoulders, meaning, *I'm old enough, thank you*. No one could read her lips except for the two of us. There were even dried chestnuts, which had long become impossible to find in Egypt, and here they were strewn on tiny tables in that large living room, where a dozen or so relatives were seated comfortably, chatting away. I don't know why but I was totally impressed by the huge thick curtains in the living room that reached to the floor and blended with the upholstery throughout the room. I had never noticed, much less been interested in, curtains or upholstery before.

The head of the household greeted me by shaking my hand, and then kissed my mother's hand, and then, unable to resist, hugged her in a tender and earnest embrace. Ancona had never met my mother before but had heard so much about her, he said, asking me to translate from Italian to French for her benefit. I usually overdid my mouth movements when speaking to her, but that night I tried to avoid distorting my lips too much, all the while making sure she understood. Only once did she ask me to repeat what I'd said to her sotto voce, so no one might know. Ancona's wife greeted us in French, as did their son, who was dressed in the latest, tight Italian fashion, whereas I was dressed in the traditional British manner still fashionable in Egypt: blazer, gray trousers, white shirt. Among those assembled was an Italian university professor of architecture and his wife, who, like her sister, taught French in a high school. They, too, stood up to greet us. I later found out from Flora that they were very wealthy and were rumored to own several buildings, including the hotel where some believe Freud liked to sojourn whenever visiting Rome.

What I liked about some of these people was that, despite their wealth, which was so apparent in their furniture, their clothes, their hospitality, even in their heedless, debonair manner, they spoke Italian with a distinctive Roman accent. It made me realize that Romanaccio was not just a patois spoken by poor, uneducated people working in the marketplace or yammering on crowded public buses, but a language that suddenly acquired a stylish, patrician panache. My uncle's old-world attitude did not sit well with these people, who never welcomed him into their midst. They despised him and made sure he knew it.

Uncle Claude was related to Aunt Flora in two ways: her brother had married one of Claude's sisters, and Claude had married Flora's cousin, Lella. Lella, who was much older than Flora, had shuttled between Rome and Alexandria for years until settling down in Rome. Claude had married Lella to benefit his wallet, not his heart or any other organ. In their midst, my uncle was considered an interloper and a thief, and, yes, a *pistacchio chiuso*. Toto, who was Aunt Flora's nephew, couldn't contain himself, whispering to me, "What an asshole," which he followed with an obscene gesture by shaking his fist several times. I had grown up with Toto in Alexandria and was forever fond of hearing him relate the most outlandishly filthy jokes.

At some point the host, holding a teacup and saucer in his hand, said they should begin the meeting. "And, please," he said turning to my brother and me, "eat something." We did, my brother first, then I.

Uncle Claude reiterated what he had told the director of the sum-

64

mer institute. He reminded everyone that we had always attended English schools but he never mentioned a word about my American school, the very concept being too *déclassé* in his view. He also added that our knowledge of Italian was at a grade school level.

"So, this is the situation that brings us here tonight. Seeing that these boys are Italian nationals and will probably want to work here and never go back to Egypt, they have to adapt as fast as they can to today's Italy. Yes, they will have to lose a few years of schooling and put aside their hobbies, which they can always pick up again after they've distinguished themselves as engineers, which is what our new world asks of almost everyone. They speak three languages already and could still parlay these when it comes time to landing a good position. I've always been partial to engineering, and this is where my son, as you know, made a life for himself and is living quite happily in Turin."

"Your son happy?" interrupted the host. "I would never have put it that way. That, however, is an entirely different discussion, and this is not the moment to take it up. What your poor boy had to struggle through with you as his father merits an entire epic."

"The point right now is this: is he self-sufficient today? The answer is yes. Does he have a secure position? Yes. Does he have future prospects? Of course. And this in the end is clearly what matters. There's no need for long epics or witty epigrams here. If I had wanted a child forever dependent on Lella for spending money, the situation would have been different. But his mother is gone, poor woman, and I had to make decisions for both him and his sister, and frankly they are both managing very nicely on their own. There's no more to be said on the subject."

Claude's daughter, whom I had never met but had heard spoken of many times in Egypt, was sitting in the very living room that evening next to Ancona's seven-year-old daughter, known to be highly intelligent. Moments before sitting down, my mother had recognized in her the little girl she had once seen at the large family estate in Alexandria that belonged to her mother's family, bankers and landowners.

What I hated was that I agreed with every word my uncle had spoken, even if everything he said ran counter to my own inclination. I'd fallen in love with the poetry of Rupert Brooke, Alfred Noyes, and Walter de la Mare, and here I was ready to sign their death warrant.

Now the professor decided to speak.

"What you say is very logical, but here logic, *carissimo Claudio mio*, proves completely irrelevant. We've heard that the young man loves literature and antiquity, and you want him to set that love aside to become an engineer knowing that his heart and his mind are set elsewhere. The same applies to his brother, whose interests haven't quite defined themselves yet. Why not have them aim at law school the way you did, or maybe think of studying law abroad? I had no idea that I would be inclined to study philology until I was twenty! And as for you, you would have walked in one of your brother's footsteps to become a mere auctioneer if your other brother hadn't enticed you to turn to law instead. We are here to explore better ways than engineering."

I found myself agreeing with him as well.

Then the host started to speak. "I'm an antiquarian and I know enough about the arts to suggest that art is not irrelevant, so if he wants to be in a *liceo classico*, then we must put our minds together and help him enter a school even if we have to pull strings—which I've done for all three of my daughters and you, *Claudio mio*, have done for your daughter, who is with us tonight. You would have preferred her to be a secretary but she was admitted to the Sapienza because she knew what she wanted, as do your grandnephews."

My problem was that I agreed with each and every one of them and knew that this could not be so. How could I become a lawyer when even those who held opposing views earned my vote? I couldn't even argue with Flora—and now I was going to become a lawyer and argue with another lawyer, when I was totally incapable of constructing a persuasive argument about whether I wanted coffee or tea?

My uncle's position was not as iron-clad as he had let on. "I am not saying engineering is the be-all option. I was offering it as a viable possibility. Of course, I will bring to bear all my friends and contacts when the time comes for the boys to find a good school. In my view, the sciences are the wave of the future. However, I'm an old man and I am willing to listen to better views."

His flexibility surprised me because it suddenly gave his voice a new, human register. I saw that behind his barking and belligerence, he was perhaps a far more docile man than I believed. And perhaps Aunt Elsa was right in liking him as much as she did. I wondered what his daughter, who hadn't uttered a word, thought of her father. Did she fear him and cower before his temper tantrums as poor Rosalina the cook probably did? Or did she despise him and consider him a double-dealing ogre? Or was she no different than he was but had simply learned to hide it better?

Aunt Flora asked to say a few words, because, she said, her thinking was headed in an altogether different direction. "Who in his right mind would want to stay in Italy if they had a choice to go elsewhere? Italy is still a small, troubled, and backward country. Australia, Canada, South Africa, Mexico are better places than Italy—and this even if most of you have come from elsewhere and are resolved to remain here, as I, too, have decided to stay. Our relatives who live in South Africa may be compelled to leave Johannesburg to move here, but they're doing it against their will. Italy is not their dream. Then there's the United States, of which not a word has been spoken tonight. As you already know, these young men have been attending American schools in Egypt, and it seems criminal to take them off the American schooling system because someone has determined they must now live here as engineers, when in fact I know that their sights are pointed altogether elsewhere, principally New York. Why scuttle their trajectory to bigger things under the illusion that Italy has anything better to offer? It does not. If they want to stay in Italy, let them decide, not you, Claudio. Let them become familiar with Italian grammar this summer but let us not spoil their chances of aiming high as opposed to so low that all they'll spot are the roaches scampering as soon as you turn on the light at night. They should enroll in American schools here in Rome."

"What about an English school, St. George's?" said Signor Ancona.

"Why not St. George's?" Flora replied.

A rush of palpable satisfaction swept the room and almost all stood up to refill their wineglasses.

"St. George's has always seemed so distant and unreachable, but now that I think of it, perhaps we should have sent our son there," said Ancona's wife.

"Maybe. Maybe," said her husband.

"Is everyone agreed, then, St. George's?" This was Uncle Claude.

"I think so, yes," said our host.

Watching Flora smile told my mother that the meeting had gone our way, not Claude's.

But I knew Aunt Flora's mind. She had accepted St. George's, but she knew that this was only to buy time until we found a spot in an American school in Rome. In her view, and from all I'd heard her say for years, she had always set her hopes on America, not England.

What I didn't know that night was that the evening meeting in Marsilio Ancona's living room would change the entire course of my life.

Claude's daughter drove us home. She had a small Fiat and drove with maniacal dexterity. My mother could sense we were happy and I explained to her what had transpired. His daughter, it turned out, cautioned us not to be swayed by her father's humble little peroration. "I don't always trust my father," she said, but she'd said this with a timid chuckle in her voice that undid the stifled warning of her words. "He's always got a card up his sleeve."

Early the next morning Uncle Claude rang our doorbell. "Put on your good clothes, we're going to St. George's."

"But are they expecting us?" I asked, totally baffled by the sudden turn of events.

"Yes, I made an appointment a week ago."

"But what you said last night . . . ," I began.

"What I said was for effect. I knew they'd cave in as soon as someone mentioned the English school. Do you think I am an idiot? I had them in my pocket while they were all babbling and jabbering away. Get dressed, the two of you, and you too," he said to my mother. "I have other errands to run, you know."

I should have thanked him for all the trouble he'd taken on our account. I never did.

— 3 —

Mendicants

The thought of attending an English school kept me up that night. I felt that after the evening's meeting, there was a good chance I'd be spared enrollment in our neighborhood Italian school, where the elementary students wore those wide, fluttering pre-war black overalls for which I'd nursed a dislike, especially when I noticed that these grade-school aprons were fastened by what looked like oversized black butterfly knots. But I also knew I'd be back to the English school system, which I'd outgrown in Egypt. True, the English system in Egypt was unenlightened and barbaric and unshakably rooted in the dated mold of Victorian public schools, where caning and other forms of corporal punishment were the rule. Still, at the large meeting, I'd inferred that St. George's required all students to wear a red blazer. I liked the American freedom to wear sneakers, T-shirts, and jeans at school.

In the car on our way to St. George's that morning, my uncle told us that following our interview with the headmaster, the school was going to take our measurements for the school uniform. He had not only planned our meeting with the headmaster but had arranged for our uniforms as well—everything was already established long before the previous night's gathering. If no one had mentioned the English school, Uncle Claude would never have raised the subject and stuck to his original plan to enroll us in an Italian school. But he had already staked his bet at an adjacent roulette table in the event that the meeting took a different turn. He would beat you at a friendly poker game each and every time and still let you think either that he was unusually lucky or that you'd simply been dealt terrible cards.

But then I remembered what people had said about him when we were still in Egypt: his entire career was spent siding with two contending parties, the Fascists on one side, the Allies on the other, which explained why he and his brother Vili had thrived as double agents before, during, and after the war. He'd lived a prosperous life in Egypt and simultaneously amassed a sizable fortune in real estate in Italy, most of it thanks to his wife's money.

Uncle Claude parked his car in the pebbled parking lot of the English school. Some of the very neatly parked cars were dirty, beaten-up jalopies that had been driven all the way from Britain and had come to expire in Italy. I guessed they belonged to some of the teachers. It had never occurred to me that teachers were poor enough to own such decrepit wrecks or that they felt confident enough not to care what their cars looked like. Probably running away from Britain in search of sunlight and warmth. I'd read enough English poetry to know what drew them to Italy.

Uncle Claude had his own view of the English. Over the years, he had known many Englishmen and regarded them as a strange breed, rigorous to a fault, overly unctuous when they remembered to show a human face, and always eager to teach you a captious, nit-picking little lesson, yet able to turn shockingly informal once they've gotten to know you. They are all so *complexés*, he'd said, using the French word for people who are so inhibited and repressed that it takes them forever to emit a hearty laugh. They just smile the way they speak, with their teeth clenched.

Once he'd parked, he turned off the engine and simply sat there in a sudden stupor, imposing a rigid silence in the car as he stared at the steering wheel, trying to recollect himself. I had seen him do the exact same thing the night before when he drove us to Marsilio Ancona's home. He reminded me of an actor before the curtain rises, rehearsing the attitude he means to strike as he strolls onto the stage, running through his lines, straightening his back, clearing his throat a few times, assuming the posture of his role. "Brits can be overly familiar sometimes. Don't be taken in by their mealy smiles." Then, turning to my brother, "And don't ever cross your legs when speaking to someone, and never put your hands in your pocket. You did that last night." Everything about Uncle Claude was performance. It scared me, but I admired him.

Then he did something that shocked me. He told my mother, who was about to get out of the car, to remain in it. She obeyed, realizing that her deafness and her raucous voice might interfere with the tenor of the visit Uncle Claude wished to have with the headmaster. Though it felt exceptionally cruel, I realized that he was doing something I myself might have wanted when trying to hide my mother from my friends, my teachers, my friends' parents, the universe itself. But my father, who had never quite accepted her deafness and did not always introduce her by telling someone that his wife was deaf, would never have asked her to stay in the car. I felt terrible for her and feared that my awkward gnawing feeling, which was an admixture of profound pity knotted up with guilt, would possibly cast a pall on my visit. It felt as though my mother had been put in detention. "What an asshole," I thought, remembering Toto's phrase of the previous evening. Then I whispered Toto's words to my brother in English. It put us in a good mood.

On our way to the main office, Uncle Claude put his hand on my shoulder.

Pure performance.

He spoke English with a marked British accent that contrasted with the one we had acquired in our American school. He had met the headmaster before and there was initial talk of golf between them, so I presumed that the headmaster was a member or guest of the golf club. They exchanged a few wry smiles to bolster the tone of pleasantry. Then my uncle, speaking to the headmaster as if to draw him aside—another performance—explained that my brother and I were refugees from Egypt and that our father was still held in Egypt. The word *held* was not precisely true though *held* lent an aura of drama and urgency to our presence in the room, which was, as I soon gathered but wouldn't have guessed, Claude's way to initiate talk of possible tuition abatement at the prestigious school. He said he was aware that the eldest son of someone who, as they both knew, had to remain nameless was enrolled in the school, as were the children of the ambassador himself. (*The* ambassador, of which country no one would ever know, was a wild guess he later confessed with the gusto of a poker player who can't resist confiding his bluff for the sheer pleasure of showing how easily he'd bilked his fellow cardplayers.) The headmaster agreed that the price of tuition was high but reminded my uncle that full scholarships were no longer possible, given the school's budgetary crisis. "There was a time—" began the headmaster. "I know," interrupted my uncle, "those days are long gone. My son wanted to study at LSE, but the cost of travel and lodging had become prohibitive. Fortunately, another institution in England was able to house both him and, later, his sister. I hope you are able to arrange something similar here."

I knew that Uncle Claude's son and daughter had never studied in England and had been compelled by their father to take degrees from universities in Rome and Milan that did not charge a penny. I had no way to tell how much of what was transpiring between the two men was a sham. But I liked Claude's diabolic sleight of hand.

The interview went well. I was asked a few perfunctory questions, which I answered without difficulty. Did I like Rome? Yes, very much. Had I read Shakespeare? Yes, I had. Did my brother and I have plans for Christmas? Undefined yet, I answered before my brother could say a word. The headmaster seemed to like my word *undefined*, little realizing that I had intentionally used the word to suggest we had several options but hadn't settled on one in particular, whereas, had my forthright brother answered, it would have been starkly obvious that we didn't have the shadow of an option other than to spend our first Christmas on Via Clelia.

After our meeting with the headmaster, we were asked to see what must have been the school nurse-seamstress, who would take our measurements for school uniforms. Father would have liked the idea of a uniform. He had never been partial to our free-for-all American look that sometimes made us seem headed not to school but to the beach. We took a brief walk, visiting the dining commons, where a huge contingent of older boys turned their gaping, ruddy faces at us and would have shouted out obscenities if we hadn't been accompanied by the headmaster. I could almost feel their surly contempt.

And then one thing turned me off completely. For two years now I'd been used to American classroom chairs, each with its extended writing pad. At St. George's every student had a mini-desk in front of him. It reminded me of my awful days in English schools in Egypt, with their cramped air, their gaping, missing inkwells, and their wooden desktops into which generations of boys had etched obscenities, all of which came right back to me when I saw the small desks rigidly lined up one next to the other exactly like the teachers' cars outside in the gravel parking lot where my mother was still waiting. I had liked how American students sometimes pushed their chairs back then slouched with their legs spread out before them, even when speaking to their teachers. There was a sense of expansive freedom in their disregard for posture or grace that had always struck me. I didn't particularly like the way they leaned their chairs back on two legs and dangled while speaking without ever falling back, but I grew to like and envy the freedom of their bodies.

Uncle Claude paid for the red jackets on the spot. Most people purchased two jackets for each boy, said the Italian nurse-seamstress. Boys unavoidably got them stained and dirty. But Uncle Claude paid for one jacket each. The seamstress lady understood, or at least was polite enough to know she shouldn't insist.

The jackets would be mailed to us sometime in early August. I was impressed. When we finally reached our car and my mother emerged, I explained to her that we'd been admitted and that our jackets were going to be mailed from Britain. She, too, like my father, didn't dislike the idea of a uniform. At least we weren't going to attend an Italian school, she said.

Uncle Claude was pleased with the result of the meeting and was the first to congratulate himself. Sending us to St. George's had been his impulse all along but he'd had his doubts. Then he said he had to see his lawyer now—as always that damned hotel of his, he growled—but he would be happy to drive us to the main bus terminal, from which he was sure we knew which bus to take far better than he did. We did not object, as pleased to be rid of him as he was of us.

But as our bus tottered its tired way on that scalding late June noon and crossed the marketplace of Piazza Vittorio and then on to the arches of San Giovanni in Laterano, finally picking up speed on Via Appia Nuova, I was filled with a riot of contradictory feelings that I would never be able to resolve. I kept thinking of what a far cry the English school had been from my American high school in Egypt, how rigid, how unwelcoming. At the same time, I couldn't deny that, despite the enduring whiff of freedom that America represented, I still couldn't dispel the fantasy I nursed about England. I loved England, or at least my fantasy England, an England I was encountering in my very recent readings of Evelyn Waugh and Katherine Mansfield, a world intensely serene if self-satisfied, with its stiff afternoon tea rituals, its perpetual wet pavements, and its autumnal evenings that lasted far too long before resolving into dinner. My encounter with Joyce's "Araby" wouldn't let go of me, even if it was set in Dublin, not London, and my readings of Virginia Woolf, who reminded me of Aunt Flora, took me back to those afternoons when, together in my grandmother's home in Alexandria, Flora and I would read *Mrs. Dalloway*, thinking we were slipping out of Egypt back into an old England that we missed and ultimately belonged to, knowing all along that it had never really existed or been our home.

Two weeks later a letter came addressed to my mother from the headmaster of St. George's welcoming us to the school. I read the formal acceptance and tried my best to convey its meaning to my mother. In the letter, the headmaster reminded us that books would be available to purchase in late August, that arrangements needed to be made with the school bus if we wished to be taken to and from school every day, and finally, would we be bringing our own lunch or sign up for the school's? As for the cost of tuition, when I saw the figures, I realized that we were never going to be able to afford St. George's. Uncle Claude's bandied pleasantries with the headmaster were nothing more than a flimsy game of patty-cake that produced no discount at all. We thought we were playing him; instead, he had played us. It was then that my brother gave me an ironic glance and said five words: "Undefined plans for Christmas, right?" That one word, *undefined*, had made the two of us look like spoiled patricians when I should have allowed my brother to reveal that we were nothing but paupers begging to be doled out a serious discount. My call to Uncle Claude to break the news got him upset. "You have been more trouble to me than I ever thought. Either find the funds or start looking for an Italian school yourselves, and good luck to you."

He hung up the phone.

My mother was upset with the school, with Uncle Claude, but above all with me. She blamed me because I should have projected conviction during the interview, and this I hadn't done. My brother told her about my *undefined* Christmas plans. And this enraged her.

I hadn't wanted St. George's when it was being offered, but now that the offer would be rescinded I was just as miserable.

That afternoon, as we were walking to my Italian tutorial, we saw a dead dog lying in the middle of the road; it had been run over by a car. Someone had covered its face with a newspaper, but you could see that blood was still trickling from its ears. I didn't like Via Clelia, didn't like my Italian tutorial, didn't like Rome. I belonged elsewhere, but I didn't know where.

Perhaps Uncle Claude was right the first time, when he told me to set aside my fantasies and accept that we were settling in Italy once and for all. His once-and-for-all Italy seemed more damning now when I remembered how five or so minutes after setting foot on Italian soil I was already thinking of America. This was not unusual. We were not once-and-for-all people. I wasn't. Neither was my father, nor Aunt Flora. We were elsewhere people.

~

By our fourth week in Rome, my brother had made friends with a boy who lived across the courtyard. At first my brother felt awkward speaking to someone in Italian, but eventually the two would meet outside the locked garden in the courtyard and would sit and chat while rocking on a thick metal chain that linked two short posts to prevent cars from entering the courtyard. They became friends because all the boy did during the early-afternoon hours when the rest of Italy seemed to nap was bounce a ball on one foot, pick it up with the other, and pass it back to the first without letting it hit the ground. My brother was curious about the maneuver and, after watching the boy perform, came downstairs and asked the boy to let him try. He tried and failed but the boy, sensing from my brother's accent that he was a foreigner, spoke slowly and explained to him that it took practice but could be learned. I saw them sitting as they swayed back and forth almost every afternoon on the chain and realized that one could make friends with Italians, an idea that had never crossed my mind but seemed entirely plausible to someone like my brother. Did one become friends or did one just chat—or was there really no difference? I was not good at becoming friends with someone simply because he bounced a ball from one foot to the other. The trick was to land the ball between one's shoulder and neck and to keep it there, but even Attilio—that was his name—wasn't always good at it. My brother asked my mother to give him some money so that he could buy a ball. He ended up buying not a soccer ball but a cheap rubber one, and he turned out to be a much more agile shoulder catcher than Attilio himself. Neither of them took naps, but as the afternoons wore on, and the daily beggar with the terribly off-key operatic arias came and went, more youngsters their age joined them. They spoke a lot about *calcio* and Italy's principal players, whose names I'd learn from my brother. Occasionally, the boys would leave the area around our courtyard and disappear to the park of Villa Lazzaroni, which abutted Via Clelia across the Appia Nuova. There, they sat together and chatted, teased girls, smoked cigarettes stolen from their parents, all of them whiling away the hours before returning home for supper. This was where in all likelihood, and without realizing it, my brother started to acquire a Roman accent. He liked them. I preferred to think they were simply our neighborhood riffraff but I envied him.

From them he was able to learn a few things about the neighborhood that he passed on to me. While I was busy reading novels in my room—hiding, really—he was learning Rome. There were two barbers on Via Clelia. They were always full on Sundays, and I was to avoid the fat barber, because my brother learned he was mean. The girl at the small grocery store always gave you money for returning empty mineral water bottles. The older owner of the shop gave less, especially if you walked in with a bag from another grocery store. He learned that the Trianon was a cheap movie theater—but we were never to go alone at night. "Why?" he'd asked. "You'll see," they replied, with a smile almost meant to mock him. You could buy loose cigarettes at such and such a *tabaccaio*, but never at the one on Via Tuscolana. They pointed out the wine cellar where their parents bought wine. You brought an empty bottle and the owner would fill it up for you, white, red, or fizzy—few in our neighborhood bought bottled wine. My mother liked fizzy wine, and this is where my brother and later I purchased it, despite the squadron of dragonflies in the shop. Next to the wine store was a shop whose rolling shutters were always down during the day. This was where, at night, two *puttane* plied their trade. I had seen the two before; they were old and fat, one with frizzy blond hair, the other with frizzy black hair, both cheaply dyed. I had seen the two hobbling along together but never realized they were prostitutes, nor could I bring myself to believe it later on. In the evening, sometimes, I would pass by their tiny "shop" and give a hasty look inside before walking away. I never saw clients there, but obviously they must have had them; they even had a telephone in their one-room shop, and I caught one of the two talking on the phone while sitting on the bed, dangling a loose mule on her chubby foot. Next to her sat a startled fat doll with her pink, swollen rubber legs splayed as though waiting for the day when she'd be old enough to practice the same trade. I was sure there must have been something like another room or a large alcove behind the opaque cloth curtain. Sometimes, in the evening, you could make out a muted red light behind the curtained French doors.

What surprised me was the speed with which my mother, too, got to know the neighborhood. Within a few weeks, she knew the names of most streets and alleys, corrupting their names to suit her French reading of them. She was already known by several vendors in the marketplace and had picked up Italian words, in good part because gestures and exaggerated labial movements helped. They were even happy to extend her credit, though she hadn't asked for it. She roamed the neighborhood by herself, knew where to find a cobbler, a pharmacy, a place to buy zippers and cloth, and a grocer who had products unavailable at the supermarket. She bought milk that came in a carton shaped like a pyramid. She had even found a place that sold spooled wool, as she was determined to knit thick sweaters for us this winter. She liked the colors that were fashionable in Italy that year. How she knew all this, I'll never know. But her best discovery was bread, the darker the better, as most Italians preferred hollow white rolls. She also loved prosciutto, which we'd never had before.

She grew to love Italy, or simply accepted it, and within her first month had already established a routine, saying hello to people she'd gotten to know in the street or in the market, knowing where to find good meat for my brother and good cheeses for me.

My mother never compared Italy with what we'd known before. She didn't look back, had no complaints, and, unlike Flora, nursed no need to refashion the world to fit a mold that agreed with what she'd had to let go of. My mother told me one morning that she had dreamed she was on a train and that one of the stops was labeled *Alexandria*, but that she was not getting off there. She stood by the open window in the train, felt a welcoming warm sea breeze waft through her hair, then shut the window and watched the city drift away as the train pulled out. She would not step foot in Alexandria again until two decades later.

When we went to the beach late one Sunday morning with Aunt Flora, my mother did not complain that the trip to Ostia took at least an hour and a half. In the old days, the walk on the sandy road leading to the beach in Alexandria took less than five minutes, even when you added the time it took to stop for a quick cold cola along the way. You never ate at the beach; at best you bought a sweet sesame biscuit, sometimes two, but nothing more, because our cook would have lunch already waiting at home the moment we took off our bathing suits and changed, often without showering. I loved my mother's egg, tomato, and black pepper sandwiches, which she'd have ready for me after my swim. Now, at the beach, we would buy a whole roasted chicken, which Flora, my mother, my brother, and I would cut up with a knife brought from home and eat along with roasted potatoes sold separately. I still preferred my egg-and-tomato sandwiches.

Five weeks after we had settled in Rome, our thirty-one suitcases arrived at Via Clelia to the astonishment of the neighbors, who came out to see so many huge valises piled on the sidewalk. The deliverymen were unwilling to bring them up the two flights to our door. So my mother tipped them and begged them to help. The tip amounted to money that was going to go to tomorrow's movie tickets, and Uncle Claude was once again away at Montepulciano, so we'd be unable to ask him for money. My mother would have to borrow from someone else. But she never would have dared ask Flora; she asked Grazia instead.

~

Sometimes on those early-summer days, my brother and I would jump on a bus and head downtown, where the two of us would get to know or, as I liked to think, to understand Rome. There were faces everywhere, on the bus or the tramway. I was almost tempted to speak to them, become friends, as my brother had done in our neighborhood, but something always held me back. A couple of times, after visiting a site, we'd stop for a bite to eat. Late one morning my brother walked into a *forno* and suggested we each buy a *supplì* (from the French word *surprise*). I had no idea what a *supplì* was and followed him reluctantly, but I quickly learned to like those oblong fried rice balls with a light dash of tomato sauce and that surprising piece of mozzarella tucked inside. What I could not register was that each time we went out for a quick errand, there'd be loads of things to discover about Rome of which I had no notion or which I had almost intentionally shunned. In the same way, he helped me discover tiny little squares of pizza with oil but no tomato—*focacce*—to fill those late-morning cravings that won't kill you if you fail to quell them but, from what he told me, yielded a very palpable pleasure without disturbing your appetite at lunch. Thus, too, in the fall he returned with my mother after buying persimmons, which they adored but I wouldn't touch, because these soft, faded orange fruits looked to me like rotting tomatoes. It took me weeks to taste my very first one, and of course I adored it, but by then it was the end of the season and I would have to wait a full year before tasting another.

These days, when I arrive in Rome in mid-autumn, the first thing I do is buy a *supplì* at Roscioli and then proceed a few steps away to the bustling marketplace on Campo de' Fiori to buy persimmons. My mother one day brought fresh walnuts and almonds. Until then, I'd known only dried almonds and walnuts; these, too, took me a long while to adore. Today, the very scent of fresh almonds can take me right back to those evenings on Via Clelia when the three of us would pass around the only nutcracker we had to break open fresh nuts of many sorts that tasted so different from the kind I'd known elsewhere. Much as I hated life on Via Clelia, being taken back there through the senses summons great joy, something I still don't understand but have grown to accept as one of the most pleasurable inlets to memory. As Virgil says, "A joy it will be one day, perhaps, to remember even this."

On other days, my brother and I would walk into expensive record stores and pretend we were buying American records but needed to hear them first. They'd install us in a glass booth and there we'd listen to three or four songs, though we'd previously agreed to make a face on hearing the first song to let the saleswoman infer that we were not going to buy this song but might very well buy the next on the list. At the end of our little charade we'd walk out of the record store without buying anything but with just enough coins to split a tiny gelato cup at Giolitti, which I still revisit each time I'm in Rome, thinking back to my brother as a fourteen-year-old. He was nimble, bold, and forever curious. He loved Rome. I'd told him that I couldn't understand how Italians still pronounced Tide laundry soap *Teedé*, or Colgate *Kolgaté*, and Palmolive *Palmolivé*. I was being difficult, he said, just my usual ornery self. I listened and tried to learn from him. He was the one who taught me how to stop by a watermelon vendor, pick up a slice of the fruit for the two of us, and with a pointed knife, which the salesman lent you, pick off the seeds while gorging ourselves on watermelon. Sometimes we each got our own slice.

I liked ambling about with my brother with no goal. I liked being shown places I had never visited before, liked stepping into the heart of the Colosseum my first time because he led the way, liked taking the bus back and arriving home to a wonderful supper prepared by our mother. But these visits to the record store, followed by an ice cream or by a *supplì*, were things I would much rather have done with a girl my age. I didn't know any girls my age, except for Amina, and taking her to the Pantheon, much as I liked the thought of taking a girl there, didn't thrill me.

Most of my time that year was spent reading. I would never have become so devoted and compulsive a reader of books had it not been for Rome, or more precisely, for my desperate need to fend off a city I didn't even want to see to imagine another. Sunlight was so intense between two and three in the afternoon that these were the only hours of the day when I'd push out the shutters to let the blinding sun stream into my room. All you saw was sunlight in the room. By four, though, I would draw the shutters in and lock them halfway to allow just a band of light to cross my bed. I liked that band of light; I could read by it. Years later when I read about the afternoon sun across a bed in a poem by Cavafy, I was transported back to those early days on Via Clelia. I was not the only one who'd known the pleasure of sunlight across a bed. But Cavafy had held a human body, I was holding a book, and I was old enough to know that the difference did not flatter me.

I was alone in those days. I could see that my brother had no difficulty accepting Rome, its people, its tempo. My mother, too, had adapted. Unlike her, though, I spoke to almost no one. She had already been asked by one of the fruit vendors to sew her a sort of work robe: long sleeves, rough brown cotton cloth, the kind you'd wash every evening after a laborious day in the marketplace. How my mother had managed to persuade this *fruttivendola* that she needed a new robe is beyond me, but my mother had had the prescience to ship her electric Singer sewing machine from Egypt, and it was readily put to the task. A day later she had finished the robe, and added two side pockets, which pleased the woman a great deal, as no one else seemed to have pockets to hide cash, a wallet, whatever. On some days I'd pass by the market, and sure enough, the woman was there selling fruit, wearing my mother's robe with fleur-de-lis ribbon ornaments sewn on the outside. There were other clients, and with word-of-mouth advertising she ended up recruiting a number of those at the market-place who wanted aprons made for them. They did not pay her with money, but with fruits and vegetables, bread, and cheese. This is how we discovered mozzarella and, a bit later, bresaola.

My mother was a very strong woman, but she cried easily, from shame, from self-pity, or when her feelings were hurt. She was so fragile that people immediately connected with her, and Italians, being a people whose language is sketched on their faces and hands, were easy to understand, as she was for them. She had once told a neighbor that she might never again see her husband, who was still in Egypt and, though officially expelled, might never be allowed to leave. Word got around and everyone felt sorry for this poor deaf woman who was trying to eke out a living with absolutely no knowledge of Italian but who, when she showed up in the market, would, however she could, chitchat with the other housewives and saleswomen. Once or twice, she met other deaf people who were happy to get to know her and whom she'd invite to tea, a somewhat unusual custom on Via Clelia but a good enough pretext for having people over.

A few hand gestures intercepted on the fly or when watching a hearing person trying to understand what someone was saying would right away tell my mother that this was most likely someone who was deaf like her, and she would make contact right away. Thus, she met an older woman who was also deaf and ended up inviting my mother to her home on the spot, scarcely three blocks away. My mother helped her carry her cheeses and vegetables. Her husband was deaf as well, but their son was not. He was in his mid-thirties, and after work he'd frequently come over to our home to pick up his parents when they were visiting. He would stay for a quick coffee, chat with me about Pascarella, whose comic Roman poetry about the discovery of America he knew practically by heart, and would leave with them, his father already hobbling quite a bit. All my mother's deaf acquaintances in Rome, as in Alexandria, had either stayed single or married people who were also deaf. My mother and another friend, Despine, were two exceptions. Both had married hearing men, and their marriages proved disastrous.

Congenital deafness was the case with the Coronari family, whom my mother met while shopping in the marketplace and whose son was deaf as well. The Avellinis, also market acquaintances, were expecting a child and were very nervous about deafness running in their family. These people would visit us in the afternoon. They were very kind to me and I took to them as well. One of them told my mother that she should join a club for the hearing impaired in Rome. Early on a July evening, the Avellinis offered to take her there. She loved it and as a result met more deaf people whom she grew to like a great deal.

Within our first few months she had managed to gather a half-dozen deaf men and women who enjoyed spending time in our apartment. Sometimes an old lady, Signora Rossi, who always introduced herself as Rossi, Giovanna—surname first followed by her Christian name, as if addressing a clerk or a functionary in a post office—would drop in, always asking if this was *l'ora del tè*, teatime. She lived on the first floor of our building. I would run into her on the stairway and would help her carry her shopping to her apartment. I also helped another woman in the building adjacent to ours when she needed a hand carrying bolts of cloth to her home. She had once promised me a shirt the second time I helped her but had never delivered.

Occasionally mother's guests would bring a cake or some biscuits, which my mother would immediately serve. To me, just hearing the distant clatter of teaspoons stirring the sugar in their teacups, which my mother had unearthed from our suitcases, was a precious reminder of that England which I, with Flora, still sought and believed we'd known and might recover someday if only we had the key.

When it got dark, I would hear our front door open, hear the voices of deaf people in the corridor, then, after shutting the door, my mother would slowly come into my room, sit on the edge of my bed, and tell me how happy she was to have made so many friends, even if one of the deaf wives was unbearable and was constantly aiming poisoned little darts at her. But that couple came frequently, and it was clear that the husband was taken with my mother, who was at least ten years older than he. The pleasure they brought my mother eventually radiated to both my brother and me, and there were days when we could actually think we were not unhappy.

Often Madame Renato dropped in, and I would be the one to start brewing a cup of coffee for her with our new coffee maker. "You are an angel," she would say. After serving both her and my mother coffee, I would sit down to listen to her litany of woes, mostly about her poor husband, who was "a *hanash*"—"snake" in Arabic, as she didn't know the word in French—"I swear to you, a true *hanash*"—and the younger of her two sons clearly shared the same curse. When my mother interrupted and asked what kind of curse she was speaking of, her answer was always the same: "He has two hair whorls in the back of his head," she would say, bringing her stubby fingers to the back of her own head, "not like everyone else, and this, madame, this is a sign." "A sign of what?" my mother would ask, trying to draw her out, knowing, as I'd already told her, that I liked Madame Renato's gossip. "A sign of . . ." She didn't want to say, so as not to scare my mother, but on being pressed again, "*C'est le diable, madame, le diable*," she would say, using the French word for Satan. "You don't say!" my mother would add, trying to look dumbfounded, so as not to laugh. "Already his eyes never look at you. When you stare at him, he immediately looks away. I am worried. Renato beats him very often, yet the boy won't change. But the worst is that he eats the wall." "The wall itself?" I'd ask, thinking this was a metaphor of some sort. "No, he scratches it and eats large flakes, like the bread you Jews eat." She would mimic a shudder, displaying goose bumps on her beefy upper arms marred by blotchy vaccine marks. "He is like his father, and frankly I don't know who of the two is more possessed by Satan, because they are fifty-fifty." She would turn to my mother with a totally bewildered expression on her face, while neither my mother nor I knew what *fifty-fifty* meant. But then, giggling mischievously and covering her mouth with the back of her hand as if nursing second

87

thoughts each time she went a little too far in disclosing the horror-filled dungeons of her life, she always ended by saying, "More than this I'd better not say, better not say, otherwise people will say I'm lying."

When one day she brought along her two sons, I made a discreet effort to spy on the back of her youngest son's scalp, and sure enough, there before my eyes were the two whorls his mother had mentioned, something I'd never thought to look for in anyone before. But then this was precisely why I loved Madame Renato's stories. Like dreams, they were gnarled, implausible, and almost fabricated. She didn't necessarily believe her stories, but the very telling made them believable not just to us, but to her as well. Every item about her immediate family or, as I was soon to find out, about the strange, distorted lives of the people in her building, whose shameful secrets she'd unload as soon as she had her coffee with my mother, was, at best, the relentless gossip-mongering of a concierge and, at worst, the prurient prying into secrets most people normally wish to conceal from the all-seeing eye of God Himself.

"She says bad things about everyone. So just imagine what she says about us," said my mother, once Madame Renato had left our apartment. It was then I realized that if she felt at liberty to spill all manner of personal secrets gleaned on her job as the *portinaia* of her building, it was because we welcomed gossip, but also because we, too, were willing to rat on others. My mother wasn't a person given to talking much about other people; but I loved Madame Renato's gossip. Mother frequently accused me of being a *mauvaise langue*, an evil tongue. I loved nothing better than comparing notes with Madame Renato, not because she knew anyone I knew, but because our pleasure lay in assessing the faults of people in general and comparing what made us dislike or distrust so many. I liked having her correct my reading of peoples' motives by adding another, more sinuous layer than I would have imagined, just as I liked suggesting an additional twist to why one of her upstairs tenants always hid her garbage in complicated knotted plastic supermarket bags. "It's not that I need to see her garbage," she'd say. "What would I want with her garbage,

God forbid—but if she hides it every time, it must mean there's something in there she doesn't want anyone to know about, and this kills me, don't you see?" Then, as though to justify her compulsion, "I don't need to know," she'd claim, "but I want to know."

Madame Renato finally met Uncle Claude one day when he came to pick up his twelve artichokes. She looked at him with the seemingly simpleminded stare of a silent, senseless, ignorant, gawky woman who was entirely intimidated by as august a personage as the *dottore*. She played the part of the woman who mops the stairway every morning, top floor to bottom floor, and who'd come to borrow one of my mother's slim knitting needles because, poor absentminded woman that she was, she had no idea where she'd lost hers, given, if he only knew, the infernal chaos in her home. No sooner had he shut the door behind him than she said she knew his type. Right then and there she deplored how he showcased a whole bundle of large bills before giving my mother his measly one thousand lire and then pretended to want to stand and chat when any fool could see he couldn't wait to take his precious artichokes and run along with them, vicious man that he was.

I told her that elsewhere in the family he was called *pistacchio chiuso*. Trust me, she said, he is not *chiuso* at all down there. That conniving look on her face presaging a racy thought was right away followed by a hasty snicker and that unmistakable back of the hand languorously applied to her mouth, as though she regretted having said something off-color but also underlining her sauciness by feigning that she meant to take it back.

Once Madame Renato was gone, it felt like evening had suddenly fallen over our lives, and while my brother was still out playing soccer and my mother was preparing supper, I went off to read. I knew I was hiding and, in the words of a writer I was reading at the time, *insufficient to myself*. I was obsessed with other people, with those I happened to cross on the sidewalk, in a store, or on a bus and who would stare at me, as I would stare at them not just because I wanted them too but because I didn't want to want them.

My mother, seeing my door closed, which she knew was meant to keep her out, would sometimes lose her temper. Her crises were like a squall that could break through every bulwark placed in its way. My brother, who hated her bouts of ill temper, would intervene on my behalf and would suddenly bear the brunt of her yelling. There was no containing her once she started to yell. She would find something we'd not explained, something I'd done wrong or he'd forgotten, or just about the most trivial errand that had failed to make her life easier as a mother, a cook, a seamstress, a cleaning lady—a charwoman, she'd yell—and suddenly she'd unleash numberless reproaches she still wished to hurl at my father for living in Egypt while here we were, refugees, left to starve and borrow money from the janitor, the janitor, of all people! She threw things, broke things, and if things broke, well, they broke. She slammed doors, she banged the medicine cabinet and the refrigerator door, she cursed out the kitchen window when with no warning a wind would hurl it shut and shatter the frail windowpane, which went crashing down to the ground two floors below with a sound I'll never forget and which she couldn't hear or know about until she came back to the kitchen and, after sweeping the floor and removing the shards, sat at the kitchen table with both elbows resting on the ugly tartan oilcloth and cried.

In Egypt, I had heard her scream at the servants, at the maids, at our blind washerwoman, at the sellers in the marketplace. I'd grown up with her eruptions. Now when we were alone in the evening, there was sometimes no other solution but for my brother and me to leave the house and hope she'd calm down in our absence. We took hopeless walks down Via Clelia, then onto Via Camilla, then to Via Furio Camillo; sometimes our silent, brooding walks took us as far as Via delle Cave and into Via Turno, where we tried to avoid running into the Renatos, who'd most likely ask what we were doing there and force us to make up a lame, last-minute errand when all we had in our pocket was a key and not a single lira. Sometimes I wished she'd die when she got that way. But I never dared tell my brother this. One time, though, he said they should put her away. Finally, I couldn't help myself and told him you could love someone and still wish them dead.

~

My father had instructed Uncle Claude to give us a monthly sum from which he could deduct the rent owed him. He did this on the first of each month, but was frequently away, which necessitated borrowing. Once he was back and my mother had the money, she headed immediately downstairs to pay our *portinaia* the money she had borrowed toward the end of the previous month and then right away headed to Via Turno to repay the Renatos what they'd lent us as well. We were in the black and my mother suggested we go to the movies. Since all the foreign films were dubbed and there were no subtitles, I was the one who, in the dark, would convey to my mother what the characters were saying. She would read my lips as fast as she could.

We liked going to the movies, and since there were no restrictions on late arrivals, we got to the film whenever we could and watched the end before the beginning. I got used to this and even today it never bothers me if someone tells me how a film ends. The movie experience for me lies not in the tale, but in blocking out the world and entering a new one. At the movies, one did not think, did not worry, was entirely sheltered. I liked being the interpreter for my mother. We sat through each and every advertisement, sat through intermission, and sometimes we watched the entire movie to the end even if we'd seen the end already two hours earlier. Frequently there were double features, which meant we'd spend hours hiding from Rome, from Via Clelia, from my books, from life itself. There was also a caffè-bar at the corner of Via Clelia where the men who sat around always whistled when my mother walked by, which was why she knew to cross the street the moment we left the Trianon. She was still very beautiful and men frequently turned around when she passed by.

Past ten at night, as we approached our home, what we'd run away from awaited us on Via Clelia, now dark and almost deserted. My mother did not have the strength to quell the volcano of fatigue, frustration, despair, heartache, and rage about to tear out of her lungs. My brother and I would pick up our pace to reach home before things got worse. Sometimes they did get worse.

Neighbors heard the sweet deaf woman howling at the terrible life she'd been made to live. She reminded me of Hecuba and then Niobe, women for whom the world had nothing, not a thing, to offer or promise. Hecuba howled when all her sons were killed at Troy, howled till she turned into a dog.

Grazia, who of course heard my mother's incredibly strident yelling, once told me, when she saw me coming down the stairs one morning, that the deaf she'd known in the countryside outside Rome lost their bearing depending on the phases of the moon. The deaf, she said, were the kindest people she'd ever known, but their temper was governed by the moon. What was needed was patience. I told my brother this. We decided our mother was a lunatic. Then we laughed at Grazia's nonsense. In his view, she, too, was romanticizing.

Sometimes we wanted to run away. But could we abandon our mother? I couldn't, he couldn't. She'd end up like her own mother, who on being torn away from her world and her son and daughters lost her mind and roamed the streets of Paris for three days, talking to strangers in Ladino, until she was found by the police and reunited with her son, who had given up hope of ever finding her again. She wanted to die, she kept saying, and eventually starved herself. She wasn't even sixty.

There were just the three of us in the world. There was no one else. We needed to stick together.

We hardly saw our relatives in Rome, and even when they did seek us out and invited us to their glamorous homes, we would always find an excuse to turn them down, either through misplaced arrogance, or through envy, or from simple shame at our demoted status. To visit them, we needed to take three buses—taxis were out of our budget. Occasionally, the Anconas would invite us to their large villa at Anzio. Anzio offered a magnificent beach compared with what we'd discovered at Ostia. Here they regaled us with wonderful wine and food prepared and served by their cook, whereas when we went to the beach with Flora we would purchase our usual roasted chicken and tear it apart like wolves, because sometimes neither my mother nor Flora remembered to bring a kitchen knife and both were too cheap to buy one at the *tavola calda* that sold the chicken. As for the sliced and oiled potatoes with rosemary that were sold separately, we'd eat them with our hands and then, to confirm our impoverished, degraded station in life, would suck our fingers clean, like mendicants, said Flora. Yes, agreed my mother, like mendicants.

Also that summer, probably urged by various members of the family, Uncle Claude offered to take us to his beach house at Torvaianica. His offers were more like commands but he drove us all the way to Torvaianica, a new town that had absolutely no charm or history, since all the buildings and homes were of recent construction. Uncle Claude had a villa there facing the sea and told us he was in the habit of practicing his golf along the shore using light, plastic balls. As his elder brother Nessim had done, he attempted to teach me how to hold a golf club and hit the ball. But I was hopeless. He was tolerant enough with me for a good ten minutes, but then he gave up. "This is not for you," he finally said, picking up some of the plastic balls I'd managed to hit but that hadn't gone very far. "Maybe I should try with real golf balls," I said, remembering I'd fared better with his brother. "No, this is not for you," said the sulking old man, who had clearly run out of patience. He took the colored plastic balls farther out on the beach and played by himself. After hitting balls for half an hour, he joined the three of us on the caked sand and sat with his bony knees raised, almost touching his chin. Because his bathing suit was too loose, his testicles peered out of the left side and slouched on the sand, followed later by their leering third companion, a sight Mother, my brother, and I pretended not to notice but that brought a grin to our faces. Eventually, he stood up and said he was going to sunbathe on his terrace. But we should know he sunbathed in the raw, so we shouldn't be shocked—he was a modern man, he said, leaving us quite uncertain whether this was a warning or a lure. We looked at one another with bewildered smirks without exchanging a word, determined it was wiser not to climb the stairs above the first floor of the villa, fearing we might encounter his nakedness, which he wanted us to infer was prodigious. A dead sparrow surrounded by white hair, I said. No, a baby carrot, with a thick vein, was my mother's contribution. A slim asparagus with two quail eggs, my brother couldn't resist.

On our list we already had pistachios, artichokes, now carrots, asparagus, and as a crowning joke I alluded to a mushroom called the stinkhorn. What was a stinkhorn? my mother asked. I'd show her a picture at home. My Italian tutor in Egypt had given me an illustrated guide to mushrooms, and the stinkhorn, called the *puzzolente*, the stinker, was also referred to as the *Phallus impudicus*.

The question was which of the three of us would tell him he needed another bathing suit. "Maybe he likes showing his under-twins," I supposed, remembering that the word for "twins" in Greek was *didyma*, which also meant "testicles." Maybe we should leave it alone, said my brother. It was up to his girlfriend, the *baronessa*, whoever she was, to tell him.

And with that, we went swimming for a long while, resolved to share our impressions of the sight with Madame Renato.

Uncle Claude had told my mother that she should feel free after our swim to use whatever she found in the refrigerator or in any of the kitchen cabinets to prepare something for lunch. He had no idea what was in the kitchen. The house, as he told us, also belonged to the *baronessa*, his mistress, and it was her maid who did the shopping.

After we'd dried ourselves, within minutes my mother had managed to prepare an omelet for the four of us and sandwiches with prosciutto and cheese.

When he came downstairs wearing his bathing suit again, he asked if he could have a sandwich too, but she should please remove the fat from the ham. She'd remembered this from the previous time and had removed it for him. He never ate the fat, he boasted, which was why he was a fit seventy-year-old man. We sat in the kitchen, and for one brief moment I felt that we were almost family—maybe because he seemed genuinely happy.

What were we planning for the rest of the day?

He had never asked us this before.

I was going to read, but we were probably going to the movies.

Excellent idea, he said.

What was he going to do?

Probably watch television, he said.

We'd never dared ask anything about his life.

— 4 —

The Chalabi-Hanan
Experiment

Grazia rang our bell twice. She was holding a telegram. My mother let her in and tore open the envelope. Eager to hear the news, Grazia shut our door behind her and waited inside. My father was announcing his arrival in Naples. The three of us gave a loud cheer, and once I'd explained to her the telegram, Grazia uttered a cheer as well. We had worried for him and would occasionally share our worries with her, though most of the time we'd banish the thought of his arrest or imprisonment. There had been cases of arrests followed by brutality in jail before a cringing apology for the shameful error committed by the local police.

After him there was still Aunt Elsa, and within a few weeks she'd be moving to Paris, and then we'd all be able to put Egypt behind us, forget Arabic, forget the Egyptian police, forget that some of the things whose loss I had no choice but to live with were things that had almost become part of us and that I would disown the way we disown our first teeth, our trusted blanket, or the nightstand we'd grown up with since childhood and never knew we'd ever abandon and leave behind.

I kept thinking of my father, my mother, Aunt Elsa—how would they ever account for their years in Egypt? Aunt Elsa, with her knobbly fingers ravaged by arthritis, and her macular degeneration, which everyone knew would leave her blind, or my father, long past middle age, who'd have to reinvent himself and seek out new business opportunities at a stage of life when most financially secure men were planning to build second homes either in the countryside or by the sea.

Seven months earlier, on December 31, we had all gathered at Santa Lucia, one of the best restaurants in Alexandria, to welcome the new year, and there was a band in the narrow space where my father danced with my mother and then waltzed with Aunt Elsa. My brother and I sat at our table and watched the grown-ups. What were they celebrating when everyone on the dance floor that night had been looted by the government but still came, smartly put together, eager to welcome the new year?

Now Via Clelia.

That same night, my mother decided to have me call her brother Robert, who lived in Paris with his wife and my cousins. For some reason he and she were not on very good terms, either because they'd never been close or because he and my father nursed a deep distrust, to say nothing of hatred, of each other. Uncle Robert had always stood against my parents' marriage, especially in light of the unusually large dowry his father paid for my mother. The story is that her father and brother went to visit my father's parents, who after extended pleasantries over tea and pastries began discussing the terms of my mother's dowry. My uncle, her brother, thought that the amount asked was exorbitant. Her father did not argue, but took out a huge wallet from his breast pocket and paid the dowry in cash. My uncle never forgave my father.

When I was told this story years later, her father's gesture reminded me of the Egyptian who purchased our furniture on the spot: hand in breast pocket, bulging billfold, and agreed sum at the ready. In light of the speed with which her father paid the dowry, my father was persuaded that her old man couldn't wait to foist his daughter off on the first man stupid enough to ask for her hand. My parents' blissful marriage lasted less than a week, after which each realized the mistake, though neither would untie the knot. She refused to accept the dissolution of their marriage and would not grant him a divorce. He threatened to convert to Islam if only to send her back to her parents. She told him to go ahead. They separated but never signed any formal papers, or if they did, those papers stayed in Egypt and no one was the wiser. They lived the rest of their lives in irremediable discord and regretted they'd never divorced.

Still, my mother was overjoyed to hear of his imminent arrival. Perhaps this was why she decided that same night to call her brother to let him know that the man in her life was still in her life.

But there was a great deal of resentment between brother and sister. When I was finally able to place an international call using various go-between operators, my mother was in a feverish frame of mind. The more I spoke to him to tell him that we were finally settled in Rome, the more she interrupted, wanting to know how he was; when I said that he was well, she interrupted to ask about the rest of his family—they were all well, I said, making things up because it seemed obvious and easier. "Ask him!" So I asked him, because I could tell that he was hearing her ordering me to ask what was already his foregone reply. Yes, everyone was well. Then came my mother's first little dig: why hadn't he written to her all these months? And then came the second dig: the last she'd heard from him was his Christmas card— which, by the way, had arrived in February. "Tell him!" I conveyed her complaint, because she was growing increasingly louder and hot-tempered. "I'll send her a card in December this time," he said. "Better yet, why don't you all come for Christmas this year?" And how were we supposed to do that? she asked, this time almost reproaching him for inviting her when, she explained, still louder, we hardly had enough money to buy food at the end of each month given Claude's puny allowance. "Ask your husband for money"—his turn to aim a tiny dart at his sister—"or has he robbed you of everything already?" I communicated this to my mother, while I could hear my aunt, sitting

next to her husband in their Paris apartment, telling him not to speak
that way to the son. "Leave my husband alone," said my mother, "he
could be in jail even as we're speaking." "But isn't that where he already
belongs?" came her brother's immediate second dart. "Stop it, Robert," came his wife's echo, which I heard. "I'm just telling the truth,"
continued my uncle, clearly speaking to me and not just through me
to my mother. "After all he's done to make their marriage a living
hell, she still sticks up for him." I kept quiet and did not add fuel to
a fire that was already crackling between them. My mother was so
enraged with my silence, which was basically censoring information
that would have made her boil over, that in a fit of rage she banged
first her fist and then her head against the wall. "Tell him he's always
been a fat clown." I censored this outburst too. But my censoring her
exercised her even more. A dead silence fell between them. This, I realized, was how my mother quarreled with everyone. Of all the people
she'd known, the only one with whom she had never quarreled was
Aunt Flora. Everyone else she had quarreled with, from her mother,
who everyone agreed was a saint, down to the lowliest maid, to say
nothing of the butcher in the marketplace who had even threatened
to slit her throat if she ever showed her face again in his shop. "Tell
him I miss him very much," she then said. I didn't need to pass on her
message; he heard it. "I miss her too," he added. He might have been
lying, I thought, but she wasn't, unless he came from the same place
as she, where loudmouthed frenetic bickering was the language of
the heart. "When is her husband coming to Italy?" he asked. I knew
the answer and said, "In ten days." My mother read my lips: "What
is happening in ten days?" I told her that Dad was coming to Italy.
"Why did you need to tell him that? It's none of his business."

My uncle said that this family *désaccord* warmed his heart but that
it was time to end a conversation that was probably costing us an eye.
"Better to speak in person when you come at Christmas. I may be able
to obtain an apartment close by." He said he couldn't wait to see us. I
said I couldn't wait to see him too. No doubt we were both lying.

Uncle Robert, nicknamed Tonton Robert, had left Egypt ten years earlier and had had a chance to find a position as a professor who had doctoral students both in France and in the United States. My father was still stuck in Egypt. Would he ever be able to rebuild his life? I did not know. Would he make us rich again? I hoped he would, and so did my mother. Uncle Claude had said he wasn't a real businessman. Why wasn't he a real businessman? I asked, never having heard anyone criticize my father's commercial acumen. "Because some strike when the iron is hot; others wait for it to cool."

~

No one had foreseen that Uncle Claude would not be available to meet my father in Naples. Though he knew Italian well, I feared that my father might not know how to handle his legion of suitcases, the refugee camp, the train to Rome, the taxi from Termini to Via Clelia. I'd never known him to have taken any form of public transportation.

As it turned out, my father was not unwilling to spend a few days in the refugee camp, perhaps to be alone for a while. I was surprised to learn, when eventually I did speak to him by phone once he'd landed in Naples, that he didn't mind the camp at all. He hadn't been alone in years, he said; why not give himself some time? Besides, he hadn't been living with us for several years and didn't hide his reluctance— but don't tell your mother!—to live with her again. I did understand, didn't I? he asked. I did understand. But I wasn't sure that I should, I said. But how could I not understand? I didn't answer. "Just don't judge, and never take sides, especially when it comes to a couple. Besides, you're old enough to live your own life, not your parents'." He'd never spoken like this to me before and it moved me.

When I asked him how life was in the refugee camp, he said it was fine. There was this Libyan-Italian woman who was happy to show him the camp. He'd been around Naples with her, he liked Naples, loved the Archaeological Museum, which he'd been eager to visit all his life, and now was as good a time as any, wasn't it? Yes, I agreed, though sensing that it would upset my mother if she could hear. The people who worked in the office at the camp recalled their hasty encounter with the man whom they still referred to with the honorific title *il dottore*. How was *il dottore*? Still terrifying? he asked, using the word he'd often used when describing the wolf in "Little Red Riding Hood." Just the same old *pezzo di merda*, I said. That bad? No, worse, I replied. I could hear him smiling as he said, "He's a big buffoon."

I found comfort in these words but I feared they might bring about a skirmish between the two men, and this was something I wanted to avoid. I knew my father's temper, just as I knew my mother's, and together they were incessantly at war. But I'd seen how my mother had instinctively cowered before Claude, and the last thing I wanted, besides a tussle of wills between the two combustible men, was to see my father compelled to shrink before his uncle, who would seize the opportunity to humiliate him.

Days later, Uncle Claude picked my father up at Stazione Termini and drove him to our home. We embraced my father several times, and each time I hugged him I tried to determine what the strange smell was that I couldn't associate with the man I'd known growing up. When I finally did ask, he confessed that everyone in the camp smoked tons of cigarettes. Did he? No, of course not—well, just a few, so as not to stand out too much, as that, too, would have been a problem. He needed to blend in. There were a lot of Poles in the camp, and they were not to be trusted, so it was better to look like them than to wear his trusted Zimmerli undershirts. We all laughed.

When Uncle Claude left soon after, we were all four finally together, which is when my mother couldn't resist breaking the news. Her sister and her brother-in-law from New York had written two days earlier to announce their arrival in two weeks. They hadn't seen each other in almost a decade. The sisters were extremely close and wrote to each other at least once a week, back and forth across the Atlantic, with pictures of us and of my cousins. Couldn't she have delayed their visit by a few more weeks? asked my father. "You know how they are," she said; her whirlwind sister imposed her whims on everyone. They had already bought their tickets for the only day Pan Am had seats available for Rome. My father didn't really seem to mind, though I remembered he had disliked his American brother-in-law no less than my mother's brother in Paris. In which hotel were they going to stay? asked my father. My mother didn't even hesitate. Here, she replied. "But is there room for them here?" I was going to give up my room and sleep in the living room, which had become my brother's bedroom and which was where—I couldn't resist adding—my uncle's so-called prestigious clients sat drinking espresso while waiting their turn. My father wasn't sure he understood the reference. This was not really a home for regular people, my mother added. What kind of people, then? asked my father. The kind who spend at most an hour and then disappear. My brother, who knew the ins and outs of the neighborhood better than I, couldn't help but laugh and explained there were two aging examples of the profession down our block. My father finally got my brother's meaning. "So is this where we'll be living?" he asked, amused, baffled, and horrified. "Yes, here," said my brother, laconic as ever.

The two men must have spoken on their way from Termini to Via Clelia. Uncle Claude had rescued some of the money that had been stolen by my father's once-trusted courier. Claude had been a very deft lawyer, but my father needed clarity and Claude was being evasive about the measures he'd taken to recoup some of the stolen funds. My father was reluctant to expand on the matter until he was in possession of more accurate facts—these were not and would never be forthcoming.

My father was pleased to see that I was busy setting the table for supper that night. Knife on the right, fork on the left, and since Mother was preparing soup, a soup spoon to the right of the knife, plus four napkins. Before supper, my father said he wanted to take a shower, and asked me to bring two clean towels. But I did not know where my mother kept the towels. I asked my brother, but he didn't know either. When I asked her, she replied half-distractedly, "Where the towels always are." It was then that my father gave us both a quick, sharp look that cut through the joyful feeling I was hoping might last the evening. "So this is how you've been helping out?" he asked after my mother had told him how much she appreciated our giving her a hand in managing household affairs. "Who washes the dishes every day?" he asked. "She does." "And who does the laundry?" "She does that too." "And who mops the floor?" "She." And I did what exactly? he finally asked. "They do what they can," she interrupted, handing him two clean towels with a hasty, dismissive gesture that seemed to say, *Happy now?*

⌒

I liked when my father and I used to sit together and talk, just talk, about books. I liked being treated like an adult. I told him that in my spare time I'd read the diary he'd kept as a young man when he was just a few months older than I was. Why didn't he write, I asked him, why not start now? His answer never changed. In another lifetime, maybe, not now.

A week later, my father asked me to accompany him to meet someone. We took a bus to the meeting spot near Termini station, but we were to say we'd taken a taxi. We got into the man's Citroën DS and he drove us to a factory twenty minutes from the station. The man introduced himself as Antoine Chalabi and he spoke with a familiar Alexandrian French accent, though highly singsong, which betrayed his Syrian origin. He was like us, Jewish, though his family, unlike ours, did not speak Ladino and had, just as I suspected, come from Aleppo, as had my mother's father. By the way he gesticulated, smiled, and felt a constant need as he spoke to reach out and touch my father, who was sitting next to him in the car, I could tell that this man was of humble origin, despite his extremely well pressed beige cotton suit, the turquoise shirt with its sharp cutaway collar, and cuff links. Everything about him—his Dunhill cigarettes, his references to the Parioli district, where he lived, to say nothing of his car—bespoke wealth. My father had told me that in Alexandria the man had been a small-time owner of a shop for zippers, ribbons, buttons, men's underwear and women's brassieres, and all manner of notions. He had sought out my father in Alexandria about dyeing underwear. But my father had told him he only dyed spools of cloth, not individual items. And that was the end of that.

As Chalabi drove us to his factory, I heard his whole life story. He'd had the shrewdness to leave Egypt without telling anyone, not even his trusted second-in-command, who'd kept his books and been with him for almost twenty years. His underlings would most likely open his shop the next morning, find everything as they'd left it the previous evening, but Monsieur Chalabi (that's how he referred to himself) would be nowhere in sight. "And with good reason, don't you see?" he added. In fact, after bidding everyone good night the evening before, he and his family had sailed on the next ship to Bari. What he'd done on the sly for two long years, without the knowledge of his servant, who slept in a little room in the back of their tiny apartment, was to save his money in various hideaways at home along with the large bundles of bills that his father, a cobbler by profession, had given him before dying. He had to show there were funds in his bank accounts, and these he knew he'd have to forfeit and leave behind in Egypt once he'd made his getaway. Abroad, he was able to convert the cash he'd smuggled with him into foreign currency at a great loss, but he'd brought enough to make a new life for himself in Rome. His devious trick was to give his trusted servant of many decades an extended vacation to visit his dying mother in distant Upper Egypt, where he'd tend to her and stay with his two brothers and, with God's help, come back in two months to his old job at the Chalabi residence—"With God's help." He laughed, recalling the words he'd told his servant, who would eventually return to the Chalabi home, only to find it lined with furniture he'd never seen before and strangers sitting at an unfamiliar table drinking coffee, and realize that the Chalabis had left the country without even saying goodbye after he had given so many years of service both to them and to their parents. "That sits on my heart," said Antoine Chalabi, tapping his chest several times with a flattened palm. "But we needed to have the house to ourselves without letting on to my friends that we were leaving, without telling our children even, for fear they'd tell their friends at school, and of course without the intrusive gaze of our servant, who'd report us to the police in no time. We sent him away for his protection too, you see, so if questioned by the police about our whereabouts, he could say in all innocence that he was away visiting his mother."

Unbeknownst to his young children, who'd been told not to enter the living room where the suitcases were lying about, his wife undid the stitches binding the thick two-ply leather sides of each suitcase and stacked as many bills as she could ever so neatly between them, then restitched their double layers. Luckily they had his father's leather sewing machine, which they'd kept in the house without even foreseeing how vital it would turn out to be. So they managed to pack everything they owned, except for the furniture and the rugs. "And the sewing machine?" I asked. "Ah, your son is brilliant," he exclaimed, turning to smile at me with that huge Aleppo smile that I hadn't seen except on my grandfather. "We had to leave that old contraption behind. Still," he continued, talking to my father, "I was terrified that the noise would alert the neighbors. But you see now what comes of the extraordinary cunning that God gave me?" He turned around again as he drove to watch my reaction, beaming with self-satisfaction. "Except for our suitcases, we left everything in the house and were picked up by a small truck before dawn and driven to the port so as not to arouse the suspicion of the neighbors. Everything on the q.t.," he added, "that was my father's way, and it's been mine too. You'd be surprised at the trouble we had with the porters when we asked them not to bang the suitcases against the banisters in the stairway. One of the porters even asked me why we needed everything done so quietly, like thieves. I told them with anger on my face that I was not a thief, but that the neighbors would throw scenes of weeping and utter loud mournful cries that would scare our children. They pretended to believe me. But, *hamdulillah*, I paid these porters well. I am sure we were not the first or the last to leave in the middle of the night, and these good porters must have known why."

He hummed an Aznavour song as he drove his luxurious Citroën. "The irony is that even though the stitching was perfect, we needed to avoid any bulges in the leather, so we had to use more suitcases but we didn't own enough things to put in them. So my wife suggested I load them with underpants and brassieres." Did I know what *irony* meant? he asked. I said I knew. "The other irony, because there is always a second irony when you've already uncovered one"—he was clearly very happy with himself—"is that these pieces of underwear had to look as though they'd been used in case the people at the customs desk, suspecting contraband, would ask us why we were traveling with so many underpants and brassieres. I was scared to death. But I bribed them well beforehand, so none of our suitcases were even opened. I swear to you, *baruch hashem*," he said, finally reaching the end of his tale, "I didn't have a moment of peace until all the suitcases were on board, and until the ship raised its anchor." Momentary silence. "Until the ship raised its anchor." He clearly liked repeating this expression.

A longer silence followed. "We'll be there in five minutes," he added finally. Then, turning to my father, "You see, Monsieur Henri, we desperately need your expertise in our factory. But you will see for yourself. I don't want to be accused of forcing anyone's hand."

I could tell that my father disliked this man, with his trimmed and polished fingernails, his overpowering pine aftershave, and the treacly self-adulation punctuating his narrative every few minutes. But I refrained from exchanging a single complicit look with my father for fear it would arouse laughter in one or both of us.

The purpose of the visit that day was for my father to see the underwear factory. It produced budget underwear, mostly for popular department stores, but Italian boutiques liked the Egyptian cotton, which, unlike many of his Italian competitors, Chalabi was able to import from his remaining friends and former colleagues in Egypt and have shipped via Lebanon. "They still call it Egyptian cotton," he added, "but that no longer exists. But who's to know this?"

Once we stepped out of the car and took a look inside, I noticed that the factory was not very large and had big windows that allowed plenty of light to permeate the premises. Outside the building there were a few small trucks, while a foreman kept ordering people about as they loaded large corrugated boxes into them. The trucks read CHALABI & HANAN with a spunky colored logo that bore a yellow crown. The boxes boasted the same logo but without the colors. When we were escorted inside by the foreman, I saw there were about twenty or so men and women manning sewing machines. Not exactly artisanal, but still small enough to produce what I suspected was a good product. Chalabi led us into an office space where at one very large table sat a bookkeeper, a couple of secretaries, and a person who I assumed was mailing out batches of letters and invoices bearing the company's colored logo. In short, a thriving business. In a year's time, Chalabi explained, they were going to build a large annex where they planned to start dyeing men's underwear, since people these days liked colored underwear and brassieres. He smiled at my father and added, "Hint, hint, Monsieur Henri." They were also starting to export to Scandinavia and Brazil and Mexico, which would mean hiring at least ten new sewers. "We didn't go looking for these businessmen from South America, they came to us. And the good thing," he added, "*sono tutti ebrei comme nous, yaany*" (mixing French, Italian, and Arabic), they're all Jews like us, see?

Inside we were led to one of the two corner offices, one of which belonged to Mr. Hanan, clearly the other partner. Hanan, my father later told me, had owned a tiny cloth shop in one of the poorer neighborhoods in Alexandria. He wore a determined frown and was very formal, clearly not interested in pleasantries with me or for that matter with my father, though he made a passable show of goodwill when he let us into his office. His handshake was limp and wimpish, usually a sign that someone is either entirely duplicitous, deliberately rude, or just simply stupid. He, too, like his partner, didn't want to sound too pushy, started with a formulaic "We don't want to insist but we would surely welcome you among us." Then, surprising me, he asked about my hobbies and interests, but as I started to tell him, he was interrupted by one of the secretaries, who apologized to Signor Hanan but needed to pass on a client from Spain. Why did I think this was a choreographed interruption?

What my father hadn't told me—and he was right not to have

done so earlier, to avoid swaying my judgment—was that the two partners wanted him to join their company not as an employee in charge of
their dyeing works but as a partner who would oversee their unfledged
plans for the future. No more detours through Lebanon, they said,
no more waiting months for deliveries. The man who would head all
dyeing and bleaching would be living in Rome, a car ride away from
the factory. Chalabi & Hanan would be responsible for the cutting and
sewing of all items—they were in fact already developing new articles
of clothing—while my father would be in charge of dyeing the cloth
before it was cut and sewn. "Simple," said Chalabi, opening up his big
smile. Hanan looked at his partner with a furrowed brow, as if to quib-
ble with the alleged simplicity of things, but he went along with the
latter's version for the benefit of the newcomer. "*Yallah, Monsieur Henri,
tout marche ici, non è vero?*" he said in Arabic, French, and Italian—a
desperate attempt at good fellowship among tight comrades who spoke
the same language and were only too glad to bridge the divide that had
once stood between them in Egypt. Translation: Come on, Monsieur
Henri, everything works here, no? The contrived geniality was unmistakable, if only by its false note.

He took us around the factory, where my father was sincerely impressed by the way everything was set up, from the main office down
to the factory workers and the intake and delivery areas, all perfectly
scrubbed and clean—thanks to Hanan's desire to keep everything
streamlined and neat. To prove the efficiency of how things were
done, Chalabi gave one of the workers a piece of cloth and within
minutes he produced a man's T-shirt, which Chalabi grabbed and
handed over to me. It was perfect and clearly my size.

Chalabi's good fellowship lasted all through the morning until he
drove us back to an area I liked best, around Piazza del Popolo, from
which I planned to show my father parts of the city I was familiar
with—Baroque and Renaissance buildings and my favorite bookstores. Chalabi said he'd have loved to have us over for lunch but not
today, as his wife wasn't well, and was resting—"Women, what can
you do? But another time, real soon," he added.

When the doors of Chalabi's white Citroën closed behind us and my father and I were out on the sidewalk, I still holding the paper bag with my new undershirt, my father asked me, "Well, what did you think?" He said he was to see the partners within a week's time to tell them whether he was interested in joining their firm, but meanwhile he wanted to know my opinion.

My verdict was personal. This was what he wanted, he said. I felt that it was strange he'd want an opinion from his withdrawn, quiet son who had a very flimsy knowledge of the outside world, and even less of business. But I knew he trusted me. He wanted a reaction, possibly because he didn't always trust his own judgment. Still, I relished that my opinion mattered.

The men would obviously ask him to join their company as a partner, and to join he'd have to contribute a hefty amount of money, correct? Correct. But what would happen once they learned every dyeing technique he had perfected over the years? Why would they need him then? Or, put otherwise, what reason would he have to trust them if, at that point in a year or two, they decided to dissolve the partnership? Would they give him his money back? And where would we be without that money? More to the point, I added, if he did join their partnership, we'd be committed to staying in Italy. Was this what he wanted?

"Clearly you don't."

"I'm not sure," I replied.

"I don't know either," said my father.

Plus, I added, I didn't like either of them.

The fact is that neither of us trusted them. "Two skunks trying not to pass for foxes," said my father.

He had never really liked dealing with men like them. To him they remained small-time shopkeepers who'd made a point of looking poor and who lived miserable, frugal lives the better to elude the eye of the Egyptian government out to seize the assets of anyone who seemed remotely well-off. Besides, they spoke Arabic at home, said my father, which is why he had never traveled in their circle and wouldn't have known them had they not reached out to him. They knew French the way Madame Renato knew French or I knew Arabic—you picked it up but you didn't know it. Their French was riddled with mistakes. As was their Italian. They were, he finally said, not without laughing, two brachycephalic fops. Hadn't I noticed how flat the backs of their heads were? I hadn't.

Turkish Jews always made fun of Syrian Jews because of that. My father said he wouldn't be able to look at the two of them without wanting to laugh. The truth is that my father feared these two because he knew he'd never outsmart them. Maybe Uncle Claude wasn't wrong about him.

⁓

Two weeks later marked the arrival of my aunt and her husband from New York. My uncle Mischa had left Egypt in 1957, probably with very, very little money. As soon as he settled in the Bronx, he found a job as a forklift operator for a trucking company, then as a clerk in a shoe store, and finally as a traveling salesman for secondhand sewing machines. Within a few years he had amassed quite a bit of money, had become a Freemason, gotten to know several influential people affiliated with Freemasonry, and in no time managed to buy an apartment on the Grand Concourse. Two years later, he sold the apartment and purchased a four-story home elsewhere in the Bronx. He became an itinerant salesman of toys whose bookkeeping was as much a mystery as was the provenance of his toys. He claimed that they were made somewhere in New York State, but they were most likely made somewhere in Asia.

My brother and I went to the airport in Rome to meet them and, on seeing them outside passport control, helped with their luggage and took them by cab to Via Clelia. Originally, they had planned to stay in a hotel, but my mother insisted they stay with us.

The first thing my uncle did after seeing Via Clelia and the neighborhood was to sit on what was now his bed and, having removed his shoes and facing my mother and me, say that this was not a life, we had to move to New York.

I wonder why it had never occurred to me, or for that matter to either of my parents, that ours was not a life. For two months now the three of us had been spinning our wheels in Rome and couldn't see that this wasn't a life. Perhaps my father's presence in Italy would change this; he kept talking of trying to find various *débouchés*, as he liked to call them—not opportunities exactly, as much as outlets that could lead somewhere. But my mother had immediately grasped the prospect of living near her sister as the ultimate solution to all our problems. My father did not think too highly of New York; instead, his hopes were set on Britain, Switzerland, and ultimately France, where we had far more relatives than anywhere else and where he felt culturally at home. My grandmother was for the time being already living in Paris, and Paris seemed to be the unequivocal solution for all of us, myself included. My mother had nothing against Paris, where her brother lived, but it was life with her sister and the irresistible exotic lure of New York City that had set her mind and my brother's spinning.

Ironically, the very next day Uncle Claude had arranged to introduce my father to someone at his golf club who might be useful in helping him find the kind of *débouché* he was hoping to find in Italy. I was also invited to that lunch. On hearing of the luncheon, Uncle Mischa told Uncle Claude that he'd love to join us, adding, with an awkward smile, that he had even brought a white tuxedo jacket should the dress code require it. Uncle Claude replied that the white tuxedo jacket would have been appropriate for more formal occasions but that this was a rather difficult meeting that had taken some time to arrange and that a third adult in the group would throw it off balance, while a younger person might serve to defuse and lighten the tension. In Uncle Claude's opinion, Uncle Mischa, with his salesman's garrulousness, would simply not be appropriate at his glamorous golf club.

The biggest irony that day was that Uncle Claude's contact had left a message apologizing that he was unable to join us for lunch given a pressing engagement.

So the three of us had lunch together. I had my first-ever *prosciutto e melone* appetizer that day and didn't understand the combination: I liked melons and prosciutto but not together. The meal consisted of pasta, slices of beef with peas, followed by strawberries. In short, more or less exactly the same meal as the one we'd had at his home on the night of the *convegno*. He said he avoided butter and fat, which I knew, and that he liked his Rosatello, which I also knew. Then he made a few jokes, one of which was quite bawdy. I had never known him to favor humor of any sort, especially when it was obscene, but in my father's presence he let down his guard and turned out to have quite a boyish, prankster side. Still, despite his loud laughter, which was a touch on exhibit for the other club members sitting out on the same patio, something like a shadow would come to veil his eyes. Something was troubling him, I could tell. He hadn't forgotten the lawyer whom we were to meet and made subsequent arrangements to have him meet my father. But these meetings were repeatedly postponed or canceled at the last minute, which my father always forgave. Uncle Claude's final reaction was a blistering handwritten note mailed to the lawyer's office. *Your cancellation the first time was totally understandable, the second time a bit less, but still forgivable, the third was an insult to my nephew, and ultimately to me. This behavior does not reflect the spirit of our club or the way we encourage club members to behave with each other, CC.*

Claude was extremely happy with his note and shared it with all of us. He read it aloud twice and then one last time in French and very slowly for my mother's benefit. Uncle Mischa thought that the behavior of the club member was entirely reprehensible but that in New York a committee would be formed to ask him to take his golf clubs elsewhere. "Italy is far more direct," replied Claude. "The man resigned from the club the very afternoon he received my note." "That's because you have a good grasp of the democratic process," said Uncle Mischa. "No, that's because we've had too many dictators. Sometimes a dictator brings about instant solutions." "But they also bring wars." "True, very true," conceded Uncle Claude. Both men decided there was no point in arguing, as both were right. Democratic process is transparent, or claims to be, but frequently leads to war. As for dictators, they invariably end up killed.

That same week all of us, with the exception of my father, visited the HIAS office in Rome for an exploratory meeting. HIAS, the Hebrew Immigrant Aid Society, which had helped my uncle and my aunt settle in America, offered to help start the paperwork for our immigration. Since my mother's sister and her husband were offering to sponsor us, the procedure seemed simple enough in those years. Besides, one of the officers in the HIAS bureau said that the times were propitious, so it was necessary to move quickly. My mother's sister had had the presence of mind to ask her to bring her passport and ours—*one never knows*. My father, they said, would have to sign his own papers. The official added that she wouldn't be surprised if by early January we were settled in New York.

I was elated by my aunt's promises. She said that she and her husband would be happy to sign all manner of financial guarantees to help speed the process. Thanks to his Freemason contacts, my uncle was going to ask for the help of a highly placed legislator who was sure to move things faster still.

Thinking of our prospects, I suddenly felt differently about the city and about the language I was hearing spoken on Via Clelia. I was, it seemed, already an American on an extended temporary stay in a city called Rome, whose people, values, and customs had never been mine. Uncle Claude, the vendors in the marketplace, the ceaseless prattle of television sets resounding till late at night, Madame Renato's unstinting screeds, and the two dowdy prostitutes who'd raise the rolling shutters after six every evening, meaning *open for business*, all had started to shed from me like an alien scent that was at best tawdry but tolerable, and at worst hideous.

I knew that Americans were no less foreign to me than my complicated Mediterranean culture was to Americans, but I spoke their language and indeed had grown to like their language, their candor, their ease in so many things, where informality was the rule, not the exception. Italy, by contrast, was twisted, ineffectual, and, to my young mind, incurably paltry.

~

Uncle Mischa opened a new world to us. It started with his grilled cheese sandwiches in the morning, which he asked my aunt to make for us as well. Then came his gift of fifty dollars for my brother and me, more money than we'd ever held in our lives. "In a week, you can easily earn seventy-five dollars in New York." We were seduced. In five years, he told us, he had become entirely American. In the bathroom, after he showered, his Dial soap left a wholesome scent that confirmed his promise of a buoyant life among the skyscrapers. Dial soap, like his bottle of Listerine and his Aqua Velva aftershave, smelled of nothing you'd ever find in nature; it was entirely artificial, but then, that is what America proclaimed in those years: that artificial was far better than natural, that America was the ur-fantasy humanity had dreamed of in Ancient Athens but was unable to reach until dental floss, ketchup, and Ex-Lax came to the rescue. The best of Earth was being not restored, not renewed, not even refitted, but thoroughly reinvented to suit a new, state-of-the-art, cutting-edge version of mankind. After Uncle Mischa was done showering, which he did every day, which also meant that the person eager to shower after him would have to wait half an hour for the water to reheat, the bathroom exuded cleanliness, uplift, and moral rectitude. Some of it did not jibe with the man we'd once known him to be in Egypt, but it stirred us because, like his artificial products, America was a place where one could scrape off the old and spruce oneself anew, sometimes with as simple a thing as Head and Shoulders shampoo and Preparation H.

This was the world that was being promised us the moment my

mother had signed papers at the HIAS office. All my father needed to do was to bring his passport and fill out his papers too.

My father was not eager to go to America. Whereupon a major quarrel erupted between my parents, into which Uncle Mischa and Aunt Rebecca had the wisdom not to intrude. My father still wanted to explore all manner of *débouchés* in Europe and was already planning to visit his many relatives in France, Britain, and Switzerland. There was even talk of visiting a relative in Milan, Claude's brother, whom my father had never met and who had left Egypt in the late twenties, never to return. That great-uncle, whom I was never to see in my life, had changed his surname during the time of the racial laws in Italy, acquiring one that, in typical family fashion, was more recognizably Jewish than the one he was born with.

Later that summer my father did go to the HIAS office and did fill out the requisite papers, though even then he hadn't given up on Europe. Several opportunities had beckoned, and he felt he'd be irresponsible if he didn't answer their call. He'd always nursed a dislike for America, which seemed a chilly, strange, uninviting planet where people chewed gum and drank too much beer. With the possible exception of Spain and Portugal, the capital of the world was still Western Europe. Our ancestors, he was in the habit of saying, hadn't fared well in Spain. They hadn't fared well in Egypt either, and we were all, according to him, paying the price for disobeying the eleventh commandment: *Stay out of Egypt*. My father didn't have to remind his uncle about Italy. Claude had narrowly escaped Mussolini's agents after he and his brother had served in Mussolini's government.

My father was a confluence of contradictions. On one hand, he wanted us to stop attending the Italian summer program—which was his way of saying that we were not going to stay in Italy for long—but he wanted us to attend an American school in Rome, though he wasn't really serious about moving to the United States. He was constantly vacillating between options he never favored and favoring contraries he couldn't reconcile. He called it his Alexandrian demon—his way of giving a deeper cast to a desire to snuggle between opposites so as never to decide anything. Eventually, he remembered that the principal of our American school in Egypt had recommended the Overseas School in Rome, so that it made sense to apply there as well, with St. George's as the fallback.

To my father's mind, fallbacks were always necessary, especially if one couldn't decide. There was always another option, carefully cultivated yet put on hold, just in case the one that seemed more likely fell through. In either case, he preferred to let fate decide. You blamed fate so as not to blame yourself.

A week after my father signed the application form with HIAS, he decided to take my brother and me to visit the Overseas School, located beyond the Ponte Milvio neighborhood on Via Cassia, the northernmost end of Rome, while Via Clelia abutted the city's southern periphery. The principal was exceptionally cordial, the person in charge of admissions was clearly eager to have us, even though I was coming in as a senior to their school and would be staying for only a year. As for the woman who asked my father to fill out a short application, she was so receptive that my father was persuaded she was attracted to him, which, to my embarrassment, occasioned the partial deployment of his charms, hardly an uncommon practice in Egypt.

But the news was not good. The tuition was expensive and my father felt that we could not afford it. The principal asked if we had other options. "Yes," answered my father, "St. George's. But this is not really a *happy* option." I had no idea why my father considered it an *unhappy* option, but he must have sensed that we'd grown used to the American system and wanted us to continue in that vein. "There is another school in Rome that might provide some financial aid." My father asked which one. Notre Dame International School. It was a Catholic school, but the Brothers of the Holy Cross were very modern and exceptionally open-minded. "It's a very good school."

So long as it was an American school, I was happy.

I was expecting my father to take us there as he'd done with Overseas. But that August he was already planning to travel to England

and then to Switzerland. He sounded like a multinational business-man handling all manner of arcane ventures, and I was proud of him. It made me feel that we were on the cusp of things that were bound to rectify our precarious status. I had gone so far as to think that even if we stayed in Rome while he found a venture elsewhere in Europe, we'd move to a better neighborhood and, if need be, perhaps put the United States on hold for a while. My father left by airplane for Milan. It was his first time on a plane.

The problem now was how to visit Notre Dame. Aunt Flora, who would have been ideal for visiting the school with us and speaking to the principal, was unable to accompany us there, as she had been asked to visit her company's Venice office for at least a week. The other possibility was for Uncle Claude to take us, but he, too, was out of town, this time at the baths of Chianciano. The only option therefore was to go with my mother, but since she couldn't speak, I'd have to do the talking for her. My job, as my mother explained to me, was to see if we were still in time to be admitted and secondly to ask for a reduction in the cost of tuition. Actually, I had better not ask whether it was too late to apply, as they might say yes. "Just say we're refugees from Egypt, and speak American to them." My mother made the two of us wear ties, but not jackets. It was too hot for ties, I objected. "Wear a tie," she said. She was in one of her moods that morning.

Our bus itinerary, as Grazia explained it to me, was going to be complicated. She thought we had to take several buses, but she wasn't sure. She'd have to ask her brother, who came upstairs that same evening to explain the bus routes. Ideally, I thought, a taxi would have been easier, but taxis were out of the question. The first bus, he said, would take us to Termini, which I'd already assumed; the second, across the Tiber to the Vatican, where we'd have to change for a third bus, which in its turn would take us to a small neighborhood beyond the Vatican, where we'd have to take yet another bus that would take us to Via Aurelia, an old Roman road that led out of the city to the school.

It was a boiling hot weekday, and after about an hour we finally crossed the Tiber and arrived at the Vatican. There we had to find the third bus. I had forgotten the number of the bus, and my brother couldn't remember it either, so I asked someone who looked as though he'd know which bus took us to Via Aurelia. This seemingly simple question was nothing more than a ruse on my part to have this person remind me of the number of the third bus that I'd forgotten. With complete self-assurance, he told us to get a bus that ended up taking us back across the Tiber. I gasped when I realized we were headed back where we'd just come from. We got off and decided to walk back to the Vatican in the blistering heat. Once back and drenched in sweat, with my mother screaming all manner of names at the two of us, I found an empty tobacco store where I hoped the owner might send us in the right direction. I remember his gum-taped glass counter where a tiny fan sat struggling meekly to cool his very dark, shabby, dun-colored store. The old gentleman pointed outside at a deserted gray sidewalk awash in litter and noonday glare. No one in his right mind would even think of standing there. When I asked the old *tabaccaio* why the stop was empty, he said because the bus must have just left. The next bus would most likely come in twenty minutes.

This was Rome all right.

So we waited under the heat with our heads uncovered. I wanted to wait across the street in the shade, but my mother told me not to move in case the bus came. The sun gave me headaches, I said. Not today it won't, she snapped. She was seething; she couldn't understand why I hadn't followed Grazia's brother's instructions, and now here we were boiling, boiling, she started to shout. I could tell that things were not going to get any better, so I tried to distance myself from her, which was also why I wanted to move across to the shade. But this made matters worse. "Don't run away from me. You belong in kindergarten—not remembering the bus number. Why didn't you jot it down?" A moment of silence. Then she began to yell at my brother for always relying on me and never taking charge of anything, because we were both irresponsible, ir-re-spon-si-ble. The yelling got worse.

She was no longer scolding us; she had become near-demented and was suddenly shrieking at the top of her lungs. A girl my age was passing by and, staring at me, seemed to ask why this madwoman was screaming at me. Then she must have realized this was my mother. Others also turned around and were looking at us. I wanted to disappear. Forget school, just slink away, take the first bus and never see her again.

"Don't you move!"

I didn't move.

"People are looking," I said.

"Let them look."

She could cook, she finally said, she could mop, she could iron, she could sew and wash our sheets, but school was not her spe-cial-ty, not her spe-cial-ty, couldn't I see that? It was her husband's. And where was he? "He's abandoned us, a-ban-doned me." And finally came her one word that expressed her inexorable, irredeemable, and unyielding despair, "*Pouwah?*" repeated several times, "*Pouwah?*" and finally yelped out, "*Pouwaaaah?*" She was saying it to us, to her husband, to everyone, to God Himself. No one would understand. But in her pronunciation, she was saying *Pourquoi?* Why? Why had things come to this, why?

My mother was delirious. She was on the verge of tears, and for the first time in my life I understood how desperate and lonely she was.

Looking at her, my brother was about to cry too.

And I knew that if he started to cry, there'd be no stopping me either.

So I lied and said our bus was coming. It was not our bus, but eventually our bus did come and the bus driver said he'd let us know when to get off but that we had to cross the street. A few stops later, the bus driver honked to a bus driver across the way, to ask him to wait for us. As we thanked him, mother gave him a silent but expansive smile, and we crossed the street as instructed to catch the other bus that had waited for us.

The new bus driver said it would take five minutes. He knew the school and the bus would drop us at the closest stop. It would require a three-minute walk to the school grounds. But the walk took ten minutes. My mother, that day, had decided to wear high heels, which slowed us down. On the tiny bus, she'd been seething but had controlled herself. When we reached our stop, she exploded again, saying, "*Yalla, yalla, fil madrassah*," to school. But she was yelling in her broken Arabic, not even in French.

When we reached the school, she said I should raise the knot of my necktie, as it had slid down when I'd unbuttoned my shirt. I had hoped she wouldn't notice. She also told my brother to tuck his shirt in, as it was slipping out of his trousers. I pulled mine as well by digging into both my pockets and reaching for the shirttail, hoping that no one saw me from the school windows.

When we reached the main office, we were told to wait for Brother Peter. Several brothers of the Holy Cross could be seen rushing about the corridor, all looking very busy, wearing long black cassocks; one was twirling his braided rope cincture, speaking to what looked like a student, while another was walking out of his office carrying a box with both hands while holding a loose sheet of paper between his lips. Strangely, I saw another brother coming out of an office, also with a sheet of paper between his pursed lips. I suddenly pictured a procession of men in cassocks all prancing about with a sheet of paper held between their lips.

One of the brothers asked if we were waiting to see him. I nodded, figuring that it would help move things along if I said yes. "I am Brother Peter," he said, leading us into his office. He asked the three of us to sit down, but there were only two chairs, leaving me to stand behind my brother, who was already seated. Crossing his lank arms almost timidly, skinny Brother Peter bid us good morning and asked why we had come to the school.

He was facing my mother as though expecting her to explain her reason for being there. This is when, for the first time in my life, I said I was speaking in her stead because she was deaf. Maybe I said this because there was no point in hiding the truth, or maybe I felt that the situation required candor, something I hadn't been taught and wasn't particularly good at. One didn't exactly lie in my family, but one obfuscated the truth, and I didn't want to obfuscate. As soon as I told him about my mother, I also found myself telling him we were Jewish refugees from Egypt, as if my mother's deafness and being Jewish were in some strange way connected. I should have weighed my words more carefully, as I was, after all, in a Catholic school, where I was certain Jews were not exactly welcome. But what I felt as soon as I uttered both truths was a sense not just of release from a silence I'd kept for who knows how many years in Egypt but of exhilaration in being reminded for the first time that perhaps I was no longer a child, bashful about my mother's impairment, but a young man who might still have things to hide from others, just not those bearing on his mother, his religion, or his parents' marriage. My father wasn't living with us, and I could tell that Brother Peter must have understood the reason, which was why he didn't even ask about my father.

Brother Peter taught me that I had chosen the right path. He then told us that I would be a senior now, my brother a sophomore. It seemed so unpredictably simple. I translated all this to my mother. She seemed relieved by the news. So there was room for us? Yes, there was, I relayed after passing her question to Brother Peter. "My mother also asks if the school would reduce our tuition?" I was making it clear that the indelicate question had come from my mother, not from me.

He did not look surprised, but listened attentively, and then fingered the keys of his adding machine with such alacrity that he seemed possessed by a demon. The machine labored, then spat out something that he read by squinting his eyes, then he shook his head as though disagreeing with its oracular pronouncement and started fingering the keys with yet more vehemence and speed until the machine obediently yielded new results that seemed to concur with what he had in mind. "We can't go beneath twenty-five thousand lire per month for each of you." We stood perplexed. My father had agreed with my uncle that we would live on one hundred and fifty thousand lire per month after paying our rent, the equivalent at the time of two hundred and fifty dollars. That was to include food, doctors' bills, medicine, electricity, gas, water, laundry, and all manner of expenses. Brother Peter reminded us that the amount would include lunch and bus transportation, but not books, which we'd be able to purchase by coming to the school in ten days, when books would be available for sale.

Another brother who was passing by and walked into Brother Peter's office, as the door was left open—he was the one twirling his cord—introduced himself as Brother Joseph, shook our hands, and said that we would be happy at the school. No one had ever spoken about happiness in any school before. I figured he was lying or was simply trying to be kind, which made me suspicious. He noticed that I had spoken with my mother without using my voice and must have inferred she was deaf. He looked me straight in the eye, nodded, then, turning to my brother, asked point-blank, "So, are you intelligent?"

I couldn't understand where such a question was coming from. No one who suspects he might be intelligent thinks, much less says, he is intelligent. But I had no idea what my brother would say. Yes, that he was intelligent? No, that he wasn't? He surprised me. "People say I might be, but they could be wrong," he said. This was positively brilliant and to the point and yet, given the circumstances, so jesuitically evasive that I was tempted to applaud.

Brother Joseph mulled the answer and seemed to approve. "Good answer," he finally said, and walked out.

Brother Peter told us that Brother Joseph liked to ask that question. It brought out an aspect of character that wasn't always visible at interviews.

So where did we live? asked Brother Peter. I told him it was around the Alberone district. This troubled him somewhat. The closest place that one of the school buses could pick us up would be at Piazza della Repubblica, about a five-minute walk from Termini. Did that work for us? Without giving the matter another thought I simply answered yes. He looked over a printed sheet at the side of his desk and said that the bus would pick us up at seven twenty every morning. Classes started at eight fifteen. The bus, he continued, never waited for people who were late.

I smiled courteously, and seeing I was smiling, my mother did the same. My brother hardly said a word. He was still under the spell of Brother Joseph's question. Later, he asked if he had answered correctly. I told him he was brilliant. Socrates couldn't have done better.

But the bus route struck a note of terror in me. A hasty estimate told me that we'd have to leave the house at six forty in the morning to be at Termini no later than seven ten, which meant that I would have to wake up at six every morning—until, I kept thinking, our papers for the United States came through. If, that is, they ever did.

On leaving the school grounds I was grumbling, and my mother, seeing I was upset, was beside herself. My brother also lost it with me. This was supposed to be good news, and here I was complaining—as always, he added.

As we waited on the opposite sidewalk for the bus that was taking forever to come, my mother changed her tune. It was good we hadn't given up on the school, she said. She was proud of me. She was proud of how Brother Peter had listened to me. What had I told him, what had he told me? I told her that I'd said she was deaf. Was that necessary? she asked. Yes, it was good to spell things out sometimes, to be frank, and put the few cards we had on the table. My brother couldn't resist. I was romanticizing again.

What never crossed my mind or my brother's was that not a penny of all our monthly expenses would go to anything our mother wanted to buy for herself. Had I thought she was aware of this? I didn't want to know. Fortunately, the thought was summarily pushed aside and didn't occur to me for a long time.

— 5 —

Roundtabling

Despite the good news, after traveling on eight buses that day, we were so exhausted that my mother decided we should have a late lunch at a small trattoria on the corner of Via Clelia and Via Tuscolana. We had passed by it numberless times but never thought to walk in. It was three in the afternoon and we were starved, and without my father in Rome, our lives seemed hollowed and rudderless. We had no idea when he'd be back; we didn't feel like a family, which was a bit strange, since we'd not lived under the same roof with him for years. But he remained central to our lives, and in his absence, we felt like dislodged bolides wobbling about the universe without orbit. In his absence, my mother was more like a stand-in parent, a squall that erupted into incomprehensible tantrums and which a sudden flip of the switch brought to her senses. My brother had his friends, my mother hers, I had my books, but we all nursed somber thoughts that we'd take to bed at night, hoping that sleep would ultimately dispel them, which it did, though by early morning they still clamored to come out like dogs who need to be taken for a walk.

I followed my father's advice to read more classics, always the classics, but I knew that I was reading his books to stay close to him, to learn his tastes, his outlook, to speak to him though he was miles away. There were also other reasons. I was reading the books he suggested not so much to educate myself, or even to travel wherever a book would take me, I was reading to escape who I was, or who I had become, even if, by a strange coincidence, I was encountering in the very books meant to shield me from myself versions of people who were none other than myself, people whose shame, whose fears, whose sense of irony and tortured, twisted minds I instantly recognized because they were identical to mine. I liked authors who understood that human nature is essentially erratic, a fitful clot of insoluble paradoxes and contradictions. I might have wanted a me that books could alter somewhat, or restore, or improve upon, a me observed obliquely, as in a play, with better lighting, a touch of makeup, and a better costume—a done-over me. I borrowed their identity provided they were not in Italy, or at least not in today's Italy. Yet none came from a dying city like Alexandria, none had a deaf mother, none was Jewish, none was as stranded as I felt that day coming back from our school interview to have lunch on Via Clelia in a restaurant emptied of everyone.

As we ate our tagliatelle with light tomato sauce and grated parmesan cheese, my mother worried how we'd tell Uncle Claude, on his return from Chianciano, that we had countermanded not just one but two of his school directives. He'd probably throw a fit. My solution was deft, intentionally muddled and evasive, though seemingly conciliatory: "We could say that Father insisted we attend an American school." "And throw the blame on him?" said my brother with a reproachful tone that he always used whenever he thought I was, as he liked to say, romanticizing, embellishing, or being my unctuous old self. In his view, I lacked the courage to speak the truth. I thought I had overcome that weakness facing Brother Peter. Had I already lapsed hardly a few hours later? Uncle Claude would of course protest and ask why my father was thinking of America and American schooling if he was out looking for business opportunities in Europe.

The explanation was at best complicated and at the very worst incidental. In our last two years in Alexandria, we had made up a verb, named after the act of us all sitting at a round table—Father, Mother, Aunts Elsa and Flora, my grandmother, my brother, and I—to discuss future prospects, decisions, and plans. "We *roundtabled* last night after supper and arrived at nothing." "All we do is *roundtable* in this family." Indeed, on the night before my father left for Milan the four of us had *roundtabled* to determine the amount we needed to live on every month, which school to attend in case we had no luck with the second American school, what we needed to purchase, with the understanding that we could not invest in too many things because chances were we might have to resettle elsewhere—subject to subsequent roundtables, of course. Most everything depended on my father's prospects and what opportunities he'd be able to find. But it also depended on this one thing that had nothing to do with decisions or plans and depended almost exclusively on hope and hap.

My mother hated the thought of hanging about until something happened. She had no tolerance for tireless roundtables. But, she wondered, as we were finishing our lunch, how were we ever going to afford this latest school? We'd have to tell my father that school tuition would set us back by fifty thousand lire each month. We'd be lucky to afford a weekly movie and my weekly Penguin Classic. We'd have to tighten the belt some more. Plus, we needed to buy winter clothing. This was something that had been tossed back and forth when my father was around but remained unresolved. I tried to calm my mother down and reminded her that our visas for the United States might arrive soon. She seemed to believe me, and because she believed me, I believed what I'd told her.

My mother picked at her bread roll and decided we should have another glass of wine, to celebrate the school. I ordered three *calici* of the house white; it probably came from the nearby wine shop, except at twice the price. The owner of the restaurant brought us three glasses, but she was clearly grumpy. She was tired and we were the only customers at this late hour. She was already setting up for dinner. We were about to order dessert, but she put on a mournful face and said there weren't any desserts left. None of us believed her, but the pasta was very good, and though we felt pressured to empty our glasses and leave, this had turned into a happy day.

As we were leaving, my mother said she couldn't wait to get home to take off her shoes. Her feet were killing her. She apologized for losing her temper earlier that day; she didn't know what had come over her on the way to school. I reminded her of the brothers walking about with the sheets of paper held between dried lips, and we all laughed. Then the demon of mimicry seized her, and for no reason at all she imitated Brother Peter with a sheet of paper between his lips punching away at his adding machine with agitated zeal. My brother blew up laughing. The wine had gotten to his head. He kept repeating, "Are you intelligent? Are you intelligent? *Ma va' fa' un culo!*" he added in solid Romanaccio picked up from the boys he hung around with.

That same evening my father called to find out how the interview had gone and whether we'd been accepted. Yes, I replied, and noted that they'd also given us a significant discount but it still amounted to fifty thousand lire per month. What were we going to do? He didn't give it much thought. We should call and say that we accepted. "Call tomorrow morning first thing." I was surprised how quickly my father had decided in favor of this new American school. This wasn't like him. I was expecting to see the issue *roundtabled*.

Where was he calling from? I finally asked. He was in a hotel in Milan, where he planned to stay for a few more days before flying to London and then Geneva. Why Milan? my mother asked me to ask. Why Milan? I asked. "Because it is the financial capital of Italy and it makes sense for me to start here." My mother, I could tell, was about to have another meltdown. "He's in Milan to stay with that woman again." My father overheard her raise her voice. "Tell her this is not the time to discuss that." "This is not the time to discuss that," I said to her. "Of course it is the time," she insisted. "Tell your mother that this woman is married now." I relayed the message as it was told.

"How does he know she's married now?" He took a moment to gather his thoughts but did not answer.

As I was to find out soon enough from his own mouth, "this woman" had been the love of his life. He was happy for her, happy that she had found a good husband. "The man she married," he added, "is my spitting image." In his mind it meant that she continued to love him. *My portrait*, he used to call him during their subsequent four decades of international telephone calls.

"Try to calm your mother," he finally said to me. I told him that I would. I always did. "She's a difficult person," he added, "but she is still your mother." I wanted to tell him she was also his wife. I sensed he knew that this retort was sitting on the tip of my tongue and was grateful I hadn't brought it up.

My father and I had always been close. We thought alike and this scared me sometimes, because his silence with me, like mine with him, was a silence of what Dante called *intendimento*, of kinship and understanding. I did not want him to see through me, just as I feared seeing through him. But I was like him, and the characters I liked most in novels were like the two of us: transient, tentative, and irresolute. As with Flora, what kept us close was our silence, our persistent second guesses that undid everything we'd believed had been firmed up moments earlier, and above all our tact—while my mother had none. She was firm and unswerving.

And then it hit me why my father had been unusually hasty in reaching his decision about our school. He wanted to get off the phone. He was not alone in the hotel room.

Brother John, who picked up the phone when I called the next day, seemed so overjoyed that the Alexandrian kids who had come with their French-speaking mother had accepted admission to the school that I found his enthusiasm totally catching. I knew I'd be disabused soon enough and that I'd discover new things every day to hold against the school, but there was something uplifting in his welcome, which I knew was not entirely disingenuous.

A few days later we returned the red jackets to St. George's and, to our surprise, were paid back in full. Our next purchase in the weeks to come would have to be winter coats, said my mother. I couldn't go to school without a coat and worried that a new one might end up costing more than we could afford. I had a winter coat made two years earlier, but I'd outgrown it, especially when I wore a sweater and a jacket underneath. And the wool sport jackets we needed to comply with the school dress code were going to cost quite a bit too. We might have to hold off buying new jackets until October, after we'd paid the first month's tuition.

Our father called again the next evening. He had not left Milan. "Figures," said my mother. He listened to our clothing problem and suggested a possible solution. I could use his jackets, his shirts, his trousers, and his shoes, but not his suits. I couldn't have asked for more. But my father had a rather strange body: he was exceptionally short but with very broad shoulders. I had a bit of a tummy and narrow shoulders and was slightly taller. This meant that mother would have to alter his clothes. The trousers might have to be lengthened—there was enough cloth in each leg—especially if my mother added a cuff to hide the mark left by the retouched seam, and the wool jackets might have to be lengthened a half inch or so. This might throw off the balance of the side pockets with the flap of the jacket, but, in my mother's words, *à la guerre comme à la guerre!*

What troubled me was not that my mother would have to redo and alter so many of his clothes, but that I knew how attached my father was to his wardrobe. Everything he owned had been tailor-made for him, his shoes, his jackets, his trousers, his shirts, down to his gold cuff links, which he'd designed himself and told me I could use. To alter these lovely jackets made of imported wool woven by the finest houses in Britain was a crime, to say nothing of the shoes that he was resigned to forfeit and never wear again. The very surrender of his things told me that a part of him was already resigned not to matter any longer, that the things he liked could easily be taken from him and become someone else's. He was, in so many tiny invisible ways and without drama, already giving up on himself, on his future, while life, like an evil croupier, had begun raking the chips back, one by one. He, too, like Flora perhaps, was born lost, long before he made then lost his fortune.

But I didn't know this, and when I opened one of the closets in Via Clelia that housed his many suits, what always struck me was the plethora of lavish colored neckties hanging from tie racks he had designed and had had especially made by his favorite carpenter. What left me feeling guilty over and above my father's clothes and my mother's determination to alter them was his gold watch, which he gave me, saying that no young man my age should be without a watch. My brother had no use for a watch and didn't wear one until much later. My father had given me that same watch a year earlier but I had returned it to him before leaving Egypt, fearing that one of the Egyptian customs officials would seize it. Now it was mine again, he said. The problem was that it had brought me bad luck. I failed every exam and test I took in Egypt while wearing my father's watch. I knew that I was being ridiculously superstitious and that I was the only one to blame for not studying as I should. But I also had acquired enough knowledge of armchair psychology to suspect that this indictment of the watch was possibly a larger indictment of my father and everything he stood for. So I made a deal with the watch. I would wear it every weekday except on test and exam days. The following year this "deal" worked perfectly. I abstained from the watch on test days and never failed another test again.

My new school sent us a letter telling us to get our new books a week before the school year was set to start. My mother offered to join us on the two-and-a-half-hour, four-bus ride to school, but I discouraged her, saying the two of us knew what to do and were not children. She couldn't really understand why we didn't want her to go with us; I'd seldom done anything without her in Rome. But on the way we recalled how she had yelled from point A to point M and then again from N to Z. We laughed when we caught ourselves echoing the words she'd babbled in broken Arabic. We didn't have the courage to say it, but we were tired of having a mother. And as we were walking after exiting the fourth bus on the deserted path of Via Aurelia, my brother shouted the word *pouwaaaah!* and we both laughed.

Mother sensed we were trying to put some distance between ourselves and her. She had no way to explain why her sons had started to dodge her than by presuming we were ashamed of her deafness and preferred not to be seen with her. But we were ashamed not of her deafness but of her temper, though we were unable to tell the two apart. Our occasional aloofness, particularly when we wanted to do things together but without her, made her feel lonely and abandoned, and this sometimes brought out the worst in her.

My mother had told me once that she realized at a very young age that her older sister, who now lived in London, was always ashamed of her. This was not the case with her sister in New York or her brother in Paris. But then, her sister in New York was not too smart, she added, laughing, as though blaming her for not being ashamed—her beloved, silly sister who had escorted her to the HIAS office to make certain we applied to move to the States.

The silly sister had come to Rome with no other purpose in mind. She had looked up the address of the HIAS office and, as I later found out, had scheduled by telephone from New York an appointment with one of the officers to begin the immigration process for the four of us. She knew that her sister's marriage was floundering and was willing to host the three of us if my father was undecided about joining or found a way to *débiner*, to disentangle himself, when the time came. One afternoon when my father wasn't home, my aunt even confessed that she would rather he decided not to join us in New York and stayed in Europe. "Your mother is young enough to find someone else," she said. My mother had just turned forty, though I, at sixteen, already considered her an old lady. I said nothing, but a new man in her life, maybe even deaf like her, wouldn't be so bad. I gave the matter further thought but all I could imagine was my mother's first row with her new American husband. When she heard of the idea of this new marriage, Madame Renato brought down the house when she imitated two deaf spouses howling at each other with yelps, hisses, and squawks, all the while saying that she was going straight to hell for making fun of the deaf like this, raising the back of her hand against her mouth to atone for the full-throated guffaw exploding from deep in her lungs.

My mother, however, would never have accepted another man in her life, especially if it freed my father. In fact, my mother would have none of what her sister was concocting. My father would have to join us in the United States or she wasn't going. Period.

That fall, however, the move to America began to stall, once my aunt and her husband were long back in New York and my father had gone, leaving us to face winter and a school year alone in Rome. One Sunday night at the Diana theater we saw *The Cincinnati Kid*, and I found myself gloomily fantasizing about American cities, because that possible outlet was dying fast as we watched sun-drenched Mediterranean Rome turn pale, autumnal, soggy, and then prematurely dark, with cold weather, ceaseless rain, and constantly frigid radiators.

One early October evening as the sky darkened, I placed my hand on the radiator and could feel nothing more than an illusory whisper of heat. The *termosifoni*, Grazia's brother said with a smirk, never work in these buildings. Still, we were told it was good to pour water into the ceramic holders hanging on the radiators. The heat would penetrate the holder and the steam was meant to humidify the room. But how could the ceramic water holders humidify anything if there was hardly any heat to begin with? "The heat is the heat there is. More than this . . . ," said Grazia's brother, shrugging his shoulders and letting his sentence trail, which is a Roman way of stating the obvious when the obvious is obvious enough. We asked him to at least take a look at our *termosifoni*. He turned the knobs one way and then the other, banged one *termosifone* with his shoe, stared at the befuddled thing that clearly didn't like being kicked, and finally shook his head. He might as well have been comparing steam to manna from heaven. *Some days God sends good news, and some days . . .*

We asked if maybe a repairman should come to take a look at our *termosifoni*.

"He'll come and tell you there is nothing wrong with them. And frankly . . ."

It was going to be a long, cold winter.

~

Getting to the school bus the first day was a disaster. We left the house at six thirty in the morning because I was nervous about missing it. My mother wanted us to finish our breakfast but I was too nervous and kept prodding my brother to finish his quickly. "You won't be late," she said, urging him to take a few more minutes with his remaining Rice Krispies. Aunt Flora had told us that our stop was among the first on Via Appia Nuova, and that buses would arrive half-empty. What caught me totally by surprise was that a succession of buses headed for Termini were crammed. Getting on one required pushing our way in before the doors closed behind us. I was almost locked out once the doors started closing, but I shoved my book bag into the bus and was helped by an older man. My brother had already managed to squiggle in before me. I eventually found a spot beside a window and paid the conductor for the two of us. But what I had not expected on such a crowded bus was that the smell of so many people could be so suffocating. It was frequently rumored among members of our family that Italians didn't bathe very often. I had watched Amina gleefully accept my mother's offer to wash her hair, which Amina said she did on Saturdays only. This, among other observations, had allowed me to infer that perhaps daily baths were not a normal occurrence among Romans living in our Appio-Tuscolano neighborhood, which straddled Via Appia and Via Tuscolana. What I found hard to tolerate was that many of the riders on the bus not only had dirty fingernails as they jammed their hands in our faces reaching for the handrail, but they also smelled of the wine they'd drunk the previous night or maybe that morning. Often, and especially when it was cold on those late-fall mornings, the smell would force my brother to lower one of the windows to let a breeze wash over his face, whereupon someone would always complain, "Who opened the windows? We're freezing in here." I feared that one day soon maybe I'd get used to that stench and no longer be repelled by it.

After many years, when I smell wine on someone's breath I am instantly taken back to those late-fall mornings when we had to stand glued to others in jam-packed buses, never daring to grab a seat if one ever was free—fall mornings I detested, though I'd give anything to experience again the unmistakable snug feeling of bodies swaying to the rhythm of the bus, seeking warmth like penguins huddled together—the grandmother going to babysit, the man with the unwieldy box, the old lady carrying a net bag of groceries and gossiping with someone she's never seen before and won't see again, people going to work, to school, or looking for work, they were on the bus too, broken and sad, always sad, angry, and scared—of the cold, of life, of your glance when they caught you staring and looked away, their ragged coats smelling of weather-beaten wool that had just been in the rain and whose damp scent I've always loved, even when it overpowers you and smells foul.

Occasionally on the bus I would hear people talk about *la partita*, the soccer game. Sometimes they discussed politics. But what astounded me months later was hearing how scandalized everyone was when one of Italy's leading singers, Luigi Tenco, committed suicide after being eliminated from the San Remo Music Festival competition. No one could begin to fathom how someone could take his own life over a song—a mere song, they'd clamor, these singers were all crazy!—strangers chattering with one another as the bus picked up speed, everyone nodding when someone finally sighed, *What's the world coming to?*

Once, on a crowded winter morning, I thought I overheard the beginnings of a subdued tussle. It grew into a bicker of loud hisses, two people arguing, until I saw the woman elbow the man once, twice, three times, clearly trying to push him away. "*Vigliacco*," she hissed, "*brutto vigliacco*," you wretched sneak, she said, complaining to the crowd that he had rubbed against her from behind. "*Sfacciato*," impudent, she screamed, waiting for the conductor to intervene, to do something and not just sit there. "If you meant to touch me, then touch me like a man, not like a thief who'd snatch my wallet instead." She was outraged, and my heart was beating because I thought they'd come to blows. "But I did nothing," said the young man, a university student, "she's making all this up." He was wearing a buttoned cardigan, carrying books strapped in a band under one arm while with his other hand he was holding a cap. "*Io non ho fatto niente di niente*," I've done nothing whatsoever, nothing, he protested. In the end, and perhaps because she kept saying he wasn't a man, the conductor asked her to kindly leave the bus. "Me, leave?" This time she grew hysterical and started yelling. She wasn't going to leave. "No, not me," she said. "He should be the one to get out, *sporco sfacciato svergognato*," shameless. In the end the bus stopped and she was compelled to leave. "*Scenda, Signora, per favore scenda*," please leave the bus, ma'am. She got off and kept yelling at the closed doors as a horde of new passengers surged into the back of the bus. Suddenly, I thought of my mother and missed her very much.

That fall, my first written assignment for English class was to describe a trip by bus, train, or plane. We were all meant to read our essays to the class. I did not tell my listeners that the trip in my essay was my ordinary morning journey to catch the school bus at Piazza della Repubblica. Instead, I let it seem that I was on a one-time early-morning bus to Montemario to visit an ailing aunt. I did not disclose where my trip originated and I made a point of saying that at Termini I'd opted to take a taxi, especially after enduring the fetid breath of those who'd been riding the bus with me. My brother proofread the piece and couldn't understand why I hadn't stuck to the plain truth about our daily rides. In his view, I was romanticizing again! He did not understand, I replied. "Oh, yes, I do," he said. "I know your mind," he added. After class, my teacher told me that in English it was better to avoid the word *stench* or *stink*, which, though related etymologically, the way, for instance, *drench* and *drink* are, or maybe even *French* and *fink*—"Just joking, just joking," said Mr. Carson, who adored France. It was more advisable to use the verb *smell*. *Malodorous* felt too archaic, no? In English, "smell" was a more gracious way of describing a bad odor, but then the noun *odor* was itself pejorative, though far less loutish than *stink*—"See my point?" I did. What I also realized was that I had acquired two new words in my vocabulary: *loutish* and *pejorative*. That same afternoon, in biology class, I learned that cells had something called the "endoplasmic reticulum." *Reticulum* had also been added to my vocabulary, as had the word *defenestration* in history class.

In one day, I had learned four words. So you could divide 25,000 lire (my share of the monthly tuition) by approximately twenty school days that month, and you'd get 1,250 lire per day, divided by four words, which meant that each word had cost my parents approximately 300 lire, almost the equivalent of fifty cents.

The real reason my composition never revealed where my bus ride originated was that I didn't want my classmates to know where I lived. All of them were wealthy, mostly Americans whose parents were either in business for themselves or worked for multinational oil companies, or for the FAO, the Food and Agriculture Organization of the United Nations. Others were the sons of diplomats who could brag of having lived in many luminous cities around the world. Some were the children of successful movie producers or actors. They would never have understood why someone chose to live on Via Clelia. I would eventually refer to our neighborhood as lying "slightly south of the Alberone district," because there used to be a huge tree (*alberone*, in Italian) that had long since disappeared. This was a polite way of avoiding telling people exactly where we lived. Most at school might have heard of the Alberone but had no idea where it stood, and when I explained that it was close to Via Appia, I hoped they'd infer I was talking of Via Appia Antica, the old Roman Appian Way, where the rich and famous lived in Rome.

Most of these well-tailored boys lived around the Parioli neighborhood, a recently developed area of Rome where mostly wealthy and upper-middle-class families lived and from which the noun *pariolino* is derived, meaning "an upper-middle-class young snob." Most of the school buses started their rounds in various corners of Parioli, and by the time they reached the spot to pick us up were already full of students. Other students were driven to school either by their parents or by their parents' drivers; one I still recall drove his own car, a beat-up black Citroën in which, it was frequently rumored, deeds of all natures took place on weekend nights once the coterie of young men had drunk enough to move on to exploits of another order. Many of these students had been together since grade school and would remain lifelong friends. They seemed to know which university they hoped to apply to, even which career they planned to pursue. They were seniors like me, but their career paths were already clearly mapped, if not by them then by their parents. Everything about them seemed ordained from birth. They were, needless to say, indescribably arrogant—which is why I feared they'd jeer at me the moment they heard I lived on Via Clelia. When they asked me which university I was planning to attend, I would right away reply, the Sorbonne. It was the only school I was more or less certain no one knew the first thing about. "It's in Paris," I'd say as though it were the most obvious thing in the world, I who had never set foot in Paris or, for that matter, France. I spoke English with a mild French accent that made my claim believable enough, though there were a few boys in the school who had either lived in Paris or were indeed French. To them, I knew better than to claim I was Parisian, since my accent would have immediately betrayed my Levantine–North African origins, so I was always careful to say that my mother was French and my father Italian. He was away from Rome, so no one would ever be in a position to know that he was born a Turk and had acquired his Italian citizenship in Egypt through the good offices of one of my mother's friends who worked at the Italian consulate. As for my mother, no one but the brothers had met her on the notorious day of our first visit to the school, and had they paid attention they would have noticed that I'd whispered to her in French.

The one person I made a point of avoiding was a boy who came from Egypt, Howard McIntire. We spotted each other right away, either because we'd seen each other several times in Alexandria or because something about us—our gestures, our instant smiles, our deferential air when we didn't know how else to behave with a stranger, the way we laughed, or walked, or even sneezed—gave us away as countrymen. I avoided him because I feared him, assuming he'd want to expose my shaky Franco-Italian fib, the way he must have suspected that I was no less eager to expose his wobbly British-Italian papers. A chill neutrality reigned between us. We never ratted on each other. We never even spoke. We simply stayed clear of each other because our years in Egypt sat like an unspeakable taboo that neither wished revealed. Egypt had scuttled our sense of identity and given it an unreliable, almost devious air. We were like children who've suffered an outrage but refuse to confide it to their parents because the shame, which should never have been theirs, was now theirs to shoulder. For us, identity was a mask, not a face. We were provisional people, born sidelined on the wrong side of history. No one was like us, which was why we hid. We were wrong people.

My brother, who never discussed him with me, had exactly the same reaction. He recognized him and hated him instantly. Howie McIntire.

One day his mother came to pick him up at school because he was reported sick. She was standing by the principal's office, and as soon as Howie saw her, he went up to her and kissed her in a totally demonstrative way, unlike most boys our age, who no longer want to be seen with their mother, much less kiss her in front of others at school. He spoke to her in English at first but what he whispered, as they were leaving the building, was Greek. They spoke Greek together. I should have known. He was really Greek the way I was still a Turk. His British papers, my Italian papers, his plan to head to Oxford, like mine to the Sorbonne, was all flimflam.

My first few weeks at school were ordinary enough. Lessons were not easy, and homework required hours. The school bus would leave at three fifteen in the afternoon and drop us off at Piazza della Repubblica around four. Then the long bus ride home, during which I always read novels while my brother managed to find a seat and, leaning his head against the window, would right away fall asleep. He was frequently queasy, so I'd let him have a seat if two were unavailable. We'd get home around four thirty. Then homework, supper, bath, and bed by ten. I'd made a point of waking up at five fifty, followed by a quick breakfast and, if there was time, tea or coffee. My brother, who had a difficult time waking up so early, was always late. On more than one morning, he'd be swallowing his breakfast on the way to the bus stop while I rushed ahead carrying his book bag and mine, because he complained it slowed him down. Many times I'd go over his homework on the crowded bus. At home I'd help him with his math and English homework. He didn't always ask me for help. Then Mother would come in and ask if I could give him a hand. "Why hasn't he come to me first?" I'd ask. "Because he doesn't want to ask you," she'd say, "so he asked me to ask you."

My mother could not help with math or any homework. But she did everything else. She ironed our clean shirts every evening, washed our clothes, cooked, made our beds. Sometimes, during the day, rather than stay at home reading French novels and magazines, she would head out to the Renatos' to spend time with them before preparing a little snack for her sons. She was learning Italian cuisine, either from the Renatos or by having people in the market explain to her as best they could how to cook their preferred dishes, always adding herbs. In Rome everything tasted better with herbs.

Alone at home, though, she never heard when a sudden gust slammed our kitchen window against its frame and the glass shattered. Being deaf, she also wouldn't hear the water running from a faucet and would sometimes flood the apartment. Then she'd have to leave whatever she was doing and soak up the water everywhere, towel after wrenched towel, all by herself. When I thought of her this way, something like love and pity and a rising sense of guilt were so intricately coiled together that I'd be paralyzed until nothing at school, no class, no test, no one, could take my mind off her. "Did you think of her?" I'd ask my brother when I'd occasionally run into him in one of the school corridors. "Don't start," he'd reply.

Early that winter, my mother took us to a department store near Via Clelia to buy permanent-press shirts and asked if we wanted to buy a record. We decided on a Beatles 45.

My mother asked if we liked the song. We liked it very much.

She was sorry not to be able to hear, as she would have liked to listen to the music, just to understand what it was we liked so much.

"It's nothing so special," my brother said. She knew why he'd said this, and I knew she knew. She would watch us play old records we'd brought from Egypt and the two or three 45s we'd purchased in Rome and would never understand what records are, what music does, or what it meant to play "Eleanor Rigby" again and again.

The old turntable we had brought from Egypt eventually experienced a voltage overload. My mother immediately removed the plug from the wall but we were sure we'd seen the last of the record player. The room stank of blown wiring. We needed to call the electrician, because we didn't want to bother Grazia's brother again. But like the glazier and the plumber for the *termosifoni*, the electrician would need to be paid in cash. No movies on the weekend, she concluded. When the electrician came, he laughed at us, saying we'd used a 220-volt outlet for a 110 record player. He was surprised the wires hadn't burned sooner—this was bound to happen, he said, looking at the three of us as if we were fools. He fixed the damaged wire, but would need to bring more wire for our old Grundig radio. We paid him for his work, but before he was set to leave, I asked if he could do something about the window that the sudden gust of wind had slammed shut, shattering its glass. Was there perhaps something wrong with the frame itself, since it refused to shut properly? He was an electrician, he said, not a glazier. "*Non è di competenza mia*"—in short, not my job! He never came back. Eventually we'd have to ask Grazia's brother to replace the burned wiring. We paid him with several glasses of wine, which he liked, though I could tell he was being kind and had accepted that form of payment because he knew we were always short of cash. Had we lived on a farm, we would have been paying our doctor with chickens, eggs, and freshly dug turnips. The wine was cheap. I had bought it at the wine store that my mother designated as the one *du côté des putains*, next to the whores.

Meanwhile, we were without "Eleanor Rigby" and we weren't going to the movies that weekend. We stared at our kitchen window, half of its glass still in place, while the large top half had shattered. The glass was temporarily replaced by a large olive-colored towel thumbtacked to the frame to block the cold wind. We didn't have enough money for a new glass panel that month. It would have to wait a few weeks. Meanwhile, brewing coffee in the early morning when the *termosifoni* were not working was like boiling water in an igloo.

Madame Renato had come with her husband and sat speaking quietly with my mother, but when her husband said he had to leave, Madame Renato gave my mother a sidelong glance meaning she knew all too well what he was up to. "In less than an hour he'll drink a whole bottle and then he'll slip away to gamble with his neighbors upstairs. He loses my money to these people and in the morning I'm the one who mops their landing. Is this fifty-fifty?"

In these moments I'd put aside my homework to eavesdrop on Madame Renato's lamentations. I loved her stories—because that was what they were, stories, but always interminable and unresolved, filled with distress, humor, and the most remorseless character studies that stirred her plangent, mischievous giggling. Never mind that her jeremiads repeated themselves; there was always either something new she'd forgotten to bring up, or on hearing the same tale again, I was like a child who wants the same old story retold every night, mindful of changes when one or two are slipped in. At some point, she'd turn to me or my brother, and with a wink and just a gesture, wonder if either of us could find a tiny moment to brew a *tout petit* espresso for her. An easy price to pay for her to stay seated and continue with her stories, which all three of us had grown to love.

Once I begged her to sew a button for me, and she did so with pleasure, wetting the thread in her mouth and then passing it through a needle. The thought that her spit was on my shirt horrified me and I did not wear the shirt until it had been washed.

When she left I always felt invigorated and inspired to return to my homework, which I'd neglected for her sake. I was reading Dostoyevsky that winter, yet here was a living Dostoyevsky, in our Appio-Tuscolano neighborhood, which gave her yarns the inimitable feel of bulletins sent out with the printer's ink still dripping from her rag-and-bone shop.

She complained about her daughter, Regina, who worked in a seamstress's shop but dreamed of becoming a model. "I adore my daughter, but how can she be a model if she is shorter than I am, and I am the shortest person this side of San Giovanni? You see what I have to put up with?" As it turned out—and there were always surprises with Madame Renato—she had come to ask my mother to speak to her daughter, to make her see reason and encourage her to study to become a dressmaker. "She's already working with a seamstress, so the jump from that to a dressmaker is fifty-fifty. She's good with people, and we are willing to pay for her to study. Plus, she speaks French—true, her French is not as good as mine but I could coach her. Please, reason with her," she'd beg my mother.

My mother took it upon herself to speak to Regina. But within a few weeks of inspirational talks, Regina announced she was getting married, and—as only luck could arrange it—her fiancé's name was none other than Renato, like her father's. Everyone wished her well, but no one could hold back their laughter when they overheard her calling her beau Reno, which is what Madame Renato called her husband. Reno Junior operated a competing dressmaker's shop, and she became the manager there even though she had never picked up a needle, much less sewn on a button. The final irony was that none of the dressmakers in the shop would deign to sweep the floor, so it fell to Regina the manager to do exactly what she had done in the old salon.

Maybe marriage was not such a great idea after all. Regina was very perplexed. She spoke to my mother about what she referred to as *the situation*. No, she didn't mind sweeping up after the clients. It was not degrading. After all, her mother had been plying the same trade for almost a decade. Still, there was *the situation*.

The situation? asked my mother.

My mother eventually grasped what the situation was and advised that the quicker the wedding took place, the better. Who knew what her father would do in one of his drunken stupors—kill her, or kill Reno Junior? Regina wasn't sure. Wasn't sure about what? asked my mother. Did she not love her beau? She loved him fine. Then what? Regina hesitated, then confided that he might not be the father. Did she mean there was another man? She blushed, then finally confessed and said that he lived in her parents' building. And? And she had always loved him, since forever, but he was married. Plus, he's the man who gambles with my father at night.

My mother told her to get married and not tell anyone, not Reno One, not Reno Two, the gamblers in the building, or Madame Renato.

When I got back from school that afternoon, my mother could not hold back and told me the whole story. I had to promise not to breathe a word to anyone. Whom would I ever tell? I asked. No one I knew had the foggiest idea who the Renatos were. This is what gossips always claim when trying to allay the concerns of someone confiding a delicate secret. There was no one to tell. Nevertheless I told many of my classmates at school. My mother, usually so discreet, couldn't hold her tongue either. She told Aunt Flora when she met her on a late Sunday morning before going to see a free film at the French Institute, then she wrote everything to my father, who had known Renato in Alexandria. She even told Grazia, which was like broadcasting the news around the neighborhood, since Madame Renato was as much a *portinaia* as Grazia, and if Grazia told the mailman, who was her friend, then surely the mailman would spread the rumor to all the *portinaie* in the world.

I never found out if the news actually got out, but in typical fashion, my mother regretted opening her mouth: *I shouldn't have.* She feared that the rumors would reach the Renatos and they would learn what their daughter had never told them.

As for me, my mother's warning couldn't have been clearer: *Don't ever get yourself in a situation!*

If only, I thought.

~

One Sunday at noon, a man rang our bell and stood at the doorway, hesitating and holding a bottle of uncorked *vin santo*. He was an elegant, slim, tall, patrician-looking man whom it took me a few moments to recognize. Monsieur Leo or, as I later called him, Signor Leo. I'd met him two years earlier in Alexandria at a birthday party for Despine's daughter, who must have been three or four at the time. He, too, was deaf, but he signed in my mother's far simpler sign language than the one Italians used, and the conversation simply flew between them. He stayed for lunch because my mother had asked him to come after meeting him at the club for the deaf a couple of weeks earlier. We moved to the small living room, where the bridge table was located, and for the first time since our father had been with us, we were four for lunch. I had a test the next day, but I enjoyed the conversation, even if much of it escaped me. I said that I remembered Despine's mother, who used to serve Greek sweets on a spoon, and that I still recalled her father, who had taught me the Greek alphabet one afternoon when I was very young. Signor Leo seemed interested and understood everything I was saying. A few randy topics were broached here and there, and those were not hard to miss, especially when he told my mother rumors about their friend Despine, whose life had essentially fallen apart when her husband disappeared to Greece without leaving a trace. He left her their child as well as their dog, which she had called Marie, which had totally outraged my nanny, who was herself called Marie. Despine, who had been a classmate of my mother's in their school for the deaf, came from a prosperous Greek family. She had never worked, and when her father's property and bank accounts were nationalized before his death, she was left with hardly anything. She led a dissolute life, and was known to have slept with many men; some gave her money. Her mother had warned her about her reputation, and her friends from school had started to distance themselves, though neither my mother nor Leo had done so. But jokes about Despine abounded in our household, especially coming from my grandmother who'd known her mother. That day during lunch, after many, many apologies, Leo told us about the death of Despine's mother. She had been very sick—cancer, he thought—and was bedridden for more than two months. Despine had no choice but to be her nurse and guardian at first but eventually took to disappearing from their home for hours, leaving her bedridden mother stranded in her room. Things got worse and worse, to the point that Despine simply refused to care for her mother, her needs, her cleanliness, even her food. The mother was literally dying and knew it, living day and night in a bed that was totally soiled and fetid.

Signor Leo was coming to the point but I wasn't sure I understood and kept asking my mother to translate for me, just in case I was missing details. Meanwhile Mother and Signor Leo opened the bottle of *vin santo* and poured a small amount into two glasses.

Toward the very end, when the mother heard her daughter tiptoeing in her room, she signaled to her, and asked to give her daughter a kiss, knowing she didn't have long to live. When Despine's face was about to touch her mother's lips, the mother, who had been keeping her hands under her bedcovers, grabbed her own feces with one hand and rubbed it in her daughter's face.

The mother was taken to the Greek hospital soon after. There she was cleaned and taken care of before dying. Despine never mentioned the incident, but her mother had managed to tell the whole hospital, which is how the story had gotten around the Greek community of Alexandria, as a result of which no one wanted anything to do with Despine.

I could tell by looking at Leo's features that, despite his very sad tale, there was also a spark of guilty mirth in his narrative, as if, sordid as the story was, he enjoyed telling it. I liked this. Leo did not mimic Despine's mother's gesture or the cruelty on her face, but in his telling every muffled grimace spoke volumes. Madame Renato would never have been able to compete with that.

I couldn't put the tale out of mind and told my mother that I definitely needed to excuse myself to study for the next day's test. But as I was about to leave the room, my mother mumbled something to me. She had turned her face away from him as if to tell me something in passing, and without so much as moving her lips, said, "*Ne me laisse pas seule avec lui,*" don't leave me alone with him. I wanted to ask *Then why did you invite him?* but I couldn't without his suspecting something. So I pretended I was just about to close a window and would be right back.

Leo stayed half an hour more. My mother had almost forgotten to open up the cakes he had brought, so she rushed to the kitchen to bring them out with four small plates, one for each. Then she told him it was time to clean up and that I had homework to attend to.

I think he understood. But he promised to return the following week. My mother said she'd enjoyed his cordial.

The truth is that in Rome, my mother felt entirely independent for the first time in her life. She had lived with her parents growing up, then came boarding school for the deaf, then her husband, but now at the age of forty she was free to do as she pleased. She had no employment, she sewed and cut a few aprons for some people, knitted sweaters for my brother and me and others, and in exchange she got paid, as was usual on Via Clelia, with cheese, slices of liver, fruits and vegetables. Once a week she would take everything we'd worn to the local laundromat, where she met more people. My father considered her an irresponsible spendthrift and a scatterbrained bigmouth. "She can't keep a secret, the same way she can't keep her expenses in order," he had always complained. But my mother was far more methodical and organized than my father suspected. I seldom had to wake her up in the morning. As soon as she perceived a ray of light under her door she was up and ready to make breakfast. She and I had developed a liking for coffee in the morning, and she had purchased a half-dozen espresso cups because we refused to use the old ones found in the apartment—who knew who had left the mark of their filthy mouths on them? My brother preferred hot chocolate and scrambled eggs but I grew to like jam and butter on my favorite bread, called a *rosetta*. The *rosetta* would sometimes grow stale after a few days, but Amina had taught my mother a trick: you splashed the *rosetta* ever so lightly with water, then put it in the oven. Within minutes, you'd have fresh, warm bread all over again. Her mother would occasionally cross the street and head up to our building to deliver a bag containing around six *rosette* in exchange for my mother's injections. But my mother would have given the shots without the *rosette*, just as Amina's mother would have offered us the rolls without thinking of the shots. On rare occasions, when we had time, Mother would prepare our favorite breakfast: soft-boiled eggs, with buttered *rosette* and salt. Then we could head to the bus stop very happy young men.

There were times when, instead of riding the bus to Piazza della Repubblica, we would take the tram instead, which we preferred because you didn't have to cram into a crowded bus. We'd walk up to Via Eurialo to catch the one-wagon tram that started there. In most cases, we would find seats each and do last-minute homework or study for a test until an older person almost always asked us to yield our seat. Sometimes I would run into the portly Coronaris there, papa bear, mama bear, and baby bear sitting in a row of single seats and never budging for anyone until we reached Termini.

The real reason I wanted to take the tram on Via Eurialo instead of the bus was because there was a girl, probably eighteen, maybe older, who was always dressed in a turquoise overcoat, headed not to school but work. She was blond and beautiful and I thought of her all the time. I never spoke to her except when I offered her my seat. She accepted it and thanked me, while I struggled to find something to say that was more than a bland *prego*. She must have thought I was far younger. I felt far younger. I knew that I must have blushed. I would rush to grab a seat to offer her if she got on the tram. I'd even rehearsed what I'd say to her when the moment came so as not to fumble with words again. But I never found the courage.

I remembered Uncle Claude's words: "Some strike when the iron is hot; others wait for it to cool."

— 6 —

Paris, C'est une Blonde

I had no real friends at school. At the end of every day, I would rush to get a good seat on the public bus, impatient to get back home. I never understood why so many of the non-boarders liked after-school team sports, or why they enjoyed staying late before jumping on public transportation in a boisterous and rambunctious choir, my brother among them, arriving home just in time for supper. I was either already at home or, by late fall, had gotten in the habit of exploring the streets of the *centro storico*, the historic center of Rome. About this time, I also discovered the United States Information Service (USIS) on Via Veneto, just across from the American embassy. Instead of being dropped by the school bus on Piazza della Repubblica, I'd ask the driver to let me off by the Fountain of Moses. From there I'd go straight to the USIS library, where I'd consult the English-language books for a paper on the Existentialists. I fell in love with the library, in good part because it opened doors beyond anything remotely tied to the world of Via Clelia. The library, in the space of just a few hours, took me to Paris, to New York, and frequently, to nineteenth-century St. Petersburg, my adopted home. But the library was also my hideaway. It shielded me from the real world and was thus both a portal and a crypt. I was still alone there but in good company.

As I read about the Existentialists, I also consulted a number of encyclopedias, not just about them but about another topic far more compelling: sex, especially when sought on the sly, convinced as I was that I was the only human on our planet who liked books and encyclopedias because they revealed the universe of sex. Sex obscured by other books on my table that were constantly being shelved after I was done with them by well-meaning, chaste librarians, which is, after all, how I thought I liked sex—well-meaning and chaste—though I wouldn't have thought about it so much if it wasn't a tad indecent too, and certainly more illicit than encyclopedias made it seem. The girl on the Via Eurialo tram in her turquoise overcoat was not indecent. On rainy days, she showed up with an umbrella and accepted the seat I vacated for her, though I never dared speak to her—not indecent at all. Even Amina, good, skinny Amina, who asked *Posso?* when my door was closed and I hadn't heard her come into our home for her injection—Amina wasn't indecent either. There was, however, the Roma girl who sat on a piece of corrugated cardboard by the tram stop on Via Appia Nuova. She'd flaunt her bruised knees and allowed you to imagine *what else* lay beyond those knees, which were slightly parted; maybe she was indecent, maybe dirty too, which allowed my mind to drift to areas that encyclopedias would never dream of reaching in the dingy, white-and-black universe of Via Clelia where she sat every day begging for alms at a tram stop that has altogether disappeared along with a tram line that no longer exists today. Was I indecent and didn't want to own up to it?

And yet it wasn't indecency I was really looking for. I didn't want in-your-face indecency, but I didn't want sex cleansed and spotless either.

What was I thinking?

It was during those evenings as I strolled along its streets that Rome came to mean something as uncharted and intangible as desire itself. I found its lure on the faces of people, on the skin of their bare arms when they scarcely grazed my own, or in how they'd stare at me in ways I grew to like and learned to seek as I walked the city, thoughtless, famished, yet scared. On those early evenings, Rome became more poignant, more troubling, flooding over me like a startled admission I was still reluctant to make because it wasn't chaste but wasn't sleazy either. Weeks earlier it had the scent of pine and chamomile, then of lavender, and now of something as unnamable and vague as the musty odor of old towels and stuffy bedrooms. I couldn't tell whether what was so elusive was in the faces I kept spotting all over Rome or just in me, and this was troubling too. I desired people, but didn't know what I wanted from them or whether I even liked them. Via Veneto, the street of lights made so famous in films, and where everyone had friends and lovers strewn about caffès and bars, kept beckoning each time I left the USIS.

As I'd leave the library around six or so to go home, I knew why I had come, not for the Existentialists, not even to read up on sex in the *Britannica*. On Via Veneto when it was already growing dark in the early evening that fall, the women seemed to loiter just a bit, and always a good distance from one another so men would not fear being overheard when they came up to speak to them. I had seen them a few times already and I already knew which was my favorite, but I didn't dare to approach them.

As I walked down Via Veneto toward San Silvestro to catch my bus, I discovered by pure chance a shortcut that took me to the top of the Spanish Steps. I knew I was dawdling, and though a part of me wanted to go back to Via Veneto to see the women again, I knew they were just an excuse to tarry about and put off going home, the way I'd always head out to one bookstore and then another because books were not the purpose of my rambles through Rome. I didn't know the purpose. Or I didn't want to know.

I loved roaming the streets of Renaissance and Baroque Rome when it grew dark and the stores were open and their speckled lights spilled out on the sidewalks and I could almost imagine being hurled into a combination of Gogol's and Dostoyevsky's worlds. I didn't want to leave it behind and would reluctantly board the bus to Via Clelia.

Once home, I'd ring our bell four times as I always did so my mother would see the four flashes and know it was I. I'd insert my key, hear the click of the lock as I opened our door, hear the bottom of the door scrape the floor as it always did, and finally hear the telltale spring of the latch slipping into place to signal that I had shut the world behind me and was indeed home to the welcoming smell of my mother's cooking. It was good to hug and be hugged by someone I loved and who loved me. But I also knew, with the wretched guilt of disloyalty haunting me, that mine was not a homecoming. My mother was not a home, my brother was not a home, and Via Clelia certainly wasn't home. They were all stand-ins, but I didn't know for what.

"Go, wash your hands," my mother would say. The tablecloth, the silverware, the glasses, the cloth napkins rolled into the silver ring with my initials on it, my brother's initials on his, everything waiting.

The good news, my mother said, once we had sat down for supper, was that she had received letters from both my father and my grandmother—the letters had come in the same envelope, saying that they were arriving in Rome from Paris on the seventh, just a week or so before Christmas vacation.

A change. Something new. Anything.

My father was going to be with us for two weeks and then was going to stay in Paris for quite some time, while his mother, my grandmother, was going to fly from Rome to stay—or was it to live?—in Montevideo, where her other son had been living for fifteen years and done quite well for himself. My mother said that I would have to give up my bedroom to my grandmother. That was fine. What troubled me was sleeping on my bed after she was gone.

Within a few days, another letter arrived from Paris, this time from my mother's brother, telling us that he had found an apartment in Paris for us during the holidays. A young university professor was taking his family to visit his in-laws in the south and was happy to let us house-sit. We were invited to spend Christmas with my mother's side of the family. I hadn't seen my aunt and my cousins for a decade, since their expulsion from Egypt as French citizens in 1956. When he heard the news, my father thought it was a good idea. He would arrange for us to spend the rest of the time in Aunt Elsa's apartment. After being the last to leave Egypt, she had finally resettled in her old home in Paris. "I've locked one door in Egypt and unlocked another in France. Man is like a bird," she used to say, quoting an old Turkish proverb. She repeated these words every time she ran into someone, sometimes confusing which doors she had locked and unlocked. She was not exactly thrilled to open her door to the four of us and didn't always know how to veil her feelings.

But I was finally going to be in Paris.

Maybe Paris was our long-sought home. Everyone had said it was.

~

On December 7, the appointed day, our elevator was not working. It seldom worked, and when it did you had to put five lire in the slot. Uncle Claude had gone to meet my father and grandmother at the airport and had driven them to Via Clelia. Grandmother had had to climb three flights of stairs, and she was exhausted and out of breath. We all focused on her and gave her time to rest. During the silence that followed as she drank a glass of water in slow, deliberate sips, it occurred to me that I had never quite realized how much I'd been missing my grandmother until I saw my father standing there telling his mother to stay seated on the tiny, rickety wicker love seat by the entrance and not to rush with the water. "And so?" said my father, turning to the three of us. I was truly happy to see him. After his departure in August, when life with my mother had become utterly void of sanity, I had done my best to put him out of mind. Now I was persuaded that we were becoming a family again, dysfunctional to be sure, but no more dysfunctional than many others, though some hid it better—or so I thought.

He said he didn't know what lay ahead for him. Right now there

were a few opportunities that needed his attention in France. I asked
if these were going to be significantly different from the Chalabi &
Hanan partnership, which he had declined a few days after we'd visited
their plant. No, he said, the meetings in Paris were more significant.
"More significant than those in Milan?" asked my mother. He gave
her one of his looks, then turned to me. He wanted to see my room,
which was to become his mother's. Her suitcase lay on my bed. Her
other suitcases were going to be delivered that same night, the people
at the airport said. In the room, he asked me which books I had been
reading.

I told him that I had read *The Charterhouse of Parma*. What made
me read that book? A teacher had assigned it to his freshman class,
and since I'd never read it, I decided to buy a copy. Did I like it?
Yes, but I told him I'd preferred *The Red and the Black*. "A far better
book, in my opinion," he said, sounding no less humble than I was.
What else had I read? I gave him the short list. He was impressed. At
your age, I hadn't read any of these books, he admitted. In his diary
he frequently quoted Montaigne, whom I'd heard of but never read,
and another author whose prose he kept copying—long passage after
long passage—called Marcel Proust. Have you ever read him? No,
never, though I'd purchased the volumes in Egypt but had to leave
them there. Proust was very sensitive to smell, and it is because
of the particular scent and taste of a little cake dunked in a tea infu-
sion that he started his epic journey into his past as if under a spell.
Then my father changed the subject and asked if I'd read anything
contemporary. I shook my head. There are good living authors, you
know. I shrugged my shoulders—I liked things as they'd once been,
not as they were now.

And what about friends at school—made any?

None, really.

Was there anyone I liked?

Not really.

Sports?

Avoided them.

What else did I do besides reading all the time?

Nothing much.

You need friends. Any girls in particular? *A* girl?

No.

He said he didn't understand me. My father, possibly the closest person to me, did not understand me.

I didn't know whether I even wanted to be understood.

Did I like Rome? he finally asked.

No, I said. Then I added two words: *hate it*.

How was living with my mother?

I did not want to say anything. But I couldn't resist, because only he would understand. She is who she is. I'd been hearing this mode of answering questions all my life. It said nothing but meant everything.

My father did not respond.

Mine was a subdued conversation opener, but he seemed not to want to engage in what could easily turn into a long rant.

For another time, he promised.

I was sure he was not going to keep his word, but months later he did.

Then he took my brother into his room, obviously eager to have a private conversation with him as well.

When I looked into the entryway where the rickety wicker love seat was, Uncle Claude was sitting next to his sister, rolling the rim of his hat around in both hands. At seventy, he was still her youngest sibling.

When my father and my brother returned, we all moved to the living room. My mother took down a bottle of *vin santo* from one of the kitchen shelves and brought it to the room, ready to serve it in short glasses. We all drank to my grandmother's health. Uncle Claude said he found his sister in good health. Soon she'd be the first of her generation to cross the Atlantic. "Look at you," he said, trying to give a jovial spin to what, in the family, was called the venerable coachman's daily stops at the cemetery.

"I have no idea what awaits me there," she said, referring to Montevideo. "It's the town where the *Graf Spee* went to sink. Do you think I want to live in a place where ships go to die, or where everyone can't wait for me to do to myself what the captain of the *Graf Spee* did to his ship when he blew it up before taking his own life?"

"No one in our family has ever taken his own life. We are made of stronger stuff," Uncle Claude added, persuaded that he had, with a few strokes of brio, dissuaded the coachman from carrying off his sister.

But she was not thinking of suicide. She was scared of the family she would encounter at the airport, with whom she felt condemned to live. There was her other daughter-in-law, whom she hated even more than she hated my mother—my mother who brought her another glass of water after she finished the first. There were her three grand-children, whom she'd never seen except in pictures, and finally her own son, and let's not forget his mistress who was thirty years younger than he and whom he'd welcomed into his family, whether his wife liked it or not! How was she going to live with these hooligans, why go all the way to Uruguay when she was perfectly happy staying with her sister in the seizième arrondissement? "*Je ne vois pas la logique*," she failed to see the logic of such grandiose travel plans.

"The logic is plain to see," said her brother Claude. "You have no home because you have no money."

"I have no home," she echoed, lowering her voice. "I have no home. Of course I have no home. Clearly, you're a luminary, Claude! So now my son wants to welcome me into his home, how very, very sweet," she said with irony crackling in her voice. "An awful man, my son."

"What could he have done that was so terrible?" my brother asked.

"He doesn't know, does he?" she said, reaching out to hold my brother's wrist, because the good woman did love my brother. Her son, she explained, had left Egypt without so much as bidding a proper farewell or getting his father's blessing. His father died a few months following his escape to Uruguay. She was never going to forgive this. She couldn't, and she wasn't going to.

"You're repeating yourself, Esther!" said her brother.

"My poor husband was already sick, and possibly dying without even knowing he was dying, and I watched him slip into his final hours and took good care of him, even though I never loved him once, just as he, poor man, never loved me either—I have to be frank, even if it's in front of this young one," she said, still holding my brother's wrist. "He died without knowing whether his son had left or was still skulking in Egypt with that woman he had married, that monster who kept threatening suicide all the time, which is when my poor husband pleaded with her to 'please take your short, insipid, meaningless life and hurl it out any window you please.' Her name was Manzanita, little apple, but she was nicknamed Mazalita, a diminutive for the Hebrew word *mazal*—you see," she said, turning to me while still holding on to my brother. "You never even tried to learn Hebrew after refusing to be a bar mitzvah—*mazal*," she added, maybe losing her train of thought for a moment, "*mazal* means good fortune, but my poor husband called her *la negromazal*, bad fortune." Grandmother laughed, which made everyone laugh. And we all needed to laugh. Uncle Claude had seen Mazalita only once in his life but immediately remembered. "She is the kind who was already old when she was young, the kind who gets married and has children and then, *mirabile dictu*, becomes a virgin again."

Everyone laughed at this, and my mother laughed too when my father explained the joke to her. It had put us all in a good mood and we were all served a second shot of the cordial, which everyone agreed was very good. Uncle Claude looked at the label approvingly. He was shrewd enough to know that this was not something my mother had bought, but he said nothing, though right away I could tell what he was thinking. My mother caught his eye, then mine, and gave me a look that said, *Not a word!*

"I am sure," continued Uncle Claude, "that many married women become virgins. Take Elsa, for instance. Would you swear she witnessed the cutting of the ribbon?"

"What could you possibly mean?" asked my grandmother, startled by Claude's assertion, which came from nowhere.

"Some women lose their virginity; others find it again. Which kind are you, Esther?" he asked, clearly enjoying the ribald turn the conversation had taken.

"I am the kind who may have lost it once or twice but then never again."

She could laugh at herself. We laughed with her.

"I am sure your poor husband was pleased to see you'd found it again."

"He had other women who were happy to lose what they'd already lost many, many times before him."

My grandmother asked my mother to show her to her room, as she wanted to change.

As soon as she left the living room, Uncle Claude, who surprised me with his wicked sense of humor, picked up the same topic with my father.

"My sisters never understood the first thing about sex. I am sure our mother was to blame. I'll wager anything you want that with all their cloistered upbringing in Constantinople they never experienced a single orgasm in their lives unless by accident. Imagine this: to go through life without knowing what an orgasm is." Then, turning to me, "How many orgasms a day, young man?"

I was so flustered and shocked by such a direct question that I was unable to speak.

"You do know what an orgasm is, don't you?"

My father, sensing that I was completely stunned, tried to intercede, but Uncle Claude had already changed his tune.

"At your age, I used to have at least three a day."

"And now?" asked my father, still trying to divert the course Claude had taken.

"Now I'm lucky if it's one a month. And even then . . ." He affected a sigh. "So, what do you think I do with the *baronessa*?"

"What do you do with the *baronessa*?

"I used to think with my phallus once. Those were my best days. My phallus used to do all the talking for me. Now my tongue does the talking."

"And the phallus?" asked my father.

"The phallus is happy to sit and watch."

I hadn't laughed so hard in ages. I missed laughter.

My father recalled his first time. "My *cazzo* categorically refused to work."

"Mine is on a monthly pension," added my uncle. "But sometimes he forgets to collect." Then, turning to me and to my brother, "At your age, who even counts how many times a day?"

More laughter.

"You are a timid one," said my uncle, looking at me, though still with laughter glowing on his features. "*Mais il faut la surmonter, cette timidité,*" you need to get over this timidity. "If I could borrow three days from you, just three days, I would sleep with every woman this side of San Giovanni and leave the old and ugly for others."

Was he quoting poetry without knowing it?

By then my grandmother had returned to the living room. "Are you all done with your usual slop?"

"Yes," said her brother, at which point he said he had to leave.

When asked why he was leaving so early, he explained "*La baronessa,*" almost with the same feigned sigh he'd let loose when speaking about his penis.

As he shut the door behind him, my grandmother, referring to the *baronessa,* couldn't help saying that her brother had had an eye for the rich as far back as the Great War, adding that he wasn't even twenty at the time. He learned bridge because he knew it was what the rich officers played, whereas everyone he'd grown up with was happy with backgammon. Then he went to law school because his brother had met the future king of Egypt here in Italy, but all he met were impoverished Italian aristocrats desperate to salvage their titles, their mortgaged privileges, and the little land they still had. They taught him how to behave, talk, even laugh the way they did, how to acquire their tastes, hire their tailors and their dancing instructors, play tennis and, above all, golf. He spoke like them too, Your Excellency this and Your Excellency that, *madamina* here and *baronessa* there—but he could change in a second, and when you heard him whine in Ladino *"Mammmmmmaaaa, ande eskondiste mis kalsones muevos?"* where did you hide my new undies, you knew he was the good-for-nothing little brat from Constantinople whose real name was Chlomo, not Claude.

My grandmother was not as tired as we thought. She went to help my mother prepare something slightly more elaborate than I was accustomed to for supper. I set the bridge table for five, then my mother sent my brother and me to buy some wine, *you know where*.

When we returned and the wine was served, we were about to start the meal when the door rang; it was Amina. My mother had altogether forgotten that this was her appointed day for her injection. As soon as Amina saw my grandmother and my father, she balked, and said she would come back later. No, stay, motioned my mother. Had she had supper already? No, she hadn't, she said, they ate late in her home. She said she would come back in an hour. My father asked her to stay all the same. Then I must bring a panettone, she said, we have many in the house. She immediately rushed out, left our front door open, and was heard scurrying down across the street, and within minutes was back, pushing the door open carrying a panettone. She didn't know if we celebrated Christmas, she said, but this was an Italian dessert expressly made for the holiday. I scooted over on my chair and she sat next to me and for the briefest moment she held my hand. I knew she had done it without thinking, because moments later she let go as thoughtlessly as she had reached for it.

I liked how she had touched my hand. Not long afterward, and still under the spell of the touch, I reached for her hand and held it again. She removed it but only to twine her fingers with mine.

This was a real pre-Christmas feast. We drank, we all spoke Italian for Amina's benefit, while I translated for my mother. After dinner, she started clearing the dishes and brought clean ones, while Amina removed the cake from its packaging and began cutting slices. Would her parents be upset if she had supper without them? Not at all, she had already prepared supper for her parents while they and her brother went back to the depot to load up several of the items for the next day. My grandmother didn't exactly understand what they did for work, but I could tell something was bothering her about Amina. Eventually, I heard her mumble to my father in French, "*Mais ce sont des ouvriers,*" but they are laborers. Then, staring at Amina, who I could tell sensed she was being judged, she added, "This girl is skinny."

"This is why she gets injections?" my father whispered.

"She also knows we are Jewish," she added.

"But it's not a secret."

"It should be," she replied.

Amina was curious to know what we thought of the panettone.

"We love it," my father said. He was even going to ask for a second slice.

As she was cutting more, he told her that he and his mother had just landed from Paris and that we were all going to spend Christmas in Paris this year.

"*Non ci credo,*" I can't believe it, she said, clearly infatuated by the idea.

"We will have to bring you something from Paris. What would you like?"

She wasn't sure. She didn't know. But she was candid enough to say that she would definitely love anything from Paris.

"We've chatted enough, now for business," said my mother to Amina. She was already boiling the syringe. As always, the two went into the kitchen and shut the half-glass door behind them.

"This girl likes you," said my father while she was getting her injection.

"I know," I said. There was no point pretending otherwise. I'd suspected it since early fall.

Why couldn't it have been the girl in the turquoise overcoat? Or even the Roma girl who sat under the tram shelter with her thighs peeking out of her skirt?

Still, knowing that a girl liked me did not displease me. Luckily, at that age I felt no obligation to like her back simply because she liked me. I'd liked the touch of her hand and, better yet, the way she'd woven her fingers in mine, simply and frankly.

Everything that evening made me happy, from Uncle Claude, who could be unusually funny, impish, and irreverent when not in a position of authority, to my grandmother, who brought a sense of family cohesion into our home, to Amina, who gave the evening a younger, sprightly air, to say nothing of my father, who was finally among us. I just wished we could stay together. That night I went to bed feeling happy. In one room were my parents, in the other my grandmother, and I was in the room between them on a pile of blankets bundled on the floor of my brother's bedroom. We weren't as scattered or as lonely as we'd been for so many months.

～

Early the next morning, the serene mood that had settled on our family the night before was still with us. Everyone was unusually quiet while my brother and I had breakfast in the kitchen, as was our habit. Grandmother had found a few oranges in the refrigerator and had pressed a small glass of juice for me and my brother as had been her habit in Egypt. Then, with my brother on time for once, we left to catch our first bus. For some reason he and I walked slowly up Via Clelia, noticing for the first time that the street no longer seemed so dour and unwelcoming. The bus ride itself, always verging on the sordid, felt lighter, more spacious, and all the passengers seemed friendlier. Even school was pleasant.

Later that evening, after more research on the Existentialists at the USIS, I passed by a small movie theater and saw that they were playing *Les Parapluies de Cherbourg*.

At home, we had an intimate supper again. While discussing books with my father I mentioned that *Les Parapluies de Cherbourg* was playing near the Spanish Steps. Several days later, on the last day of school before Christmas break, we decided to see it. My brother said he was going to meet a friend from school instead, while my mother did not want to see a film that was entirely sung. Besides, she'd never liked French films, because in Egypt, French films never had subtitles, since it was assumed that everyone could understand French. Without subtitles, French films seldom made sense to her.

My father and I had seen the film a few years earlier in Alexandria in circumstances that couldn't have been more different. At the time, we had no idea what our future would be and didn't think we might leave Egypt. My father was still trying to stay, hoping to build a second factory in Cairo. I remembered how he'd driven to pick up the two friends who were to join us at the movies and for whom he'd also bought tickets. Showing a film immediately after the close of the Cannes Film Festival seemed a strange concession on the part of the virulently anti-Western government, which was allowing that year's European films to play in Alexandria for a week only. One of our guests that evening was a middle-aged woman, my father's Italian tutor, the other a Jewish girl who must have been nineteen or twenty years old and was desperately trying to lead her own life by constantly giving the slip to her extra-religious parents. For all of us, this was a festive, unusual occasion; life had suddenly opened its doors to let us peek at what was happening in Europe and remind us that Alexandria could still be a vibrant home to contemporary European culture. My father had already seen the film a few evenings before but was happy to see it again with me and his two guests. The theater was packed.

I remember how he had driven me along the coast road, Alexandria's corniche, as we listened to French and Italian songs on the radio before the film and how, afterward, he'd driven his two guests to their respective homes and then taken me back to the coast road, the two of us listening to more songs, trying to fathom why the film was—in his word—enchanting. Would we find it still enchanting this time in Rome after taking the crowded 85 bus all the way to the theater? Was Rome going to offer what a quiet car ride up and down the corniche seemed to promise, with fleeting previews of life in Europe?

Silent, as we waited for the film to start, the two of us were surely thinking back to how we'd each projected our version of a snow-blanketed Cherbourg on Alexandria so as not to see our tired and aging city that was starting to float away and drift from our grasp while still claiming to be our home. I knew we'd spoken about Rome that night, but ours was a far-fetched Rome built on yearning and dream-making. Now, in a bus headed back home after seeing the film, our Roman fantasies felt flawed, hollow, and worn out.

Maybe my father and I went to *Les Parapluies* that evening in Rome to see if we could claim that nothing really separated us from who we'd been then and who we were now, that you could castle the pieces on the chessboard all you wanted but the king was still the regal figure he'd always been, even without his crown, and the sly bishop was destined to remain the mischievous, bookish trickster he was born to be. We might still love the same film, still miss those rides up and down the corniche at night, but the two of us had lost what Jean Améry, the Holocaust survivor, called our *trust in the world*.

We arrived by way of Via Tuscolana and walked home. The street was so quiet that weekday night that we could hear our own footsteps. At the entrance to our building, Grazia was shaking a doormat that was bigger than she was. We saw the dust fly as she kept airing it with vigorous jolts. "Things get so dirty here," she said as she dropped the mat on the ground and straightened it with her left foot to align it with the rectangular first tread of the stairway. She bid us good night as she headed downstairs to her underground lodging, where, I told my father, she lived with her mother, her two brothers, and her young nephew whose mother was nursing another child.

Once inside, we saw that no one had gone to bed. My mother and grandmother were talking with my brother and were glad to see us walk in. On the coffee table sat the rest of the panettone we'd been eating several evenings before. My mother brought two small plates and cut a wedge of the cake for each of us. It was so good to come to a quiet and peaceful home where a mere piece of cake could embody a world unusually serene. We spoke about the movie, and I enjoyed being asked about it, but it was sitting in the room with the five of us that made me happy.

Paris awaited us in a few days. Father had purchased train tickets, but then changed his mind, returned the tickets, and got three seats on Air France. The only tickets available were on Christmas Eve. None of us minded.

This had been a rough year for all of us, he said, so why not spoil ourselves just a tiny bit. Grandmother would leave for Uruguay a few days later, after which my father would join us in Paris. Everything seemed to come together. I loved this.

I knew I would miss Grandmother. I had missed her while she'd been staying in Paris, and I knew there was no telling how long she planned to live in Uruguay. I might never see her again. She was past ninety at the time, and as her younger sisters used to say in Egypt, there was no reason why the venerable coachman shouldn't already have come looking for her. When I hinted to her what an unnamed someone had said about her, she answered that the venerable coachman was busy harnessing his horses but that one of the carriage wheels was seriously damaged and might require a while to repair. She wouldn't be going so soon.

What I loved about my grandmother was what she taught me about myself: that I loved laughter above so many things, that a room with a slice of cake and the residual scent of orange blossom, a fatuous conversation, be it even gossip of the most fallow sort, was of an order no less essential than those grand ideas I was struggling to master and bring into my life. Hers was a tame love, like Flora's, not the savage, mutinous, hysterical kind I'd grown up with and wished to be rid of, all the while knowing that I couldn't live without it. My mother's love was obstinate, sudden, feral, while my grandmother's was a mitigated, almost civil, cordial love that never drained the heart but didn't necessarily fill it either. Her love was restful and composed and always measured, even rationed, hence a touch skimmed. There was always hope when my grandmother was around. Hope was good enough.

My father took us to the airport and waited for us to get on the plane. We saw him waving a few times, but then it started to rain and we could no longer see him from our tiny windows. I was sure he'd gone home. He never traveled by himself in Rome, and I had no idea how he got from the airport to Termini and from Termini to our apartment. It never occurred to me that he might have taken a taxi.

This was my first time on an airplane and naturally, after takeoff and the quick snack, I took the tiny salt and pepper shakers, pocketed one of the spoons, and as for the butter, after much debate, I put the whole miniature stick tightly wrapped in aluminum foil in my pocket. By the time we landed in Paris, it had leaked through the pocket of my lovely double-breasted blazer. The stain was not all that visible—but it was there to stay.

Tonton Robert and his one daughter and Jules, a young post-doc working with my uncle, met us at the airport, and being welcomed by people who couldn't wait to see us made all the difference compared with the chilly reception Uncle Claude had given us half a year earlier. My mother couldn't hold back and started to cry, and her brother was tearing up as well, though he tried to hide it.

We had left Rome midafternoon, but Paris was already totally dark and I could see nothing of the city. We drove straight to the apartment in Saint-Cloud that was to be our temporary home while its owners vacationed in the south. My uncle introduced us to the concierge, who said she'd go inside to fetch the keys to the apartment. She spoke French to us, my uncle spoke French to her, my mother understood their French, I spoke French, and suddenly, I saw it: this was my world. Everything was in its place. I had come home, and for a tiny second, I felt I'd stepped right into *Les Parapluies de Cherbourg*, as though the previous week's film had been a rehearsal of a life to come, a life finally set right.

My uncle had wanted to come upstairs with us to test the keys, but his daughter told him that we knew where to go and that I understood the keys better than he. He snorted at himself. His student made a scoffing sound intended for his professor. They'd wait for us in the car while we went up to *débarbouiller*—wash up—after the flight. I'd never heard that verb before, and I made a point of jotting it down somewhere. I've never forgotten it.

We spent every day with my mother's family and they all took turns driving us around Paris. That Christmas Eve my Aunt Laurence had prepared dinner. They had a part-time cook who spoke Spanish only, and my uncle, who had grown up speaking Ladino with his mother and other relatives, was the only one in the family who could communicate with her. As my aunt told me when I met her, most maids and cooks in Paris in those years came from Spain and Portugal. They didn't know French and came *de la montagne*, from the mountains, which in the lingo of the family meant from ignorant peasant stock.

One of my uncle's daughters was already married; the other had broken up with her boyfriend and was still *en convalescence*, as her mother explained, wearing a smile that was doleful, all the while attempting good cheer. No one in the family had approved of her lover and was happy to see him go. She must have been four years older than I, and I remembered her playing with me at the beach when we were children. She was very beautiful, and when she kissed me on both cheeks, I tried to hide my blush. The skin on her cheeks was completely smooth and though she had scarcely brushed my lips with hers, I was in heaven. This could easily be my home. Why Rome—or, for that matter, why New York?

While we paused over dinner, my uncle spent a good half hour trying to explain the Paris subway system. His descriptions, especially of the *correspondence*, made no sense whatsoever. So the matter was taken up by Jules, who was totally clear. Then came dessert, and finally the long-awaited exchange of gifts. I got a red ballpoint pen, my brother a blue one. We agreed to exchange them once we got back to the apartment, since he liked red and I blue. Meanwhile, all my cousins and my uncle and aunt were tearing through their presents at a dizzying rate, with paper wrappings strewn about everywhere, everyone laughing and commenting on their gifts. "You shouldn't have," said my uncle to his wife. "No, it's you who shouldn't have," she replied as soon as she opened hers. "You knew I was going to get this for you, surely you knew." "I promise, I had no idea, none." And with this she kissed him on the lips. They'd been married for more than thirty years and had known each other since grammar school. I had never seen a couple still in love after so many years.

Just as I was beginning to feel awkward for not bringing any presents for the group, my mother produced from her bag three large envelopes made of very thick green paper that I knew I'd seen before but couldn't recall where. She handed one to each of her nieces and one to her sister-in-law. They immediately opened them and what was in each was not an envelope with a Christmas card as I had momentarily feared, but a scarf. The first, when one of my cousins unfolded it, showed an image of the Colosseum; the other, of a she-wolf suckling two baby twins; and the third, a florid design of the Capitoline Museum. Everyone appeared enamored with their scarves, though I suspected that their enthusiasm was a bit of a sham. My mother, I was sure, had bought these scarves not in an expensive boutique, but in one of the stalls in the marketplace on Via Enea, a few steps from the cheese vendor. The envelopes, which I finally recognized, were extras she'd brought over from Egypt and kept for gifts. They probably cost more than the scarves themselves.

After the gifts there was another surprise: a cake that my aunt had made, this time with exceptionally thinly cut, caramelized apple slices, and next to the cake, a bowl of crème fraîche. I had never had crème fraîche before, and it seemed like something prepared in heaven's kitchen, then sent down to Issy-les-Moulineaux on a dessert cart. I think I had more crème fraîche than cake that evening.

My uncle decided to walk us home instead of driving us. Jules joined us and together we crossed the bridge and stood in front of our building. Tonton had been speaking with my mother. At some point, he couldn't control himself any longer and reminded her that he had warned her about my father. She did not reply, but eventually asked me if I had the key to the apartment, then kissed him, wishing him a Merry Christmas. My mother surprised me. She very seldom held her temper, but this time she did.

~

The next morning, we had breakfast at my uncle's home. My mother wanted to spend the morning with her sister-in-law, so I said I would explore the city on my own. Tonton repeated his instructions about the métro, and before shutting the door behind me, I said I would be back that afternoon. I'd grown used to exploring Rome on my own, and this was my chance to do the same in Paris. My brother joined the boyfriendless cousin to see a Humphrey Bogart film. I had no idea who Humphrey Bogart was. Within the next five days, they managed to see all the Bogart films showing in Paris.

The whole underground system, as I'd been told by a friend in Rome, had a smell I would come to recognize and to love. Tonton Robert and his post-doc were right about the ease with which one changed trains. While going down a stairway, I froze before one of those gates that used to shut automatically as soon as a train approached the station, and to my total surprise, a woman who was rushing right behind me and clearly didn't want to miss her train shoved me onto the platform before the gate shut. The French, I realized, had a different approach vis-à-vis hesitation, coyness, and indecision. I never forgot that shove.

Soon I arrived where I wanted to be. When I finally climbed the stairs at the Franklin D. Roosevelt métro station and was standing on the sidewalk, I saw for the first time in my life what I couldn't believe had just then, and after so long, finally opened its arms to me. The Champs-Élysées. The avenue couldn't be real, though, and as I kept staring, all I could think was of movies where I'd seen it many times. It remained strangely more authentic in cinema than in life. I was looking at it but I wasn't seeing it. There was too much to see, the stores, the theaters, the restaurants, the cafés, the endless women, young and old, walking up and down the sidewalk of an avenue lined by so many trees, all decorated with Christmas lights. Above all, I watched a ribbon of red and green traffic lights in tight formation rise toward the Arc de Triomphe. I've always loved Paris on overcast days, maybe because this is how I first encountered it. Everything moved fast here. I liked the pace, the vigor and energy of Parisians. I wanted to take everything in, to stand and gawk at the Champs-Élysées, maybe because by staring I'd be taking possession of the avenue and owning it. I longed to touch something—but what was there to touch?—to anchor my experience, to give it a shape, perhaps even make a wish here to mark the experience, the way Aunt Flora did when something captivated her and she needed to hold on to it by making a wish. And so I, too, like every ordinary tourist, began to regret not bringing the camera that my father had given me on my last days in Alexandria and which my mother hated and didn't allow me to take to Paris because it was purchased in a store where my father's latest girlfriend was a salesgirl. The camera would have given me the impression that the site was not going to vanish from my grasp, that I had captured it and could eventually take it back with me to Rome.

But then this is what was so surprising. The site wasn't vanishing at all, and despite the intrusion of motorbikes and cars and the perpetual noise, the stunning impression of the Champs-Élysées was lasting longer than anything that had ever stunned me.

Reduced to my own devices, I thought that maybe one of the ways to magnify and seize this wonderful moment was to stop thinking about it and allow myself simply to experience it. But this was impossible, as my thinking about not thinking was itself already intruding on the experience. I wanted to do something with the Champs-Élysées. Perhaps I should buy something as a keepsake, to remind myself that I'd bought this key chain on the Champs-Élysées, or that cheap ballpoint pen, with which I'd take my mid-year exams a few days after returning to school in January. It would still hold something of Paris embedded in its very French royal-blue ink.

But I realized on stepping out of the Franklin D. Roosevelt métro station that I lacked the ability to grasp and take in the stunning beauty of the avenue. I felt a desire to resist it, to fight it, to name what had struck me as fast and as imperfectly as I could so as to log it and, by logging it, be done with it. I had done no differently with the Colosseum in Rome. I wanted to find and expose its frail little secret. But I disliked this resistance and remembered my father's word about Aunt Flora when he'd told me once that she needed to distrust, to deny, and then rehearse losing something only to admit having wanted it long after losing it.

Now, from where I was, I could see the Place de l'Étoile, but was this really the Arc de Triomphe I was beholding?

Because I didn't want to believe I was seeing it, I stopped a man walking by and asked him as politely as I could where the Place de l'Étoile was. He smiled, almost mocking the clumsy, indolent inflection in my speech, and, turning around, pointed to the Arc de Triomphe. There was no denying now that the Étoile was right before my eyes.

Why disbelieve the obvious? Was it to cancel it and let it spring on me each time I doubted having seen it so as to enjoy it all over again?

I did not have time to ponder why I'd stopped this stranger, when he asked if I was Spanish.

Suddenly, from thinking of myself as a young man who thought he was French and was finally in his language, in his homeland, and savoring budding manhood in, of all places, Paris, I was hurled into a universe of domestics, like the woman working in Tonton Robert's kitchen.

I told him that I was not Spanish. And I was not Portuguese either.

But I immediately sensed that I had a North African accent when speaking French.

I didn't want to feel I wasn't French.

I thanked him for the directions, then proceeded up the avenue.

I was easily distracted by all the lavish signs. I entered a large gallery and then a series of stores, with endless things I might have wanted to buy if I'd had the money.

After a long walk and so many stops along the way, I was hungry and decided, with the French money my father had given me in Rome, to stop for something to eat. But I was nervous, unfamiliar, and hesitant. It had taken me forever to decide not only what to order in Rome, but, more nerve-racking yet, how to order. I stopped by the terrace of a café where all the tables were taken. A waiter caught me looking lost and pointed to a small round table with a hasty gesture that meant he'd be with me in a moment. The table he'd indicated didn't have a chair, but he took one from one of the tables across the aisle and carried it upright by one of its legs while holding his tray with his other hand. He placed the chair in a tight spot between two tables and right away asked what I wanted to order, or did I need a menu? I figured a menu might give me time to think. A thirty-year-old couple sitting to my left looked in my direction, and the woman, thinking I must be American or English, said in English that I should simply order their *sandwich au jambon*. So I did. "And to drink?" the waiter asked. "*Pamplemousse?*" I had no idea what *pamplemousse* was, but I figured it was easier to pretend I knew. "Not everyone likes *pamplemousse*," added the same woman. I nodded to the waiter about the *pamplemousse*. Within minutes I was served a half-baguette sandwich containing one or two slices of ham, butter, and a few sliced cornichons, with a tiny container of mustard on the side. The glass of *pamplemousse* arrived, and to my delight I saw that it was grapefruit juice, which I'd always liked but had never thought of having in Rome. "But it's grapefruit!" I exclaimed to the young lady next to me.

I was in heaven—because of the food, because I was by myself in Paris, because I felt I was a grown-up. She said she suspected I was an American, but wasn't sure. She liked speaking English. I did not tell her that in Egypt we used the English word for grapefruit even when speaking French.

The irony is that I spoke English with a slight French accent, but suspected from previous experience that she was not going to be able to detect this. I did not want to speak French with her because she'd have immediately gathered that I came from North Africa, which I was as reluctant to disclose now in Paris as I'd been in Rome when fearing that Howard McIntire might reveal my Egyptian background to everyone at school.

She asked if I was traveling alone in Paris. I said I was visiting an uncle. I did not tell her that I was traveling with my mother and brother.

Where did I live? she asked.

Rome, I replied.

Was my father in the diplomatic corps?

No, he was with the Food and Agricultural Organization.

"You mean the Food and Agriculture Organization, not *Agricultural*," corrected the man who must have been her husband and had been quiet all this time. He was lighting his cigarette. He smoked Gitanes.

Mortified by possibly being caught lying, I said that, yes, he worked for the FAO, abbreviated, which is how my schoolmates referred to it, as many of their parents worked there. The couple asked what I was studying.

I said literature, hoping they'd think I was a university student, which I could tell they assumed. I didn't disabuse them.

Which authors in particular? the husband asked.

I think I was starting to sweat. I was accumulating too many lies and feared being exposed.

James Joyce, I said, but Marcel Proust as well.

Had I read *À la recherche*?

Not all of it but a good portion, I said, adding that I was particularly sensitive to his references to scent, as I thought I was as well. Scents made me travel back in time the moment I smelled something seemingly forgotten.

I was amazing both husband and wife. I was amazing myself.

Then, for some reason, I added my crowning jewel, because I loved how this was happening. I told them that after lunch I was planning to visit Shakespeare & Company, where I'd never been before.

"Because of James Joyce," he asked.

"Yes, because of James Joyce," I said with a touch of self-derision in my voice to mask, and hence emphasize, the high seriousness of my project. "I'm still a kid, you know," I said, as though coming to my own defense.

"No, we're sure you must be brilliant," continued the wife.

Silence fell between us. They were getting ready to leave. They signaled to the waiter, paid him, and left him their tip on the plate. They put on their coats, shook my hand, and asked where I came from in the States.

"New York," I replied. Good thing they didn't ask where. They confessed they'd always wanted to go to New York but hadn't yet. "One day," they said. "One day," I repeated, trying to inject a hopeful sigh in the words I echoed.

"And listen," added the husband, looking at his wife and receiving a slight nod from her, "if you have absolutely nothing better to do this evening—we're having *un petit souper chez nous*—you're welcome to stop by. There'll be people your age, as some are my students at the lycée and would be ecstatic to meet an American who knows Proust. Please, try to come. Our son is two years old, but I promise he'll be asleep." He tore out a sheet of paper from a notebook in his briefcase and wrote down their names, telephone number, address. Then they left, wishing me *joyeux Noël*. At the last minute, he turned around and said he had paid for my lunch.

I thanked them both.

I loved the French.

I was, as I looked around at the Champs-Élysées and at the note left on my table, totally in my element. This was home. Just by sitting here I'd made friends.

Half my sandwich was still uneaten and I was going to enjoy it all by myself. I slathered more mustard on my sandwich. I liked how it stung my nose. I knew I was going to order a cup of coffee but I was in no rush yet. All I kept thinking as I looked at those seated in the crowded sidewalk café was of a classic song, "Paris, c'est une blonde." And the *blonde* was clearly in love with me.

A part of me was tempted to leave the address of the couple on the table. I knew that my father would consider me crazy to forfeit the chance of meeting so many students my age. How easily had I slipped into France, he'd say. Eventually, I folded the address and pocketed it, determined to lose the piece of paper as soon as I was far enough from the café. If meeting people was so easy, there'd be countless similar encounters. These things must happen all the time in Paris.

I was wrong. I sat in many more cafés during my short stay in Paris, stood in line at various small cinemas, went into a self-service place and sat next to people at the same table, but not a word, either from them or from me. I should have gone to the couple's *petit souper*, I said days later. "Yes, you should have," said my uncle. "Life sometimes takes a sudden *virage*, a turn, and opens up pathways you never could have imagined. That *petit souper* could have changed your life, or it could have been a waste of time. But now you'll never know, right?"

After lunch I walked back down the other side of the avenue, happy that I'd had the foresight to study the map of Paris at the USIS in Rome. I knew exactly what I was going to do: head down the avenue, reach the Place de la Concorde, and from the Concorde I was going to go to rue de Rivoli, because I'd seen pictures of its endless arcade, then I'd stop a moment at Place Vendôme, get back on rue de Rivoli, after which I was going to cross the courtyards of the Louvre, not go to the museum but simply walk through it until I reached the Seine. Then I'd cut over to Boulevard Saint-Germain or walk along the Left Bank, finally reaching Shakespeare & Company. Joyce had been there just forty or so years earlier, though the bookstore had been located elsewhere in his day. If I had time, I'd pass by Notre-Dame and Les Halles. After that, I would have to take the métro to

Porte de Saint-Cloud, get myself *débarbouillé*, and go to my aunt and uncle's home.

Oh yes, I would also buy cigarettes. Gitanes. These were what I'd seen the husband smoking. You tapped the pack a few times on the table, then you pulled off the cellophane wrapper, opened the aluminum foil, took out a cigarette, and lit it, either by cupping your hand around a match or, as the husband had done, by using a plastic lighter. If I liked smoking, I would most likely want to buy such a lighter.

In a small shop next to the café, I saw the cigarettes I wanted to buy. I asked for a pack of Gitanes. Faster than the speed of light, the man slapped the pack on the glass counter. I paid. I had no idea it was this easy to buy cigarettes. The life of the senses was far easier in Paris.

I started my walk and lit my cigarette. I coughed a few times but was happy that no one saw me cough. I decided I'd change plans and walk directly to the river. The way was going to be longer but I liked the walk. It was part of my plan to know Paris, to live Paris. But within twenty or so minutes, I started to feel that I wasn't reaching the river. Walking back had become impossible; I had taken too many shortcuts and had lost my way.

After about an hour of aimless wandering trying to retrace my footsteps and not finding any métro station to get back to Saint-Cloud, I noticed it was getting dark. I had no other option but to call my uncle. I walked into a busy café on the corner of the street, asked where I could find a telephone, and, after purchasing a *jeton*, called his home. "But where are you?" he asked. "That's the problem," I replied, trying to inject a note of humor in my voice so as not to sound panicked, "I don't know where I am." "Clearly, you're from *la montagne*. Just look at a street corner, any street corner, and tell me what the names of the intersecting streets are." I was inside a café, so, cupping the receiver, I asked the garçon where we were, but he shrugged his shoulders and stepped outside to deliver two fruit juices. When I saw him come back again, I asked, "Could you tell me what street we're on?" trying to sound super-apologetic for the intrusion. "If you don't already know, no use telling you." The sheer malice of his answer shook me. I was about to place the receiver on the telephone and step outside to check the names of the streets at the crossroads when the lady at the cash register overheard my question and the waiter's blunt reply and told me the name. I reported the streets to my uncle. "But *que diable* brought you all the way there?" I told him I was trying to find a shortcut to go to the river. "But the river is in the other direction!" He burst out laughing.

His laughter made me laugh.

"Stand there. Don't move. I'll pick you up in the car."

He came in about half an hour, accompanied by my mother, my youngest cousin, and Jules. I was mortified, reduced to being the teenager I thought I'd outgrown.

I told them about the invitation. That, I figured, would restore my maturity. But I didn't say a word about the cigarettes.

"You should go to the supper," my uncle said, "or you could hang around with your *petite maman*, your Tonton Robert, and remain the good little Dédé you've always been."

~

After dinner that night, Jules said he was going to meet some of his friends. Did I want to join him? I hesitated because he was quite a few years older than I, and I assumed that his friends were his age. "Not all of them," he said, which I understood was an oblique way of avoiding answering my objection. Besides, I said, I needed to work on my final paper on the Existentialists. We had spoken a long while about the Existentialists in the car the night before, but frankly, he added, they're completely *démodés* these days. Besides, he promised to drive me back home after that evening's outing. He owned his own Deux Chevaux. Everyone in France had a Citroën Deux Chevaux— laughter, laughter—as it was the cheapest car in the world! I tried to object about the party. "Don't bother, you'll have fun. Unless you would have preferred the *lycéens* with whom you were going to drink terrible wine and gobble hard cheese on salted breadsticks."

As soon as he got into his car he took out his cigarettes and offered me one. I hesitated. "You do smoke, don't you?" "Sometimes," I replied, trying to suggest I smoked more than I cared to admit but leaving the door open for him to infer that I never smoked. "So where do you propose we go?" he asked. "I thought . . . ," I started, meaning his friends without really saying so. "You thought, you thought," he teased. "I mentioned my friends so as not to have others ask too many questions." He was quiet for a moment. "I have a brilliant idea," he said.

He was driving too fast along these narrow streets but I was reluctant to ask him to slow down. He was the type who'd speed up just to prove me a wimp. Eventually we got a glimpse of Notre-Dame in the dark, and then he turned down a number of narrow alleys until we were, as he explained, at Les Halles, the main marketplace of Paris in those years—the area I'd been planning to walk through after stopping at Shakespeare & Company.

We were on rue Saint-Denis. He found a spot to park nearby, stopped the car, and we got out. By then I had a good inkling of what he had in mind and was going along with his extravagance, hoping that after half an hour we'd be back in his car heading home. He stopped at one of those long narrow vestibules where three women stood behind a semi-closed hotel glass door waiting. What surprised me was that one of them knew him. "They call me Dalí," he whispered in my ear. "You are my guest," he added. He and the blond girl he knew bandied a few quips back and forth—the weather, Christmas, so many tourists this time of year—then she asked him, looking me over, "*C'est ton petit frère?*" Is he your younger brother? "No, a friend." She said I was *très mignon*, very cute. She said this to everyone, but I liked the easy familiarity and the welcoming tone and softness in her voice. My last time had been in Egypt with friends, and the woman, who was already lying naked, had yelled at me for taking too long to finish. I still thought Jules had just stopped for a bit of a chitchat, but then it began to appear that he was really going to go through with it. What surprised me even more is that this was not something he was doing for himself. He was doing it for me—which explains his whispered word *guest*, which I had totally misunderstood. Everything seemed to have been prearranged; there was no haggling. "*C'est mon petit cadeau de Noël*," my little Christmas present, he said to me in front of the three girls, his way of saying, to me more than to them, that there was no backing out of this. "*Tu montes, coco?*" Coming upstairs, dear? she asked me. This was a hotel, and the third girl, who was older, was the landlady, who had to be paid separately for the room. The girl who had asked me upstairs turned to me. "*Il est bien gentil ton ami*," your friend is a nice guy. She gave me her hand.

She opened the door and we entered a small room with a large bed, a chest of drawers, a sink, and a bidet. The long window was slightly open and I could hear people talking on rue Saint-Denis. She said I should undress. I took off my jacket, my tie, my shirt, removed my shoes, lowered my trousers, socks, and underwear. She made a joke saying that I had undressed before her. "*Je te plais?*" Do you like me? she asked. "*Oui, beaucoup*," I said. She must have been twenty years old. She was skinny, and when she got naked, I noticed she had very firm breasts. Without thinking, I reached out and put a palm on one breast. "Not yet, *mon coco*," she said with a mild giggle. "First I have to clean you. Come." She stood by the sink, turned on the faucet, and began to wash my penis with a bar of soap. No one, since childhood, had ever washed my penis. When I was still a boy, my nanny and my mother used to rub me everywhere when washing me with a sponge, but this was the first time someone had washed me down there and nowhere else. She held my penis in her hand, and I could tell that she was tacitly examining it. Then she dried me, very gently. "My turn," she said. She sat on the bidet, spread her thighs, and turned on the faucet to clean herself. I had never seen a woman do this. It felt so clinical, so routine, indeed everything began to feel humdrum and impersonal. I had liked being cajoled on the way up the narrow wooden spiral staircase when she called me her *coco*, trying to stir a feeling of fellowship between us. It made me want her. I even liked the sound of people passing by on the street below and chatting among themselves, one laughing loudly. I spotted a cigarette burn on the top of the chest of drawers; someone must have placed his lighted cigarette there, probably thinking he'd be done very shortly but then lost sense of time.

After drying herself with the same towel that she had used on me, she plopped herself on the bed and lay on her back, knees up, thighs parted. "*Tu viens, cheri?*" Are you coming, dear? She signaled me to the bed. I once heard a boy at school complain that the prostitute he'd been to had asked him to get on top of her, and while he was performing, he lifted his head and saw that she was eating yogurt with a spoon. There was no yogurt now, but her matter-of-factness dispelled the illusion of companionship. Besides, I could feel I was flagging, and the more I tried not to, the less I was able to get more than modestly hard. I was upset at the wasted opportunity rather than at my failure. "Let's see if you like this better," she said, attempting a new maneuver, even asking if I didn't mind her sucking me. No, I didn't mind, but I could tell she was trying her best not to give off apprehensive signals. I knew that what was failing me was desire itself. The breast that I had touched too soon no longer thrilled me; she did not thrill me. And I hated to keep Jules waiting downstairs. "I'd better get dressed," I finally said, "I am sure Dalí is getting impatient downstairs."

"I think you'll need to see a doctor, *coco*."

"I don't need to see a doctor," I replied.

"*Moi, j'ai fait ce que j'ai pu,*" I did what I could, she finally said, absolving herself, as she got up and we got dressed and walked down the spiral staircase. Jules was waiting downstairs, chatting with the landlady. The other girl was no longer there. She must have found a customer.

"Already!" he exclaimed, the moment he saw me coming down the stairs.

"It didn't work."

"It happens," he said. He didn't know what else to add to his brusque *déjà?* nor was he the type who'd have words of solace for the occasion.

Failing what to say next, I asked him how much it cost.

"Why?" he asked.

"Just wanted to know."

"Why?"

"Because . . ." I hesitated. "Because I want to come again."

"This time you're on your own."

He told me how much.

Not a fortune, I thought, but I decided not to tell him this. I thanked him for his generosity.

"Don't thank me, thank your uncle."

~

The two sides of my family who lived in Paris had nothing to do with each other. This probably went back to the days when my mother and father had begun dating twenty-five years earlier. Neither he nor she was much of a catch: she was completely deaf and had never worked except as a volunteer nurse during the war. He was hardly better: a small-time employee in a dyeing factory with hardly any prospects. He enjoyed spending his free hours in the municipal library; she preferred the beach. No two persons could have been more different or ill-suited. Her father owned a bicycle shop; his ran a billiard hall. Socially, neither party had any reason to believe it outranked the other, though her father had made a small fortune with the bicycle store, while his father smoked all day and played a lot of pool, frequently winning money but never enough to call it an income.

Each branch, of course, found ways to consider itself superior to the other. The venom that ran between the Capulets and Montagues could not have been deadlier. Bicycle shop and billiard hall could not claim to be significantly different in the arrogant eyes of my father's relatives, whose stars were Uncle Claude and his four brothers.

My grandmother's sisters, on my father's side of the family, lived in the seizième arrondissement now, one of the most prestigious neighborhoods in Paris. My mother's brother lived in Issy-les-Moulineaux, a humble neighborhood on the fringes of Paris, her sister lived in Stanmore, a suburb of London, and her other sister lived in the Bronx. Everyone lived as best they could, but the apartments in the seizième, honorable as their owners believed their residences to be, were by no means spacious, barely achieving a sort of righteous decrepitude. On my father's side, Cousin Arnaut's apartment had mirrors everywhere, so that you kept running into yourself every few seconds; their sole purpose was to make the apartment seem much larger despite having one bedroom, a living room, plus a tiny maid's room the size of a closet, where Arnaut's mother, Aunt Marta, the younger sister of my grandmother and Aunt Elsa, slept.

The enmity between the two branches of the family sprang up again when Tonton Robert drove us to Aunt Elsa's home in the seizième, where we were to spend another ten days after our brief stay in Saint-Cloud. "A big dark building like King Tut's tomb," he said while parking outside Elsa's building. Then, unable to resist, he added, "to match each one of their bedraggled faces." His wife snapped, asking him not to speak that way. "What? I say what I think. They have craggy faces because they refuse to die." I couldn't help laughing, and Jules, who had come along, joined in. Later, my brother told me I shouldn't have laughed.

Aunt Elsa's building was a blackened edifice in a deserted street, typical of the quiet seizième in the evening. After my uncle had parked his tiny car, out came his wife, his youngest daughter, Jules, my mother, my brother, and I, just like a circus act, said Jules as he stood on the sidewalk, righting himself. "I'm not coming," said my uncle. "It would be rude not to come," my aunt remonstrated. "I don't want to meet him." "But he'll be offended if you don't come." *Him* was my father, who had arrived the day before from Rome, after putting his mother on a plane to Montevideo. It was he who had arranged for all of us to sleep at Aunt Elsa's. Elsa herself had arrived in late autumn from Egypt and was very eager to be back in her apartment, which she hadn't seen in ages and was happy to find again though it had aged quite a bit, she said. From her letters, which she'd sent us as soon as she was settled in Paris, she did not sound particularly eager to share her home with anyone, especially after having hosted my grandmother for well over a month.

Eventually, Tonton Robert was persuaded to come upstairs. Barely three could fit in the tiny elevator, so I let my mother, my aunt, and my cousin and brother go up first. Eventually, the elevator returned and we went upstairs too. In the elevator my uncle, whose girth made distance impossible, had kept staring at me as if searching my gaze, while I kept averting his, sensing exactly what his wry, mischievous glance was evoking but that he'd been unable to mention in the presence of his wife and daughter. Jules had the same sly look on his face. "So, did you go back?" Jules finally asked as the elevator box inched up to the fifth floor. "Yes, I did." "And?" "Money well spent," I replied. "Where did you get the money?" he asked. I had my ways, I said.

I didn't confess to either of them, as we stood huddled in the tight elevator, that I had asked my mother for money, telling her that I wanted to buy a small present for the couple who had invited me to dinner. I pretended that I would drop off the tiny present—a big apple cake—the next day. "A big apple cake?" she asked, almost disbelieving me. The matter felt urgent enough for me to risk any lie. My brother saw right through me, smiled, but didn't say a word. We had very few secrets from each other and eventually I knew I'd tell him everything.

Earlier that afternoon, while trying to persuade myself that I still wanted to go to Shakespeare & Company, I'd taken the métro and headed directly to rue Saint-Denis. My brother offered to join me, but I told him that I was going to research quite a few things about James Joyce at the store and that he'd find this very boring. He said he'd go to the movies instead.

Meanwhile, I was driven less by the desire to be naked with a woman than by the craving to redress a wrong, with something hostile and mean-spirited directed not at the girl on the bidet, or at Jules, who had waited for me downstairs, or even at myself or the real culprit, my body; it was a vague, aimless form of revenge that I needed to exact, though I had no sense from whom or what.

I found the hotel, but saw different girls waiting in the lobby. Happily, the one I chose was also a blond and must have been the same age as the one on the previous night. She didn't clean herself in what turned out to be the exact same bedroom with the exact same old bedcover and cigarette burn, nor did she clean me. Instead, she asked that I use a condom. I didn't have one, but she produced one and said she was going to put it on me very, very gently. She waited a short while, informed me that she didn't kiss, then let it pass as though she'd never said it. I told her about the mishap in that same room the day before. She gave me a confiding smile and said that this never happened with her. Years later, when having my blood drawn, I told the nurse that no one finds my vein on the first, second, or third try. "That never happens with me," said the nurse, echoing the girl on rue Saint-Denis. And indeed, the nurse had barely tapped my arm with two fingers, when, without looking, I knew that she had found the vein. I like how sometimes people know my body better than I do. "See now?" said the girl in the tiny bedroom. "See how easy?" All she asked was for me to slow down, "*Sois pas si pressé, laisse que ça vienne de soi*," don't be so rushed, let it happen on its own. She had said it so kindly and meant it so generously, and I was so moved by her sweetness and her reluctance to hurry things along that I realized what men meant when they said they had to hold back. Later, "*Laisse, je vais te nettoyer moi*," I'll clean you. This was perhaps the highest compliment a woman had ever paid me, and I knew that, if I had the means, I'd be there again the next day and the next after that. Maybe this was why Jules knew the place so well and had no doubt befriended every woman there. If I became a regular, I'd want them to call me Picasso.

The experience hadn't changed me, I was still the same, still the kid in the family who felt no different from the person who'd been so eager to prove himself an hour earlier. It hadn't meant much. But I'd enjoyed it, and I certainly enjoyed being who I was afterward.

The one thing I wanted now was never to leave Paris.

When we entered Aunt Elsa's apartment, I hugged her very tightly. I hadn't seen her since Egypt earlier that year. I also hugged my father, who seemed a bit lost and had told my mother that he hadn't even opened his suitcase yet. Then, noticing my cousin Marianne next to him, I gave her two kisses, even though I'd arrived in the same car as she and had no reason to greet her this way. Something was telling me that I could sleep with every woman on the planet if I wanted. I didn't know if this feeling would last or could be attributed either to the girl on rue Saint-Denis or simply to Paris itself. Paris does that, I concluded. It stirs up possibilities between people who'd never have thought of them elsewhere.

The visit of my mother's relatives was short, but no sooner had my uncle and aunt and Jules and my cousin left than my father muttered, "I can't stand that man." My brother told him that my mother's brother and the rest of the family had been absolutely wonderful to us, and that, unlike my mother's sister in New York, they'd instilled in him the desire to stay in Paris for the rest of his life. "*Moi aussi*," me too, I said.

My father was not opposed to the idea. He himself had not been successful in finding business opportunities in Milan, Geneva, or London and wished above all to settle in Paris. We could, if we wanted, try to speak to the headmaster of the school around the corner, one of the best lycées in France. The idea thrilled the two of us. Living with the French language, as opposed to English or Italian or, as had been the case before, Arabic, promised to restore so many aspects of my life that had been left stranded and disjointed. I longed to be a Parisian.

The lycée, as luck would have it, was not even a block away from Aunt Elsa's home. The only problem was that I was finishing high school at an American school and was sure that the French system would set me back by a year, if not more. This was not an intolerable option but it would have to be negotiated. My brother, too, would lose a year or two.

Aunt Elsa made a quick supper for us. She boiled pasta and opened a can of tomato sauce. She also produced a slab of parmesan cheese, which she removed from a very old biscuit box that dated to before World War II, when British forces were stationed in Egypt and British biscuits were easy to find. The cheese itself looked very hard. I asked her when she had bought that cheese.

"I bought it when I bought it," she replied, which told me all I needed to know.

My mother helped prepare a salad in the kitchen. But Aunt Elsa liked her *petite salade*, which she took out of the refrigerator, removing the plate covering a small bowl containing yesterday's salad, which, she said, she liked old and soggy.

When a while later it came time for dessert, she produced star-shaped *bollos*, cheese-and-potato biscuits, her specialty. These tasted so stale that, once again, I asked her when she had baked them. Her answer was no different.

"I made them when I made them."

The next morning, when she brought out a jar of marmalade with its lid still sealed with wax, her answer was the same. She had left a label on the jar bearing her archaic nun's script that revealed the name of the fruit and the year when the jam was made. Some of her jars had remained sealed in one of her locked cabinets in Alexandria; she'd decided not to throw them out and brought them to France. Aunt Elsa wasn't going to change.

On tasting her *bollos*, my father gave me a look. My mother, quick to intercept subterfuge in anyone's glances, caught the meaning of my father's smile and right away put her *bollos* down. She said she was going to wash the dishes, which would be her way of throwing our respective *bollos* into the garbage.

My father needed to be extra careful with his aunt. Once we returned to Rome, he was going to sleep in her living room for a while. She explained that she'd be willing to put him up for a month but after that he'd need to find a place of his own. If he was able to find a business that he trusted and that needed his know-how, he'd eventually settle in Paris and have us join him, she said.

The next morning, we waited until around ten to visit the school nearby. Chances were that everyone would be away for the Christmas holiday, but nothing would be lost if we tried to speak to even the lowliest functionary there. The courtyard of the school glistened from the previous night's shower. A few students of various ages, dressed in shirt and tie, were gently passing a soccer ball around, not really playing, while others were just smoking and gossiping as they ambled about the large schoolyard with nothing to do but hang together until they headed home for lunch. The school was obviously closed for Christmas. My father asked one of the students who was smoking by himself and was more or less my age if the *directeur* was there. "Yes, I just saw him come in," he said. He did not look at me or my brother with anything approaching hostility. In fact, he walked us all the way to the *directeur*'s office. The door was wide open. "These gentlemen would like to speak with you, *Monsieur le directeur*." The man behind the desk was courteous but stiff and, despite the holiday, wore a dark jacket and tie. We introduced ourselves, and I made sure to call him *Monsieur le directeur*. My father very succinctly explained that we were in an American high school in Rome and wished to transfer to a French lycée to prepare for the baccalaureate degree. It was clear from the principal's body language that this was not the first time that he had heard a similar story. He suggested that we transfer immediately to an American high school in Paris; a French lycée was far more advanced and might require at least—*at least*, he underscored the words by rounding his pinched lips and tilting his head with assumed perplexity and obliging condescension—two years of preparation, but that these matters could only be determined on an individual basis.

My father, still unclear as to what the principal was actually saying, asked, "Please allow me to understand: you are saying that my sons should transfer right away to an American school in Paris but that in case they wanted to earn a baccalaureate degree, they might have to spend at least"—and here he, too, emphasized the words *at least*—"two years of preparation? By then of course they'd be much older than the rest of their class."

"Yes, they would be much older," repeated the director.

"So, if I understand correctly, even though my sons are fluent in French, the elder would need to spend *at least*"—this time with subdued sarcasm—"two years here to supplement his American high school degree."

"Well, he cannot spend them *here* in this school, as we are full and the waiting list is *très, très longue*."

Smile.

Smiles back and forth.

The cold stare became almost a sneer.

The director, when I asked, said he did not know whether the American school in Paris prepared its students for a French baccalaureate. "Clearly, that would have to be discussed with the *directeur* of the American high school in Paris."

What surprised me as we left the school was the number of boys smoking and, more surprising still, the number of parked motorized Solexes; each of the students had come by moped. I went to school all the way from Via Clelia to Via Aurelia, and it took almost two hours door to door. These kids were wealthy.

There was no time to waste, and that same afternoon my father took us to the American school and asked about possible transfers. Yes, they did have spots open for us but the cost was so exorbitant that it was clear this school was for the wealthy only.

When we got home, my father placed a call to a friend who lived in Neuilly. Her father had been his accountant and with his son-in-law had become a millionaire. She was a schoolteacher and her husband, a Franco-American businessman, had survived the Shoah. She told my father that the fate of people with American high school diplomas hadn't changed in fifteen years. To enter a French university, you had to have a baccalaureate degree and to obtain one you needed to spend two years in a French lycée—and entering a good lycée was no cakewalk either, she said.

My heart sank. I knew what her words implied. I will never forget that fateful evening as reality began to sink in. I was standing next to my father as he held the telephone in one hand and his fountain pen in the other as if ready to take notes that he wasn't writing down, while I clasped the listening cup attached to the same line and listened in. I saw it: our dream of France was being peremptorily dismantled right before us—the Champs-Élysées, the couple in the café, the promises I'd made myself, Shakespeare & Company, the girl on rue Saint-Denis, even the lycée with its courtyard that glistened with rainbow patterns from the previous evening's rainfall, which had seemed so welcoming, gone all of them, and with them the person I believed I might become. I looked at my brother and wondered what was going through his mind, what dreams of his were being shattered, and I saw my mother, who inferred from our looks that something was being lost the moment my father hung up the phone. There was nothing to say, nothing to add, nothing to interpret, not a word of solace. We knew we could have looked for several lesser schools in Paris, just as we knew that, had we been resourceful enough, a solution would have eventually sprung up from somewhere. We didn't want to hope because hope was costly and we couldn't afford another disappointment. Father had given up too soon. And so had we.

My American aunt was right about New York. There was no future in France either, at least not for us. Her husband was right as well: in America, I could find a job and go to school without missing a year or putting up with *that French or Italian nonsense*, as he called our quandaries on a subsequent phone call from New York.

~

New Year's Eve was a sad evening. Earlier that morning, Aunt Elsa received an express-mail letter from my grandmother. The letter, as happened in those days, was not only addressed to its recipient but was meant to be passed around, read aloud, and discussed, and therefore needed to be composed with a degree of polish, purpose, and, where needed, innuendo. It was private, but deliberately public. In it she wrote that she had landed in Uruguay a few days earlier and was happy to see her dear son whom she thought she'd never see again. Everything was perfect, the family had welcomed her like a queen, and life couldn't be better. They were very wealthy and clearly her son's decision to move to Uruguay had been a stroke of genius. She noticed that her son sometimes punished his children because they didn't want to study, but that was to be expected, seeing that there are so many things to keep them active and distracted; everyone in the family rode magnificent horses. She also reported that the mother hit her cook, but the cook was lazy and, quite frankly, couldn't even boil water. What concerned her were the series of *actes innomables*, unspeakable deeds, that she'd witnessed her grandchildren and their friends practice by the swimming pool. She was so shocked that her knees had started to tremble as they'd done when, in school, so many, many years ago, she was asked to recite the Stabat Mater in front of visiting Italian dignitaries. There are things that had better not be put on paper, she added. But, all said, her reception in her daughter-in-law's home couldn't have been sweeter. That she had not written a word about her son's life was clearly left for every reader to ponder.

That evening, in Cousin Arnaut's mirrored apartment, my grand-mother's letter was reopened and read aloud, not by Aunt Elsa this time but by Aunt Marta, who had already read it and who reached for her reading glasses after Elsa handed her the envelope to read it to everyone. Both sisters repeated that they, too, recalled having to recite the Stabat Mater in successive years at the same nuns' school, where it became a source of humor in the family: imagine, Jewish girls chosen to recite the Stabat Mater! My grandmother's letter was punctiliously interpreted by Aunt Marta as if engaged in an hermeneutic exege-sis. The *unspeakable deeds* by the swimming pool particularly caught her attention and left her no less shaken and aghast than her poor sister Esther. "I can just imagine what our sister witnessed by the swimming pool—the less said, the better, but we know, we know," she added with a complicit smirk as she removed her eyeglasses and pointed them at the letter she was holding in her other hand. After the words *unspeakable deeds* my grandmother had added an exclamation point. "Not to be overlooked," commented Aunt Marta, putting on her eyeglasses again. "Obviously!" replied Aunt Elsa. "Here, see," Marta added, showing the letter to everyone in case we didn't trust the full sweep of her arcane analysis.

Decades later, I found several notebooks that had belonged to my grandmother. In them she was in the habit of drafting letters she'd recopy and then send, noting the date of the draft and the name of the recipient. In her draft, three exclamation points, and not just one, followed her doubly underlined *unspeakable deeds*. "I am still so horrified and saddened by what I saw and am left to wither away in a tiny room from which I know there is one exit and one exit only when the venerable coachman tells me it is time to go." In her finished version, she had stifled her shock and despair by adding one timid, conciliatory exclamation mark and no underlined words, knowing that her sisters would right away infer the full scope of what she had left out.

That night, I got a belated Christmas present from Cousin Arnaut—Turgenev's *First Love*—while my brother received the soundtrack to the movie *Zorba the Greek*. Hearing that Arnaut, like everyone else in the family, including my mother, spoke Greek, I told him in passing that we'd seen the film in Egypt and then once again in Rome, though this time dubbed in Italian. He laughed and reminded me that the best scene was the last one, when Zorba teaches the narrator to dance the *hasapiko*. He explained the steps to me, but I failed to understand them, so he said he'd show me if my brother would let him play the record he had just given him. My brother agreed. Arnaut stood in the middle of the room, extended both his arms laterally, and as soon as he heard the first pluck of the bouzouki strings, started a few steps of the *hasapiko*. He repeated the steps, repeated them with his right leg, then with his left leg, then back to his right leg, then his left leg. "These are the only steps I can remember," he said, apologizing, because his repertoire stopped there. My father immediately stepped into the middle of the room and, placing an arm on his cousin's shoulder, told him to follow his steps. Sure enough, he introduced a few more steps, after which, still mimicking my father, Arnaut said, "Not everyone in the family had a Greek mistress," which he muttered hoping my mother wouldn't make out what he had just said. "The girl could certainly dance this," replied my father, locking his lips. I knew what he was doing and I didn't like it.

As it turned out, my father, too, had run out of steps, which is when my mother, the one who could hear no music whatsoever, told them, "*Pas comme ça*," not like that, and introduced two complicated steps that involved sliding the foot, kicking the ground, stepping back and finally sideways, and raising one knee then the other knee and kicking again. Everyone was overjoyed by her demonstration. Cousin Arnaut decided to uncork a second bottle of champagne, serving my mother first. Arnaut had become French, we were Italian, Arnaut's mother was still Turkish, and Aunt Elsa was German, but once the *hasapiko* played we were all Ottoman Greeks.

As I listened to the music, I remembered an old Greek grocer in whose shop Greek songs and Greek dances were always playing on the radio and where, as a child of five or six, I learned to sing along to a song that I liked about a woman with a mischievous glance and a carnation in her hair, and as I sang, the man was impressed and told my mother that I'd be a good son to her, maybe even a grocer one day, he added. He was sad because he was being forced to close his shop and leave Egypt to return to his homeland in Greece, though he'd never once in his entire life set foot there. An Armenian client interrupted him, and he climbed up his ladder to bring down one of the many cured meats hanging from the beams under the ceiling, where the flies liked to assemble. There was nothing he could do about the flies, he told the customer. "There comes a time," he said, turning to my mother, "when these cured meats have to be brought down to earth. I am no different," he continued, grabbing one of the large, oval-shaped shanks hanging from a thin cord, "at some point I don't want to be the last piece left in Egypt." He was not a good son, he added, as he wrapped the cheese for my mother. His mother did not want to leave Alexandria or move to Athens with him. His wife, on the other hand, couldn't wait to leave. "What can I do, madame, what can I do?" Then, turning to me, he added, "You be a good son to her. One day she will need you."

~

Unbeknownst to me, my mother had brought everyone the same Christmas present she had brought her two nieces and her sister-in-law. My father had brought nothing. For Christmas, they offered him a Swiss voile handkerchief in an intricate box. "*Un mouchoir— franchement!*" A handkerchief—frankly! exclaimed my outraged father hours later as he and I walked home together. "What have we come to?" I could have replied that, unlike them, he had come empty-handed. But then I realized that my father hated celebrations and rituals and had probably never paid them any heed. He was generous, but he gave presents only when he wanted to.

But this New Year's Eve dinner reminded me that displaced families who had lost their roots and their homes and whatever bound them together still needed rituals, any ritual, including those they half remembered or made up, so as not to feel unmoored without them. Even borrowing cultures that were not our own was better than nothing. We were never the main branch of anything, just a twig grafted to a short stem, trying to bear fruit.

During the festive dinner in what my father called the-tiniest-home-despite-its-mirrors, Arnaut decided to read a little poem he'd composed for the occasion. In it he applauded that all remaining members of the large family had finally left Egypt, that Egypt was becoming a vague memory destined to perish, and that now it was time for everyone to settle in France. Those in Uruguay would eventually have to return, those in Italy would cross the Alps and resettle here—*here* meaning France, he added—and those in Israel would have to be coaxed to come back to where everyone spoke one language, the language of Corneille, Boileau, La Fontaine, Racine. Arnaut's composition went on for quite a while; he closed it with his special welcome to the youngest in the family, though another, he announced that night, was soon to join, his own son or daughter—who knew what Hashem had planned? Amen.

We toasted the good news. Then we sat down for dinner, which lasted a long time and was filled with French appetizers, Turkish main dishes to recall our origins, plus an Italian second course because some of us were still locked in Italy. We closed with an Uruguayan dessert as a nod to my grandmother, who would be pleased by the remembrance. We toasted one another with a Châteauneuf-du-Pape. Aunt Elsa, the oldest in the room, seconded the toast but asked for just a finger or two of wine because the glass was too heavy for her if it held too much. There was laughter and good cheer.

After dessert, we sat to watch television announcing the close of the year. A lighter, second Egyptian delicacy followed.

This was when things fell apart.

The subject of resettling in France was a thorny one and had been touched on more than once that evening and wasn't going to subside. So far my father had not found the opportunities he'd been looking for in France and needed to stay a while longer in Aunt Elsa's apartment to explore what France had to offer. I, too, had grown to like the option of moving to Paris, and if I had to supplement our income the following year by working in a gas station, as the protagonist of *Les Parapluies de Cherbourg* had done, well, there was no shame in that. My father himself had done very well without a baccalaureate or an Abitur after attending both French and German schools in Turkey.

There was another reason my father wanted to remain in Paris, and it had nothing to do with business. Paris allowed him to keep his wife at a safe distance in Rome. He was living as a single man for the first time in his life, and I understood this perfectly, the way I understood my mother, who was also on her own for the first time.

My father explained the difficulties to everyone in the room, but especially to Aunt Elsa.

She took advantage of the others in the room to remind him that when he and her sister, his mother, had requested she put them up for a while, she had been more than happy to open her home to them, but that she was unwilling to extend her offer beyond the month she had agreed to.

My father tried to extend the deadline; she listened, understood, and though she did not appear intransigent in the tone of her voice, she stuck to her word: one month and not a day more. My father could not contain his rising temper and finally blew up.

"You are a miserable woman, you've been a miser all your life, and you'll die a miser, like your mother, your grandmother, and every one of your wretched siblings, including my mother. I was only asking for a short period and here you're talking to me about being an old lady who needs her independence. What independence are you talking about? You're almost blind, your hip is out of whack, and your hands are so arthritic that you can't even use a nutcracker, let alone hold a full glass of wine. You're a crippled old woman who farts every time she stands up. You travel the world with your old sealed marmalades like Roma housewives who carry their entire household in a shawl, babies, pots, and empty gourds. Shame on you. Be grateful that I've been running all your errands since I've been living with you. I've bought your food, brought your medicine, taken you to this doctor, to that doctor, even handled all the suitcases arriving from Egypt whose contents you opened in secret, for who knows what junk you've brought along with you. I'm the one who fetches your bottles of water from the fountain at Square Lamartine every three days, and God help anyone who sips from a bottle if he happens to be parched in the middle of the night. So keep your damned apartment to yourself, you old witch."

Arnaut's wife, who had prepared such a lavish meal for the occasion and was hoping not to have this squabble ruin her evening, tried to intervene to contain my father's wrath, but it was Aunt Elsa's turn to tell him a few things that had been rankling her ever since he and his mother had moved in with her. She took out her kerchief and rubbed her eyes because she was weeping, though everyone knew that among most members of her family tears were more often than not a symptom not of grief but of rage.

"You've been begging for everyone's help since you arrived in France with your *petite maman*, because you're a scared little beggar, just like your father. All my brothers extended a hand to help you to the best of their ability, but you've been scared to touch anything because you know you're unfit to do anything. All you've been able to find was a partnership with a clothing importer who asked you to join his firm but within weeks decided to take back his offer. Instead, you found a paltry clerical position in his brother's firm. Your degradation is complete. Meanwhile, your wife and sons are leading miserable lives in Rome while you're still busy trying to philander your way in a country whose women won't even look at you. How do I know this? Because Monica, God help her, was ready to kill you when you propositioned her. And what does Elsa do? I let you live with me. I welcome you into my home. I ironed your shirts last month. Why? Because I'm an idiot. No, a witch. I have a good mind to shut my door on you—but no, instead I let you move in with your wife and your two sons. So, one month. But not a day more."

The two had let out so much venom that they felt exhausted. Aunt Elsa turned to Cousin Arnaut and asked for a glass of water with a teaspoon of sugar to calm her down, "Otherwise, the venerable coachman might come knocking at my door and tell me it's time."

She had meant to sound funny, and it was my father who laughed first.

Arnaut had gone to the kitchen and, to show he had indeed added sugar to her glass, was busy stirring it while coming out.

"These things happen," said Arnaut's wife, who was no stranger to family brawls and was attempting to repair the damage. "Was there ever a dinner without a squabble in this family? But soon the countdown to the new year will start. Time to let bygones be bygones."

And soon, after the famous singer sang his latest hit song, the countdown did indeed begin, and within seconds another champagne bottle was uncorked, and we all kissed. My father kissed my mother, my brother, me, the hostess, and then he and Aunt Elsa exchanged kisses while she patted him on the cheek. "May this year be a good

one for you *y para muchos años*." He wished her the same in Ladino. I
could tell they meant their good wishes.

By one o'clock it was time to leave. My mother and Aunt Elsa
wanted to get back by taxi, so Arnaut called one for them. The taxi
driver said he was arriving shortly, so everyone put on their coats. My
father said that he, my brother, and I would walk home together.

I'll never forget our itinerary that early morning. Rue du Ranelagh,
then Avenue Mozart, rue de la Pompe, Avenue Georges Mandel, rue
Decamps, to rue Greuze, where Elsa lived. I liked walking with my
father, the three of us talking about so many things. I told him I'd
wandered by myself throughout the city and uncovered places I never
imagined on this planet. My brother said he knew all the tiny movie
houses in the Latin Quarter. He could live here, he said. I could live
here too, I added. "Could you indeed?" asked my father. My all-too-
hasty *yes* could have sounded too brusque for a father who might have
been reluctant to know how much I disliked life in Rome, but he had
the patience and the kindness not to argue except by saying that Rome
had its merits too. Via Clelia, as I'd told him more than once in my
letters, had no merits. Besides, I wasn't so sure that life in Rome was
significantly cheaper than Paris, certainly not easier. This was when he
finally opened up to the two of us by saying that we knew perfectly
well why he needed to be away from Rome.

Yes, we knew.

"Things with your mother and me won't ever change."

We knew that too.

A long silence followed as we crossed the empty street. Then, remembering the music we'd heard that night on television, my father
couldn't help himself: "You don't know a woman until you've danced
a java with her. To lead and whirl around with a woman who loves a
java makes you love the music, makes you love her, and if you've had
enough wine to let yourself go, you'll love who you are!" He asked if
we knew how to dance a java. "You'll find time," he said. Suddenly my
father seemed very, very young and yet quite old as well. I wondered
where he'd learned to dance a java. On the corner of Avenue Mozart

we passed by a dark old doorway from which emanated a stagnant, moldy, damp odor that felt quite familiar but wasn't unpleasant. It reminded me of the very old water pipes in my grandfather's home after he'd died. When you turned on the faucet in the kitchen, nothing came out but an explosive, bronchial sputter that hissed at you and emitted a musty, fetid air. I asked my father if he recognized the smell, which had taken me back to rue Memphis in Alexandria at the time when his parents' apartment was almost completely emptied and Grandmother had gone to live with her mother and her sisters. I must have been two then. "How can you remember?" he asked. I had no answer.

The following evening, as we wandered through a large bookstore, my father stopped and bought me the first volume of Proust's *Remembrance of Things Past*.

On our way home, I asked him if he could give me two hundred francs.

"To do what with?" he asked. But then he caught himself.

The next day, my last in Paris, I found the same girl on rue Saint-Denis.

She claimed she recognized me.

⌣

The flight from Paris to Rome was in a small Caravelle plane. Everything about the flight was frugal, down to the meaningless snacks they passed around. The message couldn't have been clearer: we were not flying out to a Christmas vacation; we were returning to Via Clelia. Tomorrow, school started. Once again, waking early, prodding my brother to hurry, the crowded bus, maybe the girl in the turquoise overcoat, then waiting on a cold Piazza della Repubblica for the school bus.

We took a bus from the airport to Termini, and from Termini my mother splurged on a taxi, the excuse being that none of us wanted to carry luggage from the bus stop a block away from Via Clelia and then walk with it to our building. It was already night and we were tired, hungry, and very sad. As our taxi raced down Via Appia Nuova, I couldn't help but notice how empty the avenue was and how meager its lights compared with those in Paris. We were returning to a small village after living it up in a grand metropolis. I just prayed that our dejected mood wouldn't turn into a flare-up of Mother's bad temper. It didn't. But I could tell how much my mother missed not being with her husband.

When we arrived, I went up the stairs to deposit the suitcase I shared with my brother outside our door, then came back down to help my brother pick up my mother's, which was heavier. After we climbed the three flights, I unlocked our door and the first thing I sensed right away, before my mother had a moment to turn on the lights, was that our apartment smelled exactly as it had when we'd first moved in after our terrible drive from Naples more than six months earlier. How strange that our own smell, our own stamp on the apartment, had disappeared and the scent we believed expunged forever had seeped right back during our absence. It had never really vanished; it had always been there, lurking under the floorboards like a sneaky hired hand who sleeps in your bed when you're away and rummages through your things, wears your clothes, reads the markings in your books, then lets his homeless friends in to remind you that all your efforts to make this home yours have been feckless. I didn't like feeling like a stranger in a home I had never considered mine. I wanted to repossess it, but to repossess it the way we still crave someone we never loved and couldn't be happier to have lost.

As soon as Mother turned on the light in the entrance hall, Paris disappeared. Not a trace of Paris in our lives. When I opened my suitcase, I found one or two things that I'd packed hoping that they'd help me keep the memory of Paris alive. The red ballpoint pen, which I hadn't exchanged with my brother because he said that he now liked the blue one better, and the copy of *First Love* and the Theodorakis album that was still my brother's but that he'd asked me to pack in between our sweaters—all three still spoke of Paris to me, but I could tell that Rome was already struggling to shake off their luster.

Why had I been so happy in Paris?

True, I had met people I hadn't seen since childhood and was happy to rediscover now as an adult. And yet I was attached to no one, not my relatives, in spite of their warmth and loud embraces. Nor was I tied to Jules, nor to the girl who had so kindly cleaned me after sex, nor to the bridges that I made a point of crossing each day, nor even to Shakespeare & Company, which I'd visited so many times because it was so close to rue Saint-Denis. Yet something did root me in Paris. Maybe it was the French language, maybe it was the Christmas spirit, or just being away, or maybe Paris allowed me to like who I was, who I could be, who I wanted to be. So many maybes, but none of them stuck. At some point I caught myself thinking of Amina. Strange, I hadn't thought of her once since we'd left Rome before Christmas.

This made me think of the Existentialists. I'd worked on that paper in Paris, and one afternoon my aunt Laurence had taken me to Gibert to buy a few used books. I had liked working on the subject in the very city where some of these writers still lived. I had not finished my paper and had a few more days left to write a conclusion. But I couldn't conclude. Now I remembered not the paper or the hours I'd spent on it but the walk down Boulevard Saint-Michel, where, without my asking, Aunt Laurence had bought my brother and me a small bag of roasted almonds from a street vendor. The boulevard at that early hour of the evening was magical, though I couldn't tell why.

Now, decades later, I think I know why. Saint-Michel at that hour in the evening when all the shops are still open reminded me of evenings in Alexandria after it had rained. Unless it's the other way around, and what I treasured in Alexandria were prescient images of a Paris I hadn't yet seen.

What struck me in our living room now was the vase of flowers. I remembered that my grandmother had gone out with my mother to buy them to celebrate the holidays. Now their stems drooped and rested limp on the rim while the flowers had wilted and their petals lay scattered around the table, dried and shriveled, and the water had entirely vanished, leaving a salty, frost-like film on the glass. They'd held on for as long as they could. They reminded me of a cat a neighbor had left behind and forgotten to feed and which, on his return many days later, was scarcely able to stand on its feet, yet still welcomed him.

The next morning, I woke up early, made breakfast with my brother, and put on my jacket and tie for school. What was she doing today? I asked my mother. She didn't know yet; there'd be something to do. It had rained the night before and the streets gleamed and the sky was quite overcast and, yes, for a moment, I was in Paris, walking to another school. When I told my brother this, he grumpily reminded me that I was romanticizing again. But the illusion was dispelled on the crowded bus with its closed windows and everyone breathing on you with their breath that smelled of last night's supper.

We were the only ones at the school bus stop, and at some point I realized that not only the old gym teacher who always waited with us but the bus itself was late. Perhaps we'd arrived later than usual and missed it, but the big clock in the arcade showed that it was late by just a minute or so.

After about a full ten minutes of panic, it occurred to us that there was no school that day. School started the next day, not that Monday. A whirlwind of emotions seized me: I could have stayed in Paris one more day, gone to the Cinémathèque, who knows what other unnamed areas I might have discovered.

It was too early to do anything in Rome. So we had better head back home.

And then I realized we had no money for bus fare and had been planning to borrow the fare from someone at school. I couldn't call home. I had no money for a phone call even if our mother wasn't deaf.

We had one option left. To walk home. What an ugly, ugly city.

— 7 —

Thinking American

I t didn't take long to pick up where we'd left off. School started in early January, the midterm exams came and went, my mother resumed her daily shopping in the marketplace, and when I returned the empty bottles that we'd left behind on the floor before leaving for France, the girl who redeemed them with small change was still there with her implacable gaze that seemed to want to scold me for being me.

There was scant joy in our lives, and the old cloud resettled far too easily on our home. This is what your life's going to be, said the cloud. Everything else returned: rowdy marketplace at dawn, packed cold bus in the morning, the streets perennially dark by very early evening, and the *termosifoni* always on the blink.

My mother had brought Madame Renato a small present from Paris and another for the Avellinis and Coronaris. Signor Leo reappeared in our home, always bringing some sort of *vin santo* each time, knowing that my mother liked it. I called him the courtier, while Madame Renato was dubbed the harridan, which would make my mother laugh, though she always came to the defense of both: "He's a good man, a poor soul, and she's gentle and kind." "A poor soul with an inheritance," I would answer. "Yes, but look what the man spends it on, *vin santo* and a few cookies," she'd reply. "And his wardrobe," I added. Everybody was a poor soul, everyone was kind. Why did I have to be so critical? she asked. Weren't we poor souls too? she added. "You never like anything," she'd say. She was right. I was drawn to nothing and liked no one. "You'll need to change," she added.

She was thinking of Amina too. My mother had bought her a Parisian scarf but asked me to give it to her. I refused, as that would be sending a signal, and I didn't want to send her any signals. So my mother offered her the scarf and said that it came from the three of us. Amina couldn't believe she'd gotten a gift from Paris and said she loved it and kissed my mother and me on the cheek, but when she came into my room and, as always, left the door ajar, she kissed me on the cheek but close enough to the mouth. I didn't turn from her and knew that if I'd wanted to kiss her, on her lips or with my tongue, it would have been the easiest thing in the world. But I refrained. The girl in Paris had given me the boldness to be more forward, if I'd wanted to go further. Amina must have read that I was wavering and simply said, "*Mo', ti lascio,*" now I'll leave you, spoken softly and gently but with resolve, though not without a show of reluctance that left me feeling quite stirred. I knew we'd possibly do more when she came back in a few days for her shot. But I wasn't counting the hours.

Later that evening, as the three of us were having supper in the kitchen, my mother said a few words that stung me but reminded me that even in her eyes I was a grown man now. "No nonsense with her. She's a good girl." Then, turning to my brother, "And as for you, make certain he doesn't do anything stupid."

In the weeks that followed, I'd ask Mother if she'd been a good girl before getting married. Her answer was always the same: "*J'ai fait beaucoup de folies,*" I did many crazy things. When I asked her to be specific, she had only one tale to tell, and it never changed: The poor boys thought they were pushing themselves on a girl who liked flirting after dancing at night. They didn't know that she was the one taking advantage of them.

Meanwhile, I had handed in my paper on the Existentialists and was assigned to select a new topic for my next term paper. I was especially fascinated by the Christian heretics martyred by the Inquisition. Mr. Carson told me to visit Campo de' Fiori and find a statue that would surely intrigue me. Whose? I asked. He refused to tell me. "Go to Campo de' Fiori and you'll see." That Saturday at around eight thirty was a clear and warm day in January. I told my mother I was going out to see a statue in the *centro storico*. She said she had some sewing to do, then changed her mind and asked, "Can I come with you?" I would have preferred my brother but I didn't have the heart to turn her down and tried my best not to seem to be acquiescing to an obligation. She was thrilled to come along, especially to go downtown, where she seldom went. We took our habitual 85 bus and from Piazza Venezia took another that dropped us a few minutes away from the *campo*. I had never been to Campo de' Fiori, and was completely surprised by how crowded was the marketplace, which occupied the entire rectangular piazza. And there, standing on a high perch, was the growling statue of Giordano Bruno, burned there at the stake in the year 1600. He was my subject. My mother asked me to translate the plaque. I did but I could tell she'd lost interest. I stared at the statue while she wandered about the market, fascinated by the assortment of fruits and vegetables that seemed far more appetizing and shinier and better displayed than those on Via Enea. I felt for Bruno. You think unusual thoughts, so they torch you.

After the *campo*, my mother wanted to head to the French Institute on Piazza di Campitelli. She wanted to borrow a few French books and asked me to borrow some as well, since there was a maximum number each member could take out. She had come to the center several times in early fall to catch up on magazines she could no longer buy, except, as usual, at the beginning of the month when we spent a bit more and kept promising to keep to our monthly budget of two hundred lire minus tuition and rent. One cinema per week, she used to say, and I would echo her resolve, which neither of us could keep to, because, good or bad or very, very bad, a film was the only real entertainment we looked forward to and would never walk out on, including commercials we'd seen a hundred times.

At the cultural center, I did some preliminary research on Giordano Bruno using the Larousse encyclopedia and began taking notes on a tiny pocket calendar that Aunt Flora had given me from her shipping company. It was meant for daily appointments, but I never had appointments, so I used it for notes. After we borrowed several books, and seeing that the weather was cooperating and that it was still early in the month, we decided to sit somewhere and order one *corso* each. I had grown to love *pasta all'arrabbiata*, she liked *bolognese* sauce. We found a small, snug place in an outside shed that welcomed tourists and sat for lunch with a glass of red wine each. We were happy. Not Paris, I told her, less buoyant, less busy, less trafficked—but not dull, she countered. I had to learn how to like things, she said. She knew about my meeting with the couple at the café and said I was lucky to have run into people who were so *gentils* with a stranger, especially with someone like me who tended to be so *mmmmm*, she added, not without a touch of irony. *Mmmmm* in her language described my reticent and reclusive temperament better than any adjective, whereas *gentil* meant welcoming, forthcoming, kindhearted. Her word for the couple was precisely the word I would have used for the girl in the Saint-Denis hotel. Some people were born *gentils*. Me? I asked. "In your own way, yes, but only when you are yourself," she said, meaning that I was not always myself. "Maybe you should have gone to their *petit souper*." I knew the real reason for not having gone to their *petit souper*. They'd have unmasked me in seconds.

Our early lunch on this very temperate day was pleasant. She liked going out. She would have given anything to sit in a bar in the evening with me, ordering just one drink each. It's not that we couldn't have afforded it; it's that I avoided it, or at least kept putting it off each time she'd implore me with a casual *Why not go out?* I knew she wouldn't be able to go by herself, and I did understand her plight, but still, it felt awkward and so utterly tedious that as soon as we'd have downed our glass we'd have wanted to pay and leave. Still, I felt sorry for her. My mother, I realized, was an abandoned woman, and after Paris, where so many in her family had sought her out, she was lonely all over again. She told me that Leo sometimes came early in the afternoon while we were at school and would bring dessert and good wine for the two of them. She didn't mind him, he made her feel young, and the good man was discreet. Sometimes they had lunch together. She didn't say more. Perhaps she hoped I'd understand, and I think I did.

After the visit to the Giordano Bruno statue, the one-hour stop at the French Institute, and the very pleasant lunch under Rome's warm winter sun, my mother said it was time for her to take the bus and head back home. She knew me well enough to read, by the slightest inflection on my features, that I had other things I wanted to do by myself that afternoon. Our outing had lasted far longer than she had a right to expect, she said, and she couldn't be more grateful for the company. I walked with her to the corner of Corso Vittorio, where she was going to take a bus to Via del Corso and shop for one or two things, provided they were on sale, before taking yet another bus home. As we walked together, I noticed her ankles. They were a touch swollen or just a bit thicker than usual. She was no longer the svelte young woman of a year earlier who'd sold all our furniture and ordered so many suitcases. I told her that I would have to spend some time at the USIS to research the paper for school. "But didn't you already research it at the French Institute?" she asked. It was her way of asking me perhaps to change my mind and take the bus back home with her. I shook my head before she had time to propose her plan. She had already dug into her purse and got out the change she needed for her bus, and holding her coin in one hand when the bus arrived, she took a second look at its number to make certain it was hers, then climbed on board. Once inside she smiled at me, and kept her eyes on me until the bus moved completely away and she was no longer able to see me. Still, she spun her head around to give me one last, lingering glance. I felt it.

She knew her way about. She had become Roman. I, too, had become Roman—even against my will.

What I didn't tell my mother was that I was headed in exactly her direction. I had resolved to cut through Corso Vittorio and lose my way in the narrow, old paved streets of the *centro storico*, where I had come to know the heart of Campo Marzio. I told myself that I was doing honest-to-goodness scholarly work in trying to get a feel for the area where Giordano Bruno met his tragic end. But scholarship was really a pretext, and I knew I was trying to drown the feeling of guilt for ditching my mother, who, after boarding the bus and standing not far from the door because she hadn't found a seat, had allowed me to read on her lips that she hoped the three of us would go to the movies once I got home. I told her it was a wonderful idea.

Without her, though, I felt free to stroll as I wished in this labyrinth of old roads, free to walk into a bookstore without her pressuring me to leave, free to look at whomever I pleased along the streets without feeling her reproof or the persistent need to look away each time I was drawn to someone.

By late afternoon, when it was already starting to grow dark and I had read what I was determined to know about the life of Bruno and how horribly he'd been tortured before being burned at the stake, I was on Via Veneto eyeing the women again, no less nervous facing them now than I'd been before my encounter with the girl on rue Saint-Denis. I'd thought that experience had unshackled my timidity, but on spotting the first of the women smoking and wearing her usual navy winter coat, I was the same as before, feckless and apprehensive. Had I become a virgin again? Inexperience was a condition one overcame, I thought. And yet, like the shame that held me back and prevented me from approaching these women or uttering a lighthearted greeting as I'd seen Jules do, something hindered me, as though my unyielding diffidence were no different from the fear of buying cigarettes the first time; perhaps it was laced into the fear of finding manhood itself unexceptional and hollow, something one looked forward to, not knowing that it is the expectation of adulthood that is thrilling, never its realization.

I knew that had any of these women invited me I would have hesitated before saying no.

But all this was moot. I had no money. And they knew it.

I walked away from Via Veneto and was headed down toward Via del Tritone, where I took my usual shortcut on Via dei Cappuccini, then onto Via Sistina, down the Spanish Steps, and up Via del Babuino, almost reaching Piazza del Popolo, the site of my favorite bookstore in the world, the Lion Bookshop. I knew that I didn't want to head home yet and was finding all manner of excuses to delay the unavoidable walk from the bus stop to Via Clelia. I had no idea what I was going to buy but knew I'd find something. Eventually, I found a novel by Lermontov, though it was a thin book and I knew that, unless I rationed the pages, I'd down it in one gulp with nothing left to last me until the following Friday.

~

My mother that week had promised to give me a haircut. The brothers at school had said my hair was getting long, and long hair was a trend among young men that the brothers were determined to curb. Brother John had spotted me in the corridor as I was leaving one class to head to another and with two fingers mimicking scissors had given me a cheerful warning. Detention was hell for someone in my shoes: I'd miss the school bus and have to take four public buses to get home.

That evening, Amina came for her shot. My mother was waiting for her, after which she'd give me a haircut and then my brother. Amina couldn't resist, took a chair right next to me in the kitchen, and said she would give anything to watch me get a haircut. I liked her bantering tone and told her she could watch provided she did not make fun of me. "Me, make fun of you?" And right away we both laughed. My mother, in addition to injections, had learned how to give haircuts and went about her job at an expert, no-nonsense pace and, as she cut, would ask me to hold a tiny round mirror with a pink plastic frame that had been purchased in the marketplace. When she was almost finished, she asked Amina if she wanted to have a try, and when she nodded my mother handed her the scissors with a nonchalant *Go ahead, be my guest* gesture, my mother's way of showing that she would have liked Amina and me to grow closer.

Amina was nervous and, holding the scissors, said she had no idea what to do. So my mother held a comb to my hair, telling her to cut just the hair that the comb had raised. But Amina was scared and even asked if she was hurting me, at which I reminded her that hair doesn't feel anything. This seemed to comfort her, but then, inadvertently, by moving the pair of scissors the wrong way she nicked my left earlobe, which started to bleed. I told her it wasn't important. My mother produced some alcohol and applied it to the cut, which burned, but I wasn't going to show any pain. Meanwhile, Amina put the scissors down and with both palms pressed against the instrument looked as though she were blessing it, when in fact she was swearing never to hold it or cut anyone's hair again. At some point, I stopped bleeding and my mother asked Amina if she was up to resuming the haircut. "*Mai*," never, she said. "*Mai, mai, mai*," she repeated.

The next evening, Friday, she crossed the street to our building and brought me a flower. "For you," she said. The three of us were about to go to the movies, and my mother asked her if she wanted to join us. She would love to but had to ask her mother first. Within ten minutes she called and told me that her mother had said yes. We picked her up at the entrance to her building, and the four of us walked together to the small movie house at the corner of the street.

The first film was an Italian comedy, and I sat between Amina and my mother. Two minutes into the film Amina burst out laughing, but seeing I wasn't laughing, she explained the Italian joke to me, which she did well, causing me to laugh but also to stifle my laughter in an attempt to relay the joke to my mother, seated at my right. Meanwhile, I'd hear Amina laugh at new jokes, which she'd explain, in the process missing more jokes herself. In the end the three of us laughed not at what was on-screen but at ourselves. "The girl has a heart of gold," my mother said. And indeed she did have a heart of gold. I held her hand a few times during the second movie, squeezed it, felt her squeeze mine, hoping my mother wouldn't see, though clearly my mother wouldn't have minded.

What I didn't fully realize was that, with the exception of my school days, the rest of my life was surrounded by Italians and the Italian language. It might have seemed unusual at first but it stopped being so as the months wore on, and from unusual it became as ordinary and unavoidable as the air you breathe. When I think of our walk home that Friday night after the double feature, Amina saying how cold it had grown as she mimicked shivering so my mother would understand, it occurs to me that Via Clelia itself, so alien at first, was becoming familiar, to the point that I was no longer able to spot anything troubling or unusual about the people who lived in the Appio-Tuscolano district. We had stopped reacting to its flaws because we had stopped seeing its flaws. This was the life we knew.

My mother had grown used to her routines, and routines shielded her. She knew the marketplace, Madame Renato, Signor Leo, her sons. My routines sheltered me no less: schoolwork, the Lion Bookshop, the Spanish Steps, the early-morning bus ride that no longer really appalled me. My brother, who'd been far more tolerant of Rome than I, was clearly putting down roots, yielding to the rhythm and to the course of our lives here. One day I caught my mother gesturing unselfconsciously in a way I'd never seen her do before: she was twisting her index finger into her cheek, to mean *Delicious*. Or another time, shaking a raised thumb and a pointed forefinger to mean *Nothing doing!* She'd learned these gestures where else but in the marketplace.

I got used to returning bottles once a week, was no longer reluctant to greet the printer at the corner of the street, or the old barber who always reproached me for reading—or, as he called it, *studying*—too much. The glazier got to know us, as did the electrician and the plumber, who told us to stop complaining about our *termosifoni*. Good people, all of them. Even the two frumps would nod hello to me. I even grew to like those nights after the movies when the three of us, sometimes with Amina, would return home as if we'd been born here and not anywhere else. I don't know if I'd accepted any of this, but I must have subconsciously resigned myself to life on Via Clelia.

The idea of the United States was still present, but in the manner of a distant mirage. You know you won't find water, but the mirage sustains you and lends your steps a hopeful pace, and the pace turns the drought in the desert tolerable enough.

It was with this aimless state of mind that I applied late to colleges in New York. Each college required an application fee that needed to be paid in dollars, which meant that I'd have to wait in line at the American Express office after school to buy an American money order for each college. I had to do this repeatedly over the course of several weeks, because at the end of each month money was scarce. So I applied negligently, took the SAT negligently, and was careless about which college might best suit me. I didn't want to think of what would happen to me after graduating from high school.

~

One late Saturday afternoon my mother showed up with two girls she had met in the marketplace. They were helping her carry various vegetables and had come upstairs to deposit the two large bags plus sundry goods. It wasn't clear whether the two worked in the market-place or had volunteered to help her upstairs. I was surprised when they entered the apartment, and what must have surprised them was seeing me wearing a cardigan I'd inherited from my father, and a shirt and tie. I was trying on clothes to see how I looked when in walked the two girls with my mother, followed just a few minutes later by Aunt Flora, who had come to help me with my college applications. Seeing me all dressed up on a day when I didn't have school, Flora was about to ask the reason for this, but when she saw the two girls standing in our foyer, she must have thought that something was afoot. In her inimitably tactful way she tried not to look surprised and said she'd join my mother to prepare dinner, leaving me alone with the girls. I didn't know what to do, felt hopelessly tongue-tied, and had no idea how to conceal feeling so visibly disconcerted by Flora in the kitchen with my mother and two girls who didn't seem eager to leave. In my brother's room, one of the two, the less pretty, came to my rescue and asked why I was home on such a lovely afternoon. I said because I had too much homework (not the truth) and because I had to type a few letters (the truth). But I didn't tell her that I was typing letters to various American colleges. Aunt Flora had read my earlier drafts that week and said I was too poetic, too ethereal. I needed to have both feet on the ground. "There's no room for your complicated, byzantine mannerisms in such letters—'*I miss my homeland, what is my homeland,* home *is a metaphor,*'" she mimicked, "none of that—I know your type," she liked to remind me. She had promised to stay for supper.

The girls were fascinated by my French accent when I spoke Italian, but more fascinated when my brother told them that we were enrolled in an American school here in Rome. "But are you French?" one of them asked. I nodded evasively without saying that I was not French. I told them that I was still quite self-conscious about my Italian and that I hated it when I lacked words, which was why "*mi geno,*" I said, meaning I felt awkward. The girls broke out laughing, and when I asked why, one of them replied that *genare* was not an Italian verb. Sabina, who had studied some French, said that I was probably transposing the French verb *gêner* and making up an Italian verb. I joined in the laughter. The other girl suggested that I could say *provo un certo disagio* or *uno sgomento*. "No," said Sabina, "*mi scoccia.*" "No, that was totally ugly," retorted her friend. There were other suggestions. I told them that if they'd all understood *genare*, then the word could easily be borrowed by Italians. They agreed, but not really.

When the girls heard that I had a typewriter, they wanted to see it. I took them into my bedroom and showed it to them. It was a very old, bulky black Royal that had been in my father's company in Alexandria and that he had taken home when it was no longer needed by his secretaries, who had newer ones. Instead of understanding why the carriage return wasn't working, I used the old mini espresso maker left behind by Uncle Claude, which we'd never used, and tied its handle to the escapement of the typewriter's carriage. The carriage no longer sprang forward unless aided by a counterweight. The typewriter was on its last legs and it must have known I would eventually have to leave its carcass behind if we left Italy.

I heard our main door open and from the kitchen I made out my brother bidding everyone goodbye. He was meeting a group of friends from school, he said. I heard him emit a stray *I don't know* before leaving. Flora must have asked him who the girls in my bedroom were and when they were leaving. Even my mother didn't quite know who they were.

What amused the two girls was the old coffee maker, which jiggled like a fish flouncing on its line whenever you struck a key. It made them laugh, for the Moka maker shook at the merest vibration in the room or when anyone stomped on the floor or, as happened with one of the girls, when you accidentally bumped against the foot of the bed. They muttered something among themselves and giggled. Which led to the other observation: why was my bed so big? Sabina, who was very attractive and surely knew it, made a joke: "Do you sleep alone on this bed?" Unable to resist what she had clearly set herself up for, I replied, smiling and staring straight at her, "Sometimes." The girls burst out laughing, and I did too, because it sanctioned the bawdy tenor settling among us. When Sabina sat at the edge of the bed and moved to cross her legs, the espresso maker began jittering. Her friend reclined on the bed and, bouncing once or twice, observed how the compliant coffee maker responded. "There are certain things I could never do with the coffee maker present in this room," Sabina said. I was poised to tell her that I would immediately remove the typewriter if she told me which things she meant. But I didn't dare. She was still laughing when I heard my mother call one of them, asking her if she knew how *saltimbocca* was prepared. I was left alone in my bedroom with Sabina. There was a moment of silence. Sabina grabbed a fountain pen she saw lying on my desk, unscrewed its cap, opened it, then screwed it back on again. "Your mother said you were in Paris this Christmas. Did I misunderstand her?" "She wasn't lying," I responded, and because the two of us were suddenly silent and she was staring at me, I was unable to resist the impulse to approach her, hold her cheeks in both hands, and kiss her as passionately as I could, not to prove anything but because she was disarmingly attractive. When I let go of her, she had only one comment: "You kiss as though you were in love with me." I did not wait to answer, even if she was snickering, though I could tell it was a forced snicker. "I could easily be in love with you. And you know it." We were, without wanting to show it, both shaken.

Her friend entered the room.

"*Ci siamo baciati*," we kissed, Sabina ratted.

"*Allora tocca a me*," my turn then, replied her friend. It was an instant reply.

To stretch the joke, I kissed her too. But I didn't enjoy kissing her, nor did I like her breath. She kissed me with more abandon than had Sabina. I opened my eyes while I was still kissing her and saw Sabina staring at us. Racy thoughts flitted through my mind. I wanted too many things and couldn't decide which, knowing all along that Flora and my mother were in the kitchen just outside my bedroom. I wanted to ask the two girls, *Possiamo ricominciare?* Could we start over? But I didn't dare, because what I really wanted was Sabina, and kissing her friend was merely a pretext for kissing her, though I also wanted her to watch Sabina and me kiss. So I let go of one girl and took Sabina in my arms and kissed her again. Only then, I remembered—or wanted to remember—the girl on rue Saint-Denis. She didn't kiss her patrons, but how sweetly she cuddled me with her whole body. Maybe it was sweetness I wanted, the raw, visceral, sweet, sexual humanity of coupling, however it came, capped when Sabina finally had put her tongue in my mouth, while

I kept thinking, even as I kissed her, that it was also her friend, plus the girl on rue Saint-Denis, and my cousin, and the Roma girl sitting on a piece of cardboard by the train station, whom I was also kissing.

"Now we're all taking off," Sabina said, with a sly, mischievous look that meant *before you really start misbehaving*. This was Rome in the sixties, teetering between affectations of modernity and the reluctance to yield to it.

Flora eventually called me to the kitchen. She didn't mean to interrupt, she said, but weren't we going to work on the draft of my letter before supper? Sabina and her friend right away stepped into the kitchen to say they were leaving. The other girl even kissed my mother twice on the cheek, but beautiful Sabina hung back a bit in my room. Then she, too, came to say goodbye and asked if she could make a short telephone call to her parents. Leaving, she said, "*Ci rivediamo*," we'll see each other again. I replied, "*A presto, sì*." Neither of us sounded in the slightest vague. I walked the girls to the door and stood there until I saw them head down the stairs. I immediately went to the window and saw them walking down a darkening Via Clelia.

~

That evening, while my mother was preparing dinner, Aunt Flora and I sat together in the small living room. She cross-examined me about what I wanted to study in college, where I hoped my studies might lead, and what I wanted my life to be. These were important questions that I needed to answer before even thinking of putting words on paper. "Above all, you must think like an American," she said, using an emphatic turn in her voice, even if I suspected she'd met very few Americans in her life and probably didn't have the slightest inkling what thinking like an American meant. "You go to school with Americans, you eat with them, you ride the bus with them, surely you must know," she said. But I didn't know. Or at least I didn't understand how Americans thought; they didn't think or feel as I did. "Speaking your mind, taking charge of who you are, thinking positively, making statements about your life even if you don't have the foggiest notion about your life," she said. "Just be declarative, not timid; assertive, not pusillanimous. Never hesitate, and never be retiring or circumspect. *Tu comprends?*"

I told her I didn't know what *pusillanimous* meant. *Never mind!* The truth is neither of us knew what *thinking like an American* meant. Then she raised her eyes from the letter we were trying to compose and stared at me. "Do you think I want you to go to America?" And, still staring at me, "I want you here. But right now we must *think American*." We laughed because she kept using the same two words and clearly neither of us knew what we were talking about. Then, because we'd started laughing, she asked me to do my imitation of how Americans spoke English, and how they spoke French. Which made her laugh even more, and I loved her loud laugh. Then, with sorrow limning her face, "Whatever will you end up doing to yourself there?" I didn't know. "They'll change you, and then what?" "It could be for the better," I replied. "No, I want you just as you are now. I won't know you when you change."

In an hour, and despite our laughter and numberless distractions, we finished the text I was going to use for my applications. Aunt Flora said she was happy with the letter but warned me not to set too much store by it. Maybe all we had done was to mimic Americans without really speaking their language. Besides, one never knows how these things turn will out. "Things backfire so frequently," she added, "that it's safer to expect they will."

This was signature Flora.

My problem was that I didn't know what I was hoping for, whether to be admitted to a college or not admitted. It's how most people think of the afterlife: they suspect it doesn't exist but live as if it might. Which is how people think of death too: you know it will happen, just not to you.

What pleased me and made me realize I had to act despite my many qualms and hesitations was not the letter we'd written that evening but a piece of paper bearing Sabina's name and phone number. She had a nice hand, confident and forthright. She'd barely had time to jot anything down while the other girl was saying goodbye to my mother in the kitchen. They told me they were going dancing, so I wasn't going to call her that evening, but I was thrilled she'd left me her number.

I had felt the stir of our kiss creep over me all the time I was working with Aunt Flora, but I kept staving it off, not because it would intrude on me or distract me from our letter, but because I didn't want to dilute the pleasure it would give me if I kept taking hasty peeks at it. I was saving her torn corner of paper for later. In bed that night, I let down my guard and thought of our kiss. Ours had been not one kiss, but two, bridged together, because as I was about to stop kissing her, she'd continued, then touched my face, and only then let go. I wondered if she was thinking of me while she was dancing that night.

～

My father was growing to accept his life in Paris, as I had no choice but to accept ours in Rome. After Aunt Elsa had asked him to find another place to live, he took a tiny apartment on the ground floor of her building and spent quite a bit of time decorating it and buying a few things here and there to make it livable, without necessarily admitting to himself or to us in Rome that he was anchoring himself in Paris for the foreseeable future. He was going to settle there, and my mother and brother and I would continue to live in Rome, until he thought it advisable for us to move to Paris—if and when. He was not likely to take well to my applications to schools in New York, which is why I kept them from him.

America, however, never quite vanished into an ethereal fantasy. My aunt and uncle in New York would occasionally call to remind me that our visas were taking more time than they thought but were bound to come through. Their calls would come at around two or three in the morning, which corresponded to eight or nine o'clock in the evening in New York. I would open my mother's bedroom door, shake her ever so gently, and, letting her see I was holding the receiver, watch her suddenly ask, as she did each time, if someone had died. "Your sister," I'd say. And right away she'd start to cry. "Is she dead?" "No," I'd say, "she's calling to tell us to be patient about the visas." My mother would shake her head. "And was this a reason to call people at this ungodly hour?" I'd signal her to be quiet as I kept listening to my aunt utter more excuses about the visas, and mouth to my mother that her sister was an American, meaning that Americans never thought that the rest of the world wasn't synchronized to their time. My mother cursed and went back to bed, still weeping from the shock, while I continued making small talk with my aunt, who truly loved us and would have roused God Himself at night if that would have brought my mother to the Bronx.

The following Monday at school all I thought of was Sabina. I was going to call her that evening. I'd find a moment while Mother was cooking in the kitchen away from the telephone and my brother busy with homework. But that evening Amina came for her injection and then stayed in my room. We listened to records of *stornelli*, Romanaccio street songs, normally with a bawdy tilt, which she hoped I understood, though I did so with difficulty and was constantly censoring my racy interpretations, only to be told that indeed her songs were far racier than I imagined. The contrast with the girl on rue Saint-Denis couldn't have been starker—how easy and untethered, how natural she had been. Sabina, however, kissed too well. I wondered if there was an undeclared Maginot Line between what we'd done in my room that Saturday evening and what I so wanted from her.

I put off calling Sabina until the next day.

The next day, I asked the school bus driver to drop me off at my usual spot, Via Bissolati, just past the Fontana di Mosè. Then, as always, I'd head to the USIS, where I planned to research Giordano Bruno in books, not encyclopedias. I'd stay until about five thirty or six and then walk down Via Veneto. Seven or so would be a good time to call Sabina.

After reading about Bruno, I closed the book and put my coat on.

I made one more turn to the encyclopedia section to look up an entry I wanted to reread because I wasn't sure I had understood it the first time. When I reread it, it was no less ambiguous than it had been earlier. The *Americana*, *Collier's*, even the *World Book*, was no clearer than the *Britannica*, as if each was timid on the subject and wanted to remain vague. I, too, was timid on the subject and was always making certain that no one saw me looking it up, but I wasn't so chaste as not to let voluptuous thoughts stir everything inside me.

The walk down Via Veneto did not change. As usual, I would stare at one or two of the girls standing away from the sidewalk, and as always they averted their gaze however I tried to catch it. I had resolved to approach one and just say hello, but I couldn't find the courage, and there was no one like Jules to strike up a conversation. I walked down to Piazza San Silvestro. I didn't want to go home yet. There stood the large remainders bookstore, where I'd sit and read at a long table before taking the bus home. Surely I'd find something on Giordano Bruno. But I was there to leaf through another book, which I'd frequently pore over and whose pre-war sexual case studies had a sort of fin-de-siècle veneer that was disarmingly erotic precisely because its bourgeois respectability was visibly factual yet shadowed over to allow readers like me to wonder if I wasn't misconstruing what seemed sufficiently obvious. Libido was everywhere in Krafft-Ebing's *Psychopathia Sexualis*, but attenuated, and its implied respectability made it all the more ferocious. I had nothing factual to hold on to, but the inferences I drew—or misread—haunted me.

The book was intended for medical professionals, and Richard von Krafft-Ebing had used complicated terms, with phrases rendered in Latin to discourage and confuse the average lay reader or young man looking for a thrill. I pored over its arcane and detailed case stud-ies on what was called inversion and sexual deviancy and was trans-fixed by its wildly pornographic stories. The individuals concerned could not have seemed more urbane, more serenely well-behaved: the young man who loved to see his girlfriend and her sister spit in his glass of water before drinking it up; the man who loved to watch his neighbor undress at night, knowing that she knew she was being watched; the timid young man who loved his cousin in ways he knew were wrong; the young man who stayed far longer than he should in public baths—I could have been any of them, like someone who reads all twelve horoscopes in the back of a magazine and identifies with every sign in the zodiac.

After reading Krafft-Ebing's case studies, I normally took the 85 bus for the long ride home, knowing that my mother would have dinner ready by the time I arrived. Lightheaded after all the case studies, I knew I'd eventually suffer from a migraine, and that the incipient migraine, coupled with the long bus ride, might trigger nausea. At the bus station was a newspaper and magazine kiosk that also sold postcards. Before boarding the bus, I'd stare longingly at the ones of male and female nude statues, then buy one, adding a few postcards of Roman vistas or of Romulus and Remus being suckled by a she-wolf to conceal my purpose. The card I loved best was the Apollo Sauroktonos, the totally feminized Apollo attempting to kill a lizard yet smiling bashfully though fully aware of his seductive beauty.

That evening, after leaving the bookstore, I spotted a large crowd waiting for the 85 bus. It was cold and it had rained earlier, so once the bus arrived, we all crammed into it as fast as we could, hurtling and jamming into one another, exactly as happened every morning on my way to catch the school bus. I, too, pushed my way in, not realizing that the young man right behind me was being pushed forward by those behind him. His body was pressed to mine, and though every part of him was glued to me and I was completely trapped by those around us, I was almost sure that he was pushing into me overtly and yet so seemingly unintentionally that when I felt him grab both of my upper arms with his hands, I did not struggle or move away but allowed my whole body to yield and sink into his. He could do with me whatever he wanted, and to make it easier for him, I leaned back into him, thinking at some point that perhaps all this was in my head, not his. There was nothing either of us could do. He didn't seem to mind, and perhaps he sensed that I didn't mind either, or he didn't pay it any heed, the way I, too, wasn't quite sure I did. I thought of the woman who had screamed on the bus. Was he going to scream? Was I? His way of holding my upper arms from behind me was friendly, the way a mountain climber might help another steady himself before moving farther up. With nothing else to hold on to, he had grabbed my arms. Nothing to it. Eventually, steadying himself a bit, he let go of me. But as the doors closed and the bus started to sway, he immediately grabbed me again, holding me by the waist, pushing even harder, though nobody around us could tell, and part of me was sure that he himself couldn't. All I knew was that he would let go of me once he'd steadied himself and could reach one of the grab bars. I could tell he was struggling to let go of me, which is why I pretended to stagger away from him, only to lean back, as soon as the bus stopped, to prevent him from moving. Part of me was ashamed of what I'd allowed myself to do to him, while another part suspected that he knew what we were both doing—but I wasn't sure. Eventually, he managed to slip between me and another passenger, which was when I got a good look at his back. He was wearing a gray sweater and a pair of brown corduroys and looked at least five or six years older than I was. He was also taller, skinny, and sinewy. He found a seat in front of me, and though I kept my eyes on him, hoping he would turn to look back, he never did. In his mind, nothing had happened: crowded bus, people slipping between people, everyone lurching and holding on to someone else—it happens all the time. I never saw his face.

He got off somewhere on Via Taranto. A sudden sickness began to seize me. The headache I had feared, brought on by the gas fumes, turned to nausea. I needed to get off earlier than I was meant to, and I walked the rest of the way home. I didn't throw up that evening, but when I got home, I knew I would never live down what had happened on the bus. All I had wanted was for him to hold me, to keep his hands on me, to ask nothing and say nothing, or, if he needed to ask, to ask anything, provided I didn't have to talk, because I was too choked up to talk. What I wanted was for him to put an arm around me in that man-to-man way that friends do in Rome.

When I reached home that evening, my mother was preparing supper with Amina in the kitchen. As she and I sat together at the kitchen table while Mother cooked, we laughed, and I could feel my nausea ebb. Amina always smelled of incense and chamomile, of ancient wood drawers with their faint, residual hint of mothballs.

But, as soon as I let my mind drift back to what had happened on the 85 bus, I knew that I wouldn't have cared what that young man smelled of. The thought that he, too, might smell of incense and chamomile and old wood furniture turned me on. I pictured his bedroom and his clothes strewn about the room, his mother complaining of the mess before he shut the door on her.

I was thinking of him when I went to bed that night, but as I let arousal wash over me, I thought of Sabina, whom I still hadn't called, picturing how she'd first unbutton her shirt and let everything she wore slide to the floor and then walk up to me naked, smelling, like him, of incense, chamomile, and old wood cabinets. I drifted from him to her, back to him and then her, each feeding off the other and, like Roman buildings of all ages snuggling into, on top of, under, and against each other, body parts stripped from his body given over to hers and then back to his with body parts from hers. I was like Emperor Julian, the apostate who buried one faith under the other and no longer knew which was truly his. And I thought of Tiresias, who was first a man, then a woman, then a man again, and of Caenis, who was a woman, then a man, and finally a woman again, and of the postcard of Apollo the Lizard Slayer. I longed for him as well, though his unyielding, forbidding grace seemed to chide my lust. As with the young man on the bus, I was filled with shame and apprehension because I'd infringed on every curve of his body. I managed to make myself think that maybe what I'd wanted on the bus was friendship, nothing more. The rest wasn't real, not real, not real.

What I didn't realize, and it came to me much later that same night, was that, as I was embracing the two as one and trying to hide each with the other, another part of me, unannounced and unwilling to show its face, wanted nothing more than to bury both.

I called Sabina the next evening. Calling, however, took far more courage than I'd foreseen. She had given me the green light, but I was still nervous. I thought I was nervous because I was trying to prevent my brother from hearing my flustered voice on the telephone or my mother asking who had called or whom I was calling; after my attempt at a few evasive answers, she'd either guess or I'd simply end up telling her. I could feel my pulse race in my chest. What was I even going to say to Sabina? How to move from the obvious— *I want to see you again*—to the conventional—*How are you today*—to the lachrymose—*Have you been thinking about me?* More important, how not to lose my breath? The more I stood holding the receiver in my hand, the more I felt winded. I said *Aaaaah* softly a few times to clear my throat and not reveal that I was too nervous to speak. After the third *Aaaaah* I could hear an improvement and felt the panting recede. I smiled to poke fun at myself for saying *Aaaaah* that way. Smiling, like whistling in the dark, helped reduce my anxiety. But what helped even more was imagining Jules's boisterous laughter on hearing me tell him about my *Aaaaah*s. Still, I forced myself to expect her to refuse. Either this was my way of courting the envious gods, who prefer to see humility and fear in us mortals before granting our wishes, or I was nervous because I wasn't nervous enough, which ended up making me nervous just the same.

Her father picked up, called out her name, and handed her the receiver. She sounded so cheerful that it caught me off guard. Maybe it was a good sign. I asked if she wanted to go to the movies. We might meet at the caffè on Via Clelia toward the Appia Nuova, near where she said she lived, and have a juice. She wasn't saying anything. *Pompelmo*, I suggested with a nervous giggle in my voice, not realizing why, of all juices, I'd suggested grapefruit, since I'd never even planned on having a juice with her. I should have rehearsed what I was going to say, should have thought this through before picking up the phone instead of practicing my idiotic *Aaaaah*s. Never improvise. With the same cheery voice, she told me she'd let me know the next day. I could sense she was busy doing something else, though I had no idea what, probably watching television with her parents. I gave her my number, but she took it down far too swiftly for someone writing it. I repeated it. "*Ma sì, ho capito*," yes, I understood, she replied, almost with a brusque, impatient rise in her voice.

Her response left me crestfallen. I'd been prepared for all kinds of attitudes but I hadn't expected the unassailable brush-off. How totally different from the girl I'd kissed a few evenings before. She and her friend had said they were going out dancing. Maybe I'd been the catalyst, the bit of naughty fun before partying into the small hours.

Or was she the cover I needed to help me push away what had happened on the bus?

I began thinking of the young man on the bus. I wanted to forget him by being with Sabina.

The next few days were troubling. I had no sense of how profoundly his touch had affected me. It wasn't fantasy. It had troubled me because it thrilled me, and continued to thrill me the more it troubled me. As I'd stood almost leaning into him, I could already sense the rise of denial worming its way into that very excitement, but not so much to dispel it, but to stoke it further, to make it fight for itself.

When I went to return empty bottles and purchase last-minute staples, I saw that a young man had taken the place of the girl who worked at that counter. I was disappointed she'd left the store, especially since we'd gotten into the habit of trading a few jokes after she'd overcome her former surly attitude with me. Sometimes she'd rub her finger on my bare arm in a manner playful enough not to seem serious. I missed her.

But I'd hardly had time to let the setback take hold when I saw her again. She and he were working the counter together. Her brother, she said. He looked like her, and she looked like him. He was older by eighteen months, she said.

He did not smile at me at first but, like her, cast a curt, dismissive glance that lingered on me as if he were contemplating an insult but wasn't saying it—clearly, a family trait. They'd been laughing about something, possibly about the customer before me, or maybe about me. I could tell he was trying to say something to me, or maybe I wanted him to say something, though I didn't know what exactly. Instead, seeing the two of them so jovial, I made a few jokes with her in my usual flirtatious tone, trying to stir her sense of humor, knowing all along that I was also trying to nudge his. That's when he interrupted us: "*E tu, come te chiami?*" And what's your name?—that *and* striking an informal camaraderie in pure Roman. I told him my name. Then he complimented me: "*Bèr nome. E chi s'o scorda,*" nice name, hard to forget.

"*E il tuo?*" And yours? I asked.

"Gianlorenzo," he said.

I couldn't help myself: "*Più bello il tuo,*" yours is much nicer.

We shook hands.

He stared at me for a short while, not knowing what to say, again with that uneasy, querulous look in his eyes that told me, I don't know how or why, that he was not upset with me but quite the contrary, that he was himself slightly at a loss for words but, unlike me, wasn't trying to hide it. Or was I imagining all this? In his world, things would never be left at that, and the words that finally came to him were simple, unstudied, commonplace words that cost nothing to say and nothing to hear. "*Sei francese, vero?*" You're French, right?

"*Sì.*" It was, as always, the easiest thing to say.

He turned around and began stacking boxes near the counter.

"*Allora se vedemo,*" see you later, he said once again in pure Roman, then left the counter.

There was something so unhindered and forthright in his speech that, once again, I found myself loving Romanaccio.

— 8 —

Domenica delle Palme

P alm Sunday in Rome. Dora and Toto, Aunt Flora's niece and
nephew, joined both my parents and my brother on a trip to
the Spanish Steps. Flora and I were more than happy they
had decided to come with us. Toto and his sister had left Egypt three
years earlier and to all appearances seemed to have settled quite well
in Rome. Toto was about to get married; Dora, who was older, wasn't
married, but then didn't have just one boyfriend. I had always loved
her zest, her spunk that caught me off guard and made me wonder
why I didn't see her more often.

That late morning, Piazza di Spagna was filled with people, but
also with flowerpots going all the way up the steps so that one had
to squeeze through the crowd of tourists and Romans enjoying the
first clear signs of spring weather. There were colors everywhere,
everything and everyone was beautiful. When I think of the French
and American painters who loved to capture large, clamorous, multi-
colored flags flapping in the wind, I am instantly reminded of this day.
I had heard of spring, but never known it in Egypt, where temperate
winters are followed by intensely warm summers and, in between, the
unmistakable promise of beach life called *good weather*. I was happy

that day, partly because school was out for about ten days, but also because my father was staying with us on a very short visit from Paris. Everything about the day felt unusual, brisk, and lively. I was wearing my blue wool blazer, a leather tie, and a long-sleeved white polo shirt, with gray flannel trousers. I was, despite the mild day, aching to remove my socks, roll up my trousers, and dunk one bare foot and then the other into the Barcaccia, Bernini's boat-shaped fountain at the bottom of the Spanish Steps, where, one after the other, young people leaned into the gushing spout to quench their thirst and wet their hair. This should have been a beach day in Alexandria, and perhaps that was why the day resonated with all of us. Three years before, we were probably celebrating the spring holiday of Sham el Nessim, about which Cavafy left a little-known poem. For me it usually marked the first giddy swim of the year. The heat, the thirst, the yearning to jump into a pool of water, any water, had seized me, and I was given to feelings I didn't know were in me.

My father and I were walking up the steps behind the rest of our party, maybe because we were sharing the same undefined longing for the beach. Toto, as was his wont, had just spoken to an English tourist who was busy looking at a map of Rome, and was helping her locate what she was looking for. He'd made her laugh several times. Typical Toto. He spoke fluent English, which seemed to surprise her. She accepted his street directions but decided to walk up the steps with us. Her name was Philippa. Flora took an instant liking to her, and they walked up to the very top together, while my mother walked with Dora, my brother, and Toto.

"He hasn't changed, twenty-five or so and still the congenital flirt he was as a boy," said my father. Flora hadn't changed either, he added, watching her go up the stairs with Philippa.

As my father and I were walking, he asked me about my own love life, my *vie sentimentale*.

I wanted to tell him that my life hadn't changed. I thought it would change after Paris but it hadn't. I remembered hinting about the girl on rue Saint-Denis when I'd asked him for money on my last day in Paris. It had made him smile. Now I was waiting to hear what he'd have to say, considering how honest he'd been about his own *vie sentimentale* during our walk on New Year's Eve after dinner at Arnaut's. He'd told me at the time that things between my mother and him had deteriorated to such a low that, after just a week with her in Rome that fall, he'd been ready to flee, knowing, as he'd told me then and was repeating now on the crowded *scalinata* of Piazza di Spagna, that he would never live long enough to forget he'd ever known her—forget her face, forget her voice, forget her body too. He must have wanted to unburden himself with me, because it flowed out of him in one sudden gush that felt so unstoppable on such a radiant and happy morning that I could do nothing but listen. There were nights, he added, when he'd much rather be in bed with anyone else, even a man, than be with her again. But then he caught himself and let out a mild snicker, meant perhaps to undermine or possibly take back what he'd just said. He was, I could tell, miserable, and I could do nothing to help.

I suspected he was exaggerating or at least wanted to give the impression that he'd overstated things, but I heard what he was saying, and I knew he was opening a subject we'd never raised before.

He asked me if I'd been with a woman after Paris. Why was he asking? Then I realized why.

I was going to tell him about the young man on the bus but then immediately brought up Sabina instead and thought the incident in my room with the typewriter and the coffee maker would amuse him, and it did. I was curious to hear what he thought. There was really no one else, I said, letting him infer that I wasn't telling him everything, either because I wanted him to believe there were other women I wasn't naming, or because of what I hoped he'd intuit without my saying a word more.

I wanted him to tell me about his years when he was my age. Even if he had nothing to tell, I still wanted to hear who he was back then, how he'd lived, what he'd wanted and maybe hadn't found.

What helped as we were talking was threading our way through the crowd and avoiding looking at each other. Everything we were saying seemed incidental, said without forethought, maybe meant to be cast aside the moment it was spoken. He told me about my mother. How a man might not enjoy a naked body in his bed was still a matter past reckoning at my age. I told him about the two *puttane* on Via Clelia. He laughed. There was a time when, with a bit of alcohol and far fewer years on his shoulders, even they, he said, without ending his sentence. We laughed.

But he quickly saw by my reaction that there might be something else I was reluctant to share. Was it the unavoidable *fiasco*? he asked. I shook my head no. Was something worrying me, diseases, for instance? I shook my head again. Was there someone special? No, there wasn't. So it wasn't Sabina. No, it wasn't Sabina or Amina, I said, forcing a smirk on my face.

He was quiet for a moment.

"So, someone else?"

"Maybe," I replied. The girl in the turquoise overcoat, I kept thinking but wasn't going to say. The Roma girl with the knees? Not her either, I thought. Surely, he must know. But he wasn't going to risk taking a wrong guess. His silence wasn't helping. Or maybe it was.

And maybe the crowd and the sun and the festive mood on that beautiful Palm Sunday helped dispel the subject. Having to watch our step to avoid the others going up the same stairs, or work our way around the countless flowerpots and by so doing continue to avoid each other's gaze, allowed our conversation to hobble about. Perhaps his mind had already drifted elsewhere, or perhaps I wanted us to share my memory of beach weather if only to shirk what we'd been dancing around and move on to something else. He asked if I knew a poem by Cavafy entitled "Η' Πόλις."

I wasn't sure, I said. I didn't want to say that I knew the poem.

"It's about our city, but it's also about all those things there's no hiding from, especially when they're in us and can't be shaken off."

He changed the conversation then, but I loved how he had opened and then closed the subject. Or not entirely closed, because over the years we returned to it, because neither he nor I forgot that we'd brushed on the topic on our way to the very top of the Trinità dei Monti. Otherwise I would never have known how honest my father was, or how delicate his candor.

And then he said something that almost undid me. "I want to love again, but I think I've forgotten what love is." I thought that one could always love someone, that finding love or being loved might be difficult sometimes but that it never ran dry. I was wrong. "I'm not even that old," he added, as though to counter my attempt to blame his condition on age. "You wanted to dance a java once," I finally threw in.

"But I need to want to dance, and right now no one makes me want to dance anything."

After our long walk back down by the Pincio we stopped to buy a cold drink and a sandwich. I liked my simple coleslaw sandwich. I liked having my father with us again. I liked feeling that those we'd been close to weren't estranged from us. Toto ordered a second sandwich, which he offered to Philippa. She thanked my father. Flora insisted that Philippa try the ice cream, which Flora also bought and tried.

A few days later my father took the train back to Paris. If I wanted to see him, I could go to Paris at the end of the school year. My brother, who wasn't a senior, had two more weeks of classes. So I'd go to Paris solo, which was my dream.

～

A week later we were back to daily drudgery.

Had I changed?

Not really. I was still a good son, still spent hours doing homework, still read voraciously, went to the movies with my mother and my brother, and remained a model student at school. Twice a week I managed to get to the USIS and, as had become our habit on Thursday and Sunday evenings, called my father to brief him on the latest developments with our applications for visas to Canada, South Africa, and Australia. But my father, I could tell, was not eager to obtain a decisive yes from any of these offices, nor for that matter was he anxious to hear from the U.S. immigration service.

He had grown accustomed to life in Paris and was looking forward to my visit. He asked about Amina, and I told him that we were good friends and that, sometimes, I liked her company, but nothing approaching what I'd told him about the girl on rue Saint-Denis. If Amina and I went to the movies together, her parents insisted that my mother accompany us. I said nothing about Sabina or about the shirtmaker in the building next to ours who lived with her sister and joked with me the two or three times I helped her into her elevator with bolts of cloth for her shirts. I told him about Gianlorenzo, whom I'd run into a few times delivering groceries to scattered buildings on Via Clelia. He had shouted a word so garbled in his Roman accent that I scarcely knew it was me he was calling. I was thrilled that he had stopped his bike and, with one foot resting on the ground, exchanged a few pleasantries with me. *Francesì*, Frenchie, he called me, with the accent on the last letter. We ran into each other a few times and he always stopped. Once, I saw him chatting with someone outside our building and was about to nod a cursory greeting and pass by the two when he stopped me, said hello, and asked, *Quanno ripassi?* When will you come by again? Wednesday, I said. When I did return bottles on Wednesday, we chatted. I told him more than I usually told people at school, he listened, even asked questions that surprised me, then told me about himself, until he caught a look from his sister and let me know there were things he needed to attend to. We became friends. He was my first Italian friend, my first friend in a long time. I told my father about him because I knew how many at school, myself included perhaps, might react on hearing that, after all my time in Rome, I had befriended no more than an errand boy. But I liked Gianlorenzo because everything came so naturally with him that to withhold anything from him was to distrust him, and I didn't want to distrust him. Sometimes I told him my sorrows, complaints, hopes, and dreams. He told me his and how he disliked working for the old lady, a job his sister had found for him. We even spoke about our grandmothers, a subject I'd never discussed with anyone outside the family. His grandmother was now living with his parents, which he found difficult to get used to; I told him I missed mine but wasn't displeased that she lived so far away. He said I was weird. I said, "I know." Talking about our grandmothers brought us close. He liked geography and knew the names of so many rivers in America. I told him he was weird too. His turn to say "I know." He wanted to travel. Where did he want to go? I asked. *Forse l'America*, he said. But first he had to learn English, and who had time for that? Sometimes we'd stop at a bar to order a quick juice free of charge; everyone knew him in the neighborhood and everyone liked him.

I'll never forget how we'd run into each other in the evening, and then he'd walk his bike, guiding it with his right hand while I walked on his left, sometimes asking me to hold it while he rushed upstairs to deliver food to older people who were unable to leave their homes, especially when it rained or was cold. I had seldom opened up to anyone without being reminded that I was either romanticizing or had failed to see things clearly. When someone shouted hello to him or interrupted us or when he was suddenly asked to move boxes elsewhere in the store while I stood there by the counter, he always picked up where I'd left off, because he cared, because he was generous, because he liked me. I didn't shorten what I was saying for fear of boring him as I did in school or even at home; I didn't talk about books; I told him about my parents' marriage, about loneliness, about the things that weren't there in my life. He knew I was unhappy. He listened and told me about himself.

The other person who had stepped into my life was a thirty-three-year-old shirtmaker called Paola. Sometimes, you could hear the quiet whir of the sewing machine at night from her building to ours.

I had seen her a few times and had helped her carry bolts of cloth upstairs when her elevator wasn't working, but early one evening as I was coming back from the USIS, I ran into her and offered to help her carry a delivery of heavy sheets of striped and colored cotton to her floor. She let me inside her apartment, asked me to deposit them by the window *over there*, and then, to thank me, asked if I wanted coffee, *o forse qualcosa di più forte*, or maybe something stronger.

Without giving her offer any thought I said *qualcosa di più forte*, thinking she'd offer me a juice. She smiled, nodded, and said that, come to think of it, she, too, was going to have *qualcosa di più forte*. She sat next to me on the sofa and offered me a cigarette, and I liked that she didn't treat me like a young man but as a man her own age. She must have known about our trip to Paris because she asked if I liked traveling. Yes, very much, I said. Did I have someone special in France? I made up something about a girl I liked who lived on rue Saint-Denis. Did I have someone else in Rome? I was flattered that she thought I could have a girl in different cities. A part of me wanted to remind her of the shirt she'd promised me once, but another part couldn't believe where this was headed. My heart was beating, and I loved every moment of it. Did I want another drink, because if I did, but only if I did, she would have one too, she said. So we had another tiny cordial. She laughed, and I laughed, and I tried not to show that I was already slightly giddy. I could have been reading everything wrong, but I caught myself saying "*Avvicinati*," come closer, using the unsuitable informal address because I still hadn't mastered the formal third-person imperative. But once I'd said it, I was committed to the rest. "*Così?*" Like this? she asked. "*Un po' di più*," a bit more. She complied right away. We kissed, and eventually she pulled me by the hand to her bedroom. Was her sister around? I asked. Her sister had her piano lesson downtown and wasn't coming back for at least another two hours. She undressed me first, she wanted to see me naked, which aroused me no end.

After we made love, she asked me again if I truly loved the girl in Rome, and all I could say about Sabina, without naming her, was "Maybe, but I'm not too sure." She loved the words and repeated them to me until I laughed, and then she laughed too, *Maybe, but I'm not too sure.* "Poor girl, she's probably in love with you *but he's not too sure.*" "Come here," she said, and we stayed glued to each other.

At some point she said, "*Dovremo separarci,*" we'll need to separate, her polite way of saying it was time for me to leave. She stood up, I followed her. "*Sei stato molto dolce,*" you've been very sweet, she added, carrying away our glasses with three fingers. From a grown-up, I'd become a toddler who'd been very sweet with his babysitter. "*Lo sai che questo non si rifarà mai più,*" you do know that this won't ever happen again. I said I knew. I was back to being an adulterous man who didn't mind knowing that certain things happened only once in life. On my way out I caught sight of two giant industrial sewing machines that reminded me of the visit to the Chalabi and Hanan establishment. She and her sister manned these machines. A side of me was still thinking about the shirt she'd promised me.

"Still, give me a kiss." And I did. She shut the door behind me, but then suddenly reopened it. "*Un altro,*" another one, and kissed me fully on the mouth, "*Sei tanto, tanto dolce,*" you're so, so sweet, and before shutting the door again, she went back into the living room and came back to hand me three tiny wrapped Lindt chocolates.

～

At school, something about me had changed. I was nursing a secret, other life. It did not make me more reticent than I usually was when others described their real or proclaimed exploits; instead, my secret made me surer of myself. Having a separate life gave my old bookish aloofness a new cast. I said nothing, but when I did speak, the inflection in my voice must have suggested something mature and not just precocious. I had another life, totally separate from my American high school. Everyone in the class could sense that behind my reticence was something new. Even my habitual ironic asides in class took on a new slant. My insights into Joyce's "The Dead" or Raskolnikov's twisted mind came, I felt, not just from good reading but from a sort of wisdom hatched both from lived experience and from an intuited sense of the depths of human paradox. From the jokes about semen that were widespread among students my age, I'd graduated to more explicit jokes than were common among them. On Friday night they'd ask me to join them at the Piper Club, a bar where many Americans hung out drinking beer for hours, which is what my schoolmates liked, still laughing on Monday mornings about the puke-fests after their endless boozing. But I never joined them at the Piper Club.

What ruined my isolation from several of my classmates was the birth of another flashy nightclub, called Kilt, located right on Via Clelia. At night sometimes I heard, or rather felt, the roar of the loud bass speakers rumbling right into my bedroom, but it was not often, and no one I knew in our building complained. Otherwise, the club hardly interfered with life on the street.

What happened soon was that those young men from school who frequented the Piper Club learned of Kilt and would talk about it at school. One of them even asked if I'd ever gone. I said no and indeed pretended I had no idea where it was. "What kind of a club?" I asked. "On Via Clelia," another classmate said. This particular student was known at school for what the brothers might have called his "dissolute" lifestyle. He was even rumored to be older by two to three years than the rest of us. He had his own car, and sure enough, one Saturday night, as I was returning from a movie with my mother and brother, I was certain I saw him leave the club and head to his car. My brother, who also knew him, even tried to call out to him. Fortunately, he didn't hear.

But I froze on the spot. The last thing I wanted was for all those snobby *pariolini* to put two and two together and see that I lived on very shabby Via Clelia. On the school list, which had been distributed to everyone in my class and where addresses and telephone numbers were listed, it would have taken nothing for my classmates to realize that I lived on the same street as Kilt. To them I was still the man who wore tweed or cashmere sport jackets and expensive custom-made suede shoes, but no one knew that these were retrofitted hand-me-downs. For all they knew I lived on Via Appia Antica but had always been reluctant to admit it because I wasn't a snob—though my very shame made me one.

~

One Saturday morning shed an enduring light on my life. Gianlorenzo, who always worked during the day, had brought his bicycle and left it outside the store. When I'd gone to buy milk early that morning, he told me that he had a lot to do at work and wasn't going to run any errands and that if I wanted to I could borrow his bicycle until that afternoon. I was beyond ecstatic. I hadn't ridden a bicycle since I'd given mine away in Egypt.

I told my mother I was going on my usual rounds to bookstores and the USIS. It was hardly the first time I'd avoided telling her or my brother where I was going, and they never asked. I said there was a book I was trying to get my hands on. What book? she asked; perhaps we could both find it at the French Institute. It was an English book; besides, I liked to browse through new books in my favorite bookstore. She did not insist, so just before nine that morning I started my journey through Rome without relying on public transportation.

Traffic was erratic on Via Appia Nuova, so I steered close to parked cars, though I had already learned in Egypt that biking close to stationary cars had its own dangers, as drivers often opened their doors without looking behind them. The Appia Nuova was not as long as I'd thought from our daily bus rides, which could take over half an hour. On a bicycle, I reached San Giovanni in less than ten minutes.

Gianlorenzo probably expected me to take his bike to the outskirts of the city, into the surrounding countryside. But I preferred to spin through the narrow streets of the *centro storico*. After San Giovanni, I rode up the street leading to the Colosseum, then up to Piazza Venezia, and before I knew it, I was riding into Piazza di Campitelli, never minding the cobblestones. And what joy to observe for the very first time the exiguous light working its way into the empty piazza at so early an hour of the morning and then softly rubbing its shiny, venerated cobblestones, called *sampietrini*, that were far, far easier to love than people.

I decided next to cut toward Campo de' Fiori, but got lost, not once but twice. I liked roaming from one side street to another, knowing that I'd eventually find a *sbocco* that would either take me back to where I'd gotten lost the first time or exactly where I hoped to be. I felt as though an untapped but far more prescient part of me had intuited the design and layout of the city's narrow, ancient lanes and all I had to do was trust my instincts, because my instincts seemed already minted in the image of Rome itself. Tourists hadn't yet invaded the city, and most students my age were still in school on Saturdays. Eventually, I stopped riding the bicycle and began to walk it, holding it exactly as Gianlorenzo did. I found a tiny place and ordered a *cornetto*, and when the vendor selected the smallest one in the bin with his prongs, I told him that I wanted *that one instead*, twice the size of the one he'd tried to pick for me, because I was famished. I expected he'd object. He didn't. "At your age . . . ," he started to say, but then didn't finish. He'd probably meant something kind, about needing to grow, staying strong, fit, or whatever. The *cornetto* was sweet, as I knew it would be, unlike French croissants. I'd skipped breakfast that morning, hoping to leave before my perennially famished brother sat for his soft-boiled eggs, but now I was hungry. I was going to eat the *cornetto* while walking my bike and meant to have it last a long time, but naturally, after a few steps I'd devoured it.

I was ecstatic. I had so much time on my hands, so much time to do nothing, not even to think, or read, or long for anyone. I wanted for nothing, I couldn't even think of wanting anything. I liked how the morning's sunlight beamed off the slate and the white marble stonework around me. *It was a clear steel-blue day* . . . How I loved the opening words to chapter 132 of Melville's *Moby-Dick*, which for me corresponded to Op. 132 by Beethoven, my favorite piece of his. What a lucky day. I held the leather seat of my bicycle with one hand. I'd been trying to push the thought away. But I knew what I was doing.

Eventually, I reached the spot I had visited with my mother and once again stared at the statue of Giordano Bruno.

I had done far more research than was expected, Mr. Carson said. In one of the university libraries I had read many pages from Bruno's books and even managed to read his play. What I also found was that Bruno had met Sir Philip Sidney, and that a character in Shakespeare, Berowne in *Love's Labour's Lost*, may have referred to Bruno himself. Yet here I was at this early hour of the morning in the heart of Rome and I wanted to think of nothing.

I walked the bike around the statue, looked at the marketplace, smelled wonderful foods, and in the end couldn't resist and purchased four small round balls of fried dough, while the man who was frying them tore out a square sheet of newspaper, twirled it into a cone, and dropped the dough into it. So old-world, I thought, but I delighted in the simplicity of his weary gesture. I touched the first piece of fried dough and it was scalding hot, so I let it cool for a few seconds and then placed it in my mouth. It was, as the smell promised, delicious and sweet. I asked the man selling them what they were called. "*Zeppole*. How else would you have me call them?"

How else would you have me call them? I liked the sound and the dismissive way he'd spoken these words. Seemingly off-putting, maybe a touch acerbic, or brazen, but underpinned by a tone of familiarity and incidental, harmless sarcasm directed at everything, the world, his job, me, and the *zeppole* themselves, as if they were little creatures that needed to be fed and tended to, otherwise they'd die, and there was no one but him left to care for them. In the end there was always an unavoidable touch of melodrama and self-pity in Roman familiarity, like that tiny crest of *panna*, whipped cream, which they hastily add with a small wooden spoon to every ice cream cone before handing it to you, on the house, as an extra favor, a concession, and a token of atonement for their unintended harshness when they grumbled hearing you order a strawberry or pistachio ice cream.

This, I realized, was how most people spoke here. Nothing they said was declarative, blunt, or assertive. It was always spoken on the slant and always yoked to its suggested yet undeclared opposite. Everything had another face, neither being entirely true or false. People didn't talk, they bantered, teased, flirted. Was I like this? I wasn't sure. But I knew that this was how I myself had started speaking. When an American student at school told me that his grandmother had died that weekend, I said *Really?* I didn't understand why he'd taken offense, since my *Really?* was not impugning his credibility but was a statement of surprise and sympathy.

Walking around the crammed stalls while pushing the bike with one hand and holding the *zeppole* in the other, trying not to finish them too soon, I thought it was strange that I hadn't smelled them when I was last here with my mother. That, too, had been an intensely translucent morning. Perhaps I should have encouraged her to join me this morning or waited for my brother to finish breakfast; he would have loved this outing. But then the bicycle? No, I liked the bicycle, and I loved the ease it gave me to revisit all my private corners within the space of a few hours without having to tell anyone.

By then I had already spent half the money needed to buy a book that week, and it was just ten o'clock in the morning. Yet nothing happened to displease me or interfere with the sudden wave of freedom coursing through my body. This happened very seldom, and if it did, only for fleeting moments, but never like this.

At a stall, I saw small wooden crates filled with many seasonal fruits. One of those crates was almost empty and at the bottom there were withered fruits that looked like oversized limes but also like dwarfed, beaten-up oranges. I'd never seen this fruit before. What were they? I asked the vendor, whose face seemed drawn by the Roman draftsman Pinelli himself. He eyed me, surprised I didn't know. He didn't say what the *zeppole* seller had said, but by the expression on his face, he might as well have used the exact same tone: *What could they possibly be?* "They're bergamots," he finally said. "Ah, yes, from Bergamo, then," I said, trying to show that I knew their provenance and wasn't entirely surprised. "*Macché Bergamo! Dalla Calabria!*" What do you mean, Bergamo! From Calabria.

How I loved that word, *macché*! Almost an expression of impatience, it, too, was underlined by a hint of scorn and spirited familiarity. He told me he was about to throw these away, as no one was going to buy them and tomorrow, Sunday, the market was closed. "Could I smell one?" I asked. "Take one—here—this is the best of the lot." I had never smelled bergamot before, citrusy but more than citrusy. It suggested numberless things without ever arriving at anything precise. I even liked the scent on my hands. Like music, it opened a universe of wonderful things, but I couldn't name a single one.

The man told me not to eat it, not even to bite into it. I pocketed the bergamot and started pedaling away, repeating to myself, "Bergamo, *bergamotto*, Bergamo, *bergamotto*."

From Campo de' Fiori I biked through the old streets of Rome, each lined by buildings coated with varying hues of ocher. I loved the play of morning light on Roman walls. When you leaned against such a wall, it left its powdery residue on your hands and clothes, which reminded me of how clay tennis courts stain your knees, your socks, and your shorts. On a day like this I'd be out in the early morning playing tennis.

Then it dawned on me why I was happy. Today was not so much a tennis day as a beach day. Not just spring weather: almost time for the first swim of the year.

I wanted the thought of tennis or of a swim to bind itself to my ride over toward the river and then up Via Giulia, where I was headed, because this felt just as good as tennis or swimming.

A few cars were coming toward me on that perennially quiet street, and I loved jolting on the cobblestones past all those splendid homes with huge portals and gated entrances through which you could peer at the old buildings, with courtyards boasting expensive foreign and domestic cars. A couple of the day students at school lived on Via Giulia, and riding on a bicycle now made passing through that street feel less daunting than walking slowly, usually with my mother or Aunt Flora, and perhaps being spotted by a classmate who'd think me an intruder stealing by on his street because it was his street and I didn't belong here. But my jaunt that day gave me an added flavor and suddenly, on deserted Via Giulia, I caught myself actually singing as I kept being jolted out of my seat by an endless row of cobblestones.

Once I reached Corso Vittorio, I was feeling so enthralled that I decided to go down Via Giulia again and head back up on Via di Monserrato. Then, changing my mind, I stopped, got off the bike, and started walking. I loved this too. I fished out the bergamot in my pocket and smelled it, then I pierced the rind with a fingernail, just the tiniest gash, and out came a powerful scent that I was reluctant to decide whether I liked or not but which cast a spell all its own on the morning and the city, as if this was what the city smelled like, or this was how I wanted to redefine its smell and was trapping its memory for who knew how many years.

I was thinking of calling Gianlorenzo to tell him . . . to tell him what? *Ti ho pensato*, I thought of you. But I didn't have a *gettone* for a call nor did I want to buy one.

After Via Giulia, I decided to head toward Piazza Navona. The sun by then was pounding the city. I took off my sweater and tied its sleeves around my neck and finally sat down on a bench right in the center of the piazza. I spread my legs, crossed my arms, took out the bergamot, sniffed it a few times until I was no longer able to smell it, and felt as though I was free of every care in my life. Nothing mattered. It was just me, the piazza, the sun, and the muffled sound of the fountains. I was in heaven.

A very fat man came to sit on my bench. He nodded hello and unfolded a newspaper. He, too, was happy with the day and, turning to me, said he could see I was surely pleased with the day. He remembered cutting classes so many, many years ago, loafing about town with his bike. I told him it wasn't my bike, but a friend's. Was my friend also cutting classes this Saturday? No, I went to an American school and we didn't meet on Saturdays. Ah, so I spoke English? I nodded. "I am Maltese," he said in English. Was I admiring the piazza? I nodded. He told me he'd spent years researching the piazza and its history, since he lived nearby and came here every day to read the paper. He pointed to the four statues in the center. "Made by Bernini," he said, "while the Church of Saint Agnes was Borromini's." The two hated each other—he went on to explain—and unlike the statues of the Nile, the Danube, and the Ganges, the statue of Rio de la Plata had an outstretched arm—"See?" he asked, pointing to the statue and imitating its raised hand—it's *inorridita*, the English word was escaping him, so I told him, *horrified*—as if either horrified by what he sees or scared that something might fall on him, and of course it's the church of Saint Agnes, built by his archrival. I liked the story. Well, it's an apocryphal tale, since the church was built quite a while after Bernini sculpted the statues of the four rivers—"After, not before, you understand?" Yes, I understood. "Rome is filled with such tales."

I thought of my grandmother who lived in Montevideo, right where the Rio de la Plata meets the Atlantic Ocean and where the *Graf Spee* met its end. As she'd prophesied, she was going to die there, just like the ship, just like the ship.

The fat man went on to tell me about the obelisks, listing all the obelisks in Rome, one after the other, reminding me that four of them were symmetrically placed in the city to form the four ends of a cross. "Rome is a Catholic city, after all, you understand, yes?"

I liked what he was saying and realized that, unlike my uncle, who during our first few weeks had provided the skimpiest, superficial details about the city, this obese old gentleman in a three-piece suit was a font of knowledge regarding a city I realized I knew nothing about. The big discovery being unveiled to me that day was that every spot in the city, down to the very *sampietrini* ("from Saint Peter, you understand, yes?"), was imbued with history, had seen all sorts of horrors and been stepped on by hundreds of millions of feet. Underneath each stone lay another stone and another under that, tiers and layers ever deeper; this city, just like us, is a multilayered labyrinth impossible to chart or resolve.

At some point I realized that I wanted to move on and, coming up with an excuse, told him that my mother was expecting me for lunch. "Will I ever see you again?" he asked, as he put his arm around me to bid me goodbye. I shrugged my shoulders, meaning something as indefinite as *Who knows?*

Later that evening, on returning Gianlorenzo's bike, I told him about the man, which made us share a good-natured chuckle. The way I parodied the fat man asking a distressed *Will I ever see you again?* was something I knew I shouldn't have enjoyed, but I did all the same, perhaps to get a rise out of him but also to let him know I wasn't the sort to like what the man had implied.

Past noon that day, as I reached the Spanish Steps, I knew what I'd come to do. I sped up Via Margutta, which was entirely deserted, and then turned onto Via del Babuino to the Lion Bookshop. It was about to close for three hours, and I had to make a quick decision. I found the book I'd been planning to buy since strolling with my family and Flora two weeks before, brought it to the middle-aged owner of the shop, who had the deep, intimidating voice of a despotic aged headmistress, and timidly asked if I could pay her two hundred lire now and the other three hundred on Monday. All of it amounted to less than a dollar. She knew me as a regular customer, knew my name by now, and knew some of my teachers, who were also her frequent customers. To prove I wasn't lying, I emptied my pockets to produce the four fifty-lire coins but had inadvertently taken out the damaged and humbled bergamot I'd been carrying in the same pocket. The coins, I could tell, smelled of bergamot. She laughed and said she trusted me. She slipped the volume into a cream paper bag with red lions rampant bearing the shop's logo and simply said, "Until Monday, then."

It was my habit now to buy a book and walk with it to the Spanish Steps. That day I dropped the package inside my shirt to free my hands while biking. Once I'd reached the steps, I carried the bike up a few and leaned it against the wall, right next to the Keats-Shelley House.

This was my spot, listening to the traffic, to the fountain down below, to the voices of a few tourists snacking and talking. But it was mostly quiet and there were spells when silence descended ever so softly over the city, as though I might have been lying down somewhere away from everything. I took out the book, knowing I had chosen it well, and started to read: *The sea is high again today, with a thrilling flush of wind. In the midst of winter you can feel the inventions of spring. A sky of hot nude pearl until midday.* I kept reading and skimming until finally I put the book down, thinking back to that Palm Sunday barely two weeks before and remembering how I had loved that day, because so many aspects of my life seemed to converge on the Spanish Steps: Alexandria, those I loved and was happy to be with, even the Alexandrian tram stops whose names and sequence I'd forgotten and was glad to rediscover almost by chance now in the pages of *Justine* that I was holding in my hands. I wished my father would read these pages and then talk to me about them, the way he always talked to me, as we'd done on these very steps. From somewhere nearby, maybe from one of the tourists sitting on the steps, I made out the scent of Aunt Flora's suntan oil. I couldn't help myself. I shut my eyes. This was the beach.

I read a good fifteen or so pages on the steps and was completely transfixed. I needed this book to think back to a city I had been burying for months and maybe even wished to scrape from memory. But I also needed this book to know who I was now and what stood behind me, as if Durrell's novel allowed me to intuit things that weren't in his book at all, but in me, except that I needed his voice and its cadence to draw closer to myself.

I wanted to read the rest at home that evening, especially since I had no plans to go out.

I took down the bicycle and carried it all the way up to the Trinità dei Monti, stopping to rest my arms periodically. I wanted to ride down the shaded Via Sistina toward Termini and then home. When I reached the top, I looked down at the city, which empties out after one o'clock in the afternoon and which was once again trying to draw me in. Eventually I thought of heading toward Ponte Sisto, maybe crossing over to Trastevere. But I changed my mind. I had no money, and I was hungry. Time to go home and return the bike to Gianlorenzo. Next Saturday he might lend it to me again. Meanwhile, my mother would have cooked a good lunch. She always made something wonderful on Saturdays, knowing it was our day at home. It would have to be reheated by now. I wanted to sit with my book in the kitchen.

I'd been happy that day.

Gianlorenzo might never know how riding his bicycle had opened up Rome to me.

～

A bit later that same afternoon, Sabina called. This was a surprise, I said. She wanted to go to the movies. Was I free? I was, I said. "I knew you weren't going to call me again," she said when we met inside the lobby of the Trianon. This took a lot of courage to say. I told her there was only one message to draw from the way she'd answered the other day. She explained that she was not free to talk at the time, because everyone in the family was in the room. She apologized and gave me a kiss on each cheek. She said she was glad I held no grudges. Then she told me about the films we were seeing. I had heard of both but hadn't seen them. "You, of course, would have preferred them in English." No, I said, I'd gotten used to dubbed films. Jack Lemmon and Shirley MacLaine sounded good enough in Italian.

We sat in the back row, where all the young couples sat. We kissed passionately, wildly, almost as soon as we sat down, just as I'd done that time in my room in front of her other friend, whose name I no longer remembered. I didn't ask if her friend minded, but I did ask how she had gotten my phone number—not from her friend? No, she said. She'd remembered it from seeing it on my telephone when she'd asked if she could call her parents. "So all this was already being planned," I finally said blithely. "Yes," she replied when I looked at her. In the dark, I heard the mischievous inflection in her voice and sensed she was smiling and trying to affect a touch of shame at being caught.

I can't remember the name of the movie we saw that evening. We were doing what the others near us were doing, kissing, petting, and talking, talking, talking in sly, smothered late-afternoon whispers. I didn't want to seem too forward with her, but she turned out to be far bolder than I when she laid her coat over both our laps and began touching me.

There was something so dauntless and unequivocal about her that it left me speechless. At intermission, when the lights came on, we were as guarded and well-behaved as everyone around us. Then, as soon as the second film started, we were back to bolder things yet. She must have done this before because she knew how to unzip a man's trousers. "*Ti piace?*" Do you like it? she whispered, licking the inside of my ear while I was almost swooning. I did not respond to her question, but when I attempted to touch her, she recoiled every time. When she asked again if I liked what she was doing, I only nodded. My eyes shut, I couldn't believe what was about to happen.

When we left the theater, I told her that I really had to get home. She uttered a semi-naughty snicker to mean she understood why. All I could think of was Leopold Bloom, who'd felt cold and clammy after watching Gerty MacDowell on the beach. We could do this again next Saturday, she suggested. I said I couldn't wait. Then she said that she, too, had to go home to change before going dancing tonight. With the same friend? I asked. "*No, col mio ragazzo,*" with my boyfriend. I gave her a comprehending, very mature smile that I'd mastered with Paola and that was meant to be as sly as hers. Then came the tiny blow—totally unintended, but it bore through me and managed to ruin everything we'd done that afternoon. When I asked where she was going, she said Kilt. On my way home, I knew exactly what was troubling me: not just Kilt, not the *ragazzo*, but the totally dispassionate, impersonal way things had happened between us. There was something so mechanical about what we'd done, like children playing with a new toy, except that the toy happened to be my body. Sabina reminded me of the first woman on rue Saint-Denis: cold, unimaginative, hasty, heartless, and ultimately a touch sleazy. But the proof was on my body. I was equally unimaginative, hasty, heartless, and sleazy. What I felt, though it came in ripples, was shame. Shame that I had revealed an aspect of my body when there'd been no intimacy whatsoever.

I was never going to call her again.

When I opened the door, my mother was washing Amina's hair. There was a slight air of partying within, which put me in a better mood. Amina, her head almost inside the deep kitchen sink, asked what I'd done that day. I told her that I'd been all over Rome and ended up buying a book I meant to read. Was she going dancing tonight? No, her parents were having relatives over for supper, so she had to stay and help. The relatives were old. They were boring. She didn't like them, she said. "But . . . ," and she shrugged her shoulders with her head still inside the sink.

I said I was going to take a quick bath. Too much walking, I explained.

Later, when I got out of the bathroom, the kitchen lights were out, and Amina had left. My brother said he was going to a school dance and was meeting a friend around San Giovanni whose parents would drive them to school. Did I want to come? "Not this time," I said. "You always say *not this time*." He threatened never to ask me again.

My mother was in her bedroom reading one of the many magazines that my father had sent by mail and which Madame Barbonne, the concièrge of his building in Paris, having taken a liking to him, would collect after the tenants had discarded them. Every four weeks, he'd bundle them up and mail them to us, which he knew was a godsend for my mother. My father, I knew, wasn't living it up in Paris the way my mother's acquaintances had claimed.

Did I want to eat something? she asked. Yes, something light, but I was going to make my own sandwich. So I took a *rosetta* and filled it with everything I could find, adding a bit of vinegar, mustard, and a dab of olive oil. I took two biscuits from one of the cupboards, put everything on a plate, and brought it to my room. I sat in my usual large armchair and started rereading *The sea is high again today, with a thrilling flush of wind. In the midst of winter you can feel the inventions of spring. A sky of hot nude pearl until midday* . . .

I was there, all right. Not my Alexandria, not the one I'd known, but a vestigial, dream city bearing the same street names and the same neighborhoods, yet always altered and seen askance. Maybe this is what I was after, not the city as I remembered it, but traces of a city that might never have existed but was reinvented and in a strange way more real on paper for me that night than was my memory of it. Maybe this was why I liked books: they were not as real as life; they offered an altered, transposed, and stylized version of the real that I liked better because it was more persuasive. It had radiance; real life never did.

It must have been two o'clock in the morning when I put down the book after hearing my brother shut the entrance door behind him and lock it very quietly, thinking I was sleeping. I called out to him. He came to my room and said he'd met a lovely girl that evening. Next time, I should go with him. So I told him about Sabina. He wanted the details, he said. I gave him the details. That was all? Yes, that was all. He was going to brush his teeth then hit the sack—his words.

When he shut my door behind him, I wanted to reread those first few pages, hoping to recover the seductive, cadenced spell they'd cast when I'd first read them on the Spanish Steps early that afternoon. My entire day in the city seemed locked in the author's prose, while his prose was locked on the Spanish Steps, and I couldn't tell them apart.

That night, I was already imagining the following Saturday. I would leave in the morning and, if Gianlorenzo lent me his bike, repeat everything all over: Piazza di Campitelli, Campo de' Fiori, Via Giulia, Via di Monserrato, Piazza Nuova, Via del Babuino, and then a long stay on the glaring sunlit steps of Piazza di Spagna, with the numberless flowerpots still there after Palm Sunday.

— 9 —

A Garden Party

Everyone knew about our meager budget. Sabina knew we had no money, which was why she paid for the movie that time; Amina definitely knew; even Gianlorenzo figured it out when he asked me if I wanted to buy a very cheap thirdhand bicycle and I lied, saying that I had my eye on a portable Olivetti typewriter instead. "*E i sòrdi, 'ndó 'i trovi?*" And where will you find the money? he had asked. I was honest enough to say I didn't know.

Toward the end of every month we'd go over our bleak finances with the passive helplessness of people who can't budget for what can't be budgeted: tuition, movies, a weekly book, the local tailor when my mother was unable to alter an item of clothing, unforeseen incidental expenses that always took a toll and couldn't be justified, food, and of course rent and utilities plus telephone, to say nothing of the cost of shattered glass, which regularly upended our monthly allotment. Unlike most households, who had mineral water delivered every morning, we purchased only as we needed. We never bought cakes. There were no treats, except for an occasional ice cream cone, which was considered a true luxury. Sometimes by the twenty-first of the month we knew we'd gone over our monthly allotment and would need to borrow money rather than trouble Uncle Claude.

One incident reminded us of how far we had sunk on the social ladder.

We were invited to Marsilio Ancona's garden party at his country home outside Rome. The occasion was the forthcoming marriage of his beloved niece, Nora, to my cousin Toto, whom I liked but rarely got to see. Toto was always jovial and easy to laugh with. His humor reminded me so much of Jules's. In fact, he and Jules had been classmates at the Lycée Français in Alexandria and shared the bawdy, boisterous bent common to all young men in those years. Now, with one in Rome and the other in Paris, they had lost touch, and when I brought up one to the other, the indifferent shrug reminded me that for them their Alexandrian comradeship was past recovery.

When my mother first told me about the reception, I said I didn't want to go. Neither did my brother, nor did she, she claimed, but we had to go. I could tell she wanted to; besides, she added, Marsilio had been exceptionally good to us and had sent us small crates filled with fresh figs from his estate, then a bit later persimmons, pears, and apples. He would also, though seldom, regale us with some of his choicest white wines. The reception was in a few days, and she had already promised Flora we were going to attend.

The reason I didn't want to go had as much to do with the ugly, dirty paupers' buses that left from the San Giovanni gate for the distant rural areas outside Rome with people carrying unwieldy wrapped packages. Not to mention arriving on these buses and then walking on the dusty roads leading to the event while everyone else, including Aunt Flora, would be arriving by car, many of them with drivers. For us the journey would take more than an hour.

We arrived exactly as I feared. The walk on the dusty, old, and mostly unpaved road was not long, but my mother was once again wearing high heels, and she needed to make her way cautiously. She said she'd always hated these shoes, and now they were all dusty too. I asked her for tissue paper, then knelt down and rubbed her shoes lightly. Meanwhile, I made a point of looking at the sign across the way to determine the time when we'd have to catch the bus back to San Giovanni.

When we finally stepped into the grounds, I was certain we looked no less haggard than anyone who'd taken the slow, crowded bus from San Giovanni. Down a long driveway flanked by very tall pine trees, I spotted Flora sipping prosecco with Philippa, whom she had brought along. Philippa was loving Italy but unfortunately was headed back to England. Bristol, *vero*? asked Flora. Brighton, replied Philippa, casting a sly, benevolent look at her as if to say, *You'll never learn, will you?*

Then Flora brought us over to Marsilio and his wife, Sara, who were glad to see us, as were the others who'd sat on the Council of Olympus nine months earlier to decide our school fate. Uncle Claude hadn't been invited, but his daughter was there, and she, too, greeted us. Then Flora led us to the refreshments, clearly intending to make us feel less uncomfortable among strangers, knowing exactly how out of place we must have felt, since she, too, must have felt out of place among these very wealthy guests. To conceal her diminished status after being wealthy once, Flora had acquired a bantering, provocative, almost peevish manner with her rich relations, which must have been a desperate ploy to appear their equal but which they now regarded as further proof of her demotion.

On watching those around us, my mother reminded me that she had been right in asking us to wear a jacket and tie. *One never knows.* People, as always, were extremely gracious with my mother, and she didn't seem the slightest bit uncomfortable, did not suppose, as I did, that we were being ceremoniously excluded even when admitted. She always took things in stride, I did not. Toto, as had been our habit the moment we caught sight of each other, made fun of the crotchety old relatives who couldn't laugh, he said, because the cork up their asses prevented them from farting. He claimed to have slept with several of the younger women present, many of them now accompanied by their husbands. I didn't believe him, but it was refreshing to hear him belittle his own wedding. "You know, after next week when I'm married to her, she'll never let me fuck another woman," he said, referring to Nora, who was talking to someone several yards away and to whom he was already referring with the heedless apathy of a married man tired of minding his wife. "At least you can have any woman here, even this old one," he said, pointing to a woman with a cane who must have been ninety, if not older, and was holding a wobbly glass of prosecco in her free hand. He stared at her: "Does your mother know you're here, dear?" he asked the old lady in an earnest and solicitous tone, which made me laugh heartily. I told him about Amina, then about Paola, then Sabina at the Trianon and what she'd done. "Did you do her too?" he asked. "She wouldn't let me." "Typical!" he said, then added, "*Pour moi, khalas, d'ora in poi, c'est tout one way,*" using the quadrilingual idiolect of our boisterous Alexandrian years, meaning: For me it's all over, from now on it's all one way. I asked if he had slept with Philippa. No, he said, she didn't like men. How did he know? "I asked her," he replied. Then he excused himself, saying he needed to kiss ass with an old couple who'd promised to help him land a job at a bank.

Toto always put me in a good mood. Flora and my mother noticed that we'd been laughing together and commented that we were surely either making fun of the other guests or making obscene jokes. Meanwhile, without thinking, and perhaps because I was still smiling after what he'd told me, I spotted his sister Dora and, seeing that no one was speaking to her, approached her and began chatting with her in Arabic. She couldn't wait to flee this band of enriched *sankaris*, she said. I had forgotten what the word meant. Plumbers, she said.

The sun was setting over the surrounding pines and I knew that the evening promised to be more beautiful yet.

Everything was moving along smoothly. More wine, more appetizers, more delicious sweets and cakes, new people to meet, many born in Egypt yet settled in Italy in the mid-to-late fifties. I was enjoying myself with so many new faces, speaking in our Alexandrian medley of words from many tongues lumped together in the same sentence, which always makes everyone laugh. I watched Marsilio circle his guests and make sure that those who weren't speaking were introduced and were served more prosecco. I watched him signal the waiters with a mere raising of his head and creasing of his brow.

I tried to draw my brother's attention but he was busy chatting about boxing. I was surprised by his impressive familiarity with the American boxing scene. My mother, too, was enjoying herself. When I was finally able to catch her attention, I signaled that a bus would be stopping in a very short while. Within minutes, and seeing that the hosts were busy speaking to their guests at the other end of the large garden, I stopped my mother from intruding on them to say good-bye, thinking that farewells from lesser relatives and peripheral guests hardly mattered and would never be noticed. I asked Flora to please give our regards to Marsilio and Sara.

Once again, my mother cautiously negotiated her steps on the unpaved, stony path to the bus stop, still complaining that she hated these shoes and should never have listened to Madame Rashidi in Egypt, who'd referred her to a new shoemaker. Once outside the stone portal to the property, I wanted the three of us to disappear as fast as we could. Good thing we were leaving, I thought. And as I hastened toward the bus stop and prayed that no one from the party would spy us waiting like three paupers for the rickety bus to San Giovanni. I wanted my mother to feel this way as well, but I could tell it was the furthest thing from her mind. I thought she was irresponsible, which was why she was trailing behind me and not hurrying.

Suddenly, from somewhere behind us we heard a voice calling, "*Ma dove andate?*" But where are you going? It was Marsilio, who had seen us leave and was rushing behind us. "*Torniamo a casa,*" we're going back home, I replied. "Just come back," he repeated, "come back. One of our drivers will take you home."

We followed him and soon it got dark and the younger guests, my brother and I and quite a few others our age, were accompanied by an orchestra of three and urged to sing recent songs on the Italian hit parade. We gladly complied. Lights were now glowing everywhere on the trees, and as we continued to sing, I began to feel that these were indeed my relatives, distant to be sure, but relatives all the same. "You've drunk a bit," said Aunt Flora, "but wine agrees with you." "Yes, it does," I said, not realizing that my quick reply was itself a sign that the wine had gone to my head.

By the time we left the reception it was past midnight. We reached home at almost one in the morning, not with one of Marsilio's elderly drivers but with one of the guests, a very dapper man who wanted to show us that his new Alfa Romeo could race through unpaved country roads and then bolt onto the freeway to Rome. He was young, full of himself, and smoked while holding his cigarette in between the fingers of the hand that barely seemed to touch the steering wheel, while the elbow of the other arm rested on the open window frame. But his manner and the way he addressed us were impeccable. Indeed, he treated us as belonging to Marsilio's inner circle. I could see that he was oversolicitous with us, and that Marsilio had given him strict orders to drop us at our door, and not before reaching our building *mi raccomando*, not before! I knew that the young man would change his attitude once I told him which street to take. But when we arrived at Via Clelia, he opened the door for my mother, helped her out of the car, then bowed before her hand. He looked at me, made a comment about my tie, and said he admired it. "Where did you buy it, if I may ask?" I couldn't resist. "In Paris." "Of course," he replied, adding, "Faubourg Saint-Honoré?" I nodded. We shook hands, then he got into his car, and I heard its thunderous roar as it sped to Via Tuscolana against traffic.

Anyone would have mistaken his laid-back, insouciant air as democratic to the core; in his conduct toward us and in the way he pretended to ignore and wasn't taken aback by Via Clelia, he was being irreducibly highborn and gracious. I admired him. I envied him. I was trying to hate him. I couldn't. He was, it hardly took a second to realize, the person I might have been had things never changed. My awkwardness was nothing more than shame disguised. My excess of courtesy when I thanked him once more was, unlike his, my way of exaggerating our gratitude the better to screen our circumstances.

~

A new blow came within days of the garden party. My mother, thanks to her deaf friends, had long since joined a social club for the hearing impaired. They gathered almost every week at a place on Via Merulana. They met in the evening, and on those days, she'd have some food prepared for my brother and me, knowing that we'd be alone until around ten o'clock, when she returned. I had told her not to bother cooking for us. My brother and I liked to improvise our supper, imagining we were bachelors, living, as Uncle Mischa had said, in the West Eighties in New York City.

At the club, they served food to help members meet and socialize. Many of the members were couples, and everyone knew that my mother's husband lived in Paris. Signor Avellini always came with his wife, and as they lived only a few blocks from Via Clelia, my mother and they were in the habit of heading to the club together and returning together on the same bus. Sometimes they would drop my mother home and come upstairs for a quick *caffè corretto*, espresso with a dash of liqueur; at other times she would go to their home. Their friendship blossomed. My mother would cut and sew something for the signora and had already knitted a jumpsuit for the baby they were expecting imminently, while the husband, who was a bookbinder, had caught sight of my loosely bound copy of *Doctor Zhivago*, took it to work, and within days brought it back totally rebound, a book I still own today. I had a copy of *Zorba the Greek*, which was being assigned for class discussion in a few weeks and which I had asked him to rebind, as it, too, was in a threadbare condition and had been found in a secondhand bookstore.

But one night Signora Avellini, whose newborn was running a low fever, could not accompany her husband to the club. When my mother went upstairs for what had become their *caffè corretto* after the club, Signora Avellini, looking very upset, started haranguing her husband for coming home late, and then, turning to my mother, started berating her as well. My mother inferred what must have upset the wife and without hesitating slapped her face, put on her coat, and walked out of their home determined never to set foot there again.

The next day, the wife called me—she spoke clearly enough even though she was hard of hearing—and told me to tell my mother that she was going to go to the police station to report the incident and that an investigation would naturally ensue.

I very cordially thanked her for the news and told her that we would be in touch with her. I had no idea what else to tell her. The incident of the *schiaffo*, the slap, perturbed me more than it did my mother.

My mother had confided the event to me as soon as she returned that night and wasn't particularly upset. But when I told her that Signora Avellini was going to report it to the police, all she could say was *Why involve the police?* Hadn't the woman ever been slapped before?

I tried to explain that, outside Egypt, one didn't slap people.

My mother was willing to swear that Avellini's wife had called her a *puttana*. When I brought the prospect of an investigation to her attention, it was clear that we would need a lawyer, and that lawyer would deplete our funds. Rent might have to wait, and I was already rehearsing what I'd tell Brother Peter to explain why I wasn't able to pay that month's tuition. I slept that night, but I had terrifying dreams.

The next morning, I rummaged through my mind for whom to dig up who'd know something about the law.

We knew no one.

But the answer was staring us in the face. "Call him," my mother said.

"No," I replied.

"Call him, I beg you. If I could, I would call him. But I can't."

"I can't either."

Finally, I think my mother was scared. She tried everything to convince me to call for her, but I wouldn't budge. Eventually, she went to her balcony and lit a cigarette, something I'd never seen her do. "You want me to beg, I'm begging you now," she said. I resolved to call Uncle Claude to explain the situation we were in.

He came within twenty minutes, and as soon as he was in the apartment, he started yelling at my mother for the first time in his life. "You don't hit people here. This is not the Middle East, or America."

What exactly happened? he asked.

My mother repeated the story. Was she one hundred percent sure she was called a *puttana*?

Yes, one hundred percent sure.

Was she looking at her when she said it?

Yes, she was.

Like a true lawyer, he did not ask for more.

He asked me to call the Avellinis.

I dialed the number, and after a few moments, which I'm sure was the time needed for the wife to put on her earpiece, she picked up the phone. "*Buona sera, signora Avellini*," I said. "*Vorrei presentarle mio zio per discutere . . .*" I would like to introduce you to my uncle to discuss . . . But Uncle Claude immediately tore the receiver from my hand and shoved me aside. "*Discutere, discutere . . . ,*" he snapped, making fun of the way I had started the phone call.

"I am the signora's lawyer and I want to come speak to you now."

Signora Avellini wanted to retell the whole incident, starting from the previous night's meeting at the club.

He didn't want to know about the previous night's meeting at the club. He wanted to meet her now.

He was welcome to see her, but she wasn't going to change her mind, she said.

He knew this, he said.

He told Mother to get dressed and right away they drove to the Avellinis', a few minutes away.

At home my brother and I were on tenterhooks. The last time I had had as much anxiety was in sixth grade when my father had gone to meet my teachers and was sure to return very upset with their report. I was right to worry that night. The report was disastrous.

At the time, I had thought that worrying was a way to placate the gods by humbling myself and placing both my trust and my fate at their altar. Worrying, as it turned out, rather than placate the gods, had incensed them further. Perhaps, then, it was better not to worry. But no, the gods would most certainly punish me for choosing not to worry. But worrying simply to win their favor might in itself be a reason for punishment.

I didn't know whether this was a sign that I was still tethered to the old world from which I believed I'd freed myself in Italy, or whether all this recursive, twisted thinking was just a reflection of my failure to trust the world. I did recall that when my father came home after speaking to my teachers that evening, he told me that my teachers were very displeased with me, with my work, with my attitude in class, and above all with my refusal to concentrate. Then came the scolding. My mother stood silently for a while and then told him it was time for supper. "The boy is hungry," she said, whereupon he lost his temper with her as well for always, always meddling and contradicting him.

When my mother and Uncle Claude returned, the two wore smiles on their faces. She told me that Signora Avellini had opened the door and welcomed them, crying and holding her sick baby in both arms and asking forgiveness. Uncle Claude had walked in with the full bearing of a renowned prosecutor eager to take matters to court.

The Avellinis had assumed that we were poor, that we knew nobody and would buckle before their threats and demands. They were absolutely right. We would have folded.

At home, Claude asked for a cup of coffee, was served right away, drank it down standing up, donned his hat again, and reminded my mother that he would return within days for the artichokes.

"And never slap anyone again," he said on his way out, without saying goodbye to me or my brother.

The truth is that without Uncle Claude we were like a hapless skiff with broken oars fending for itself in the middle of a squall. The merest wind, let alone a ten-foot wave, would topple us. He could easily have said he was busy that night or that he refused to serve as our perpetual rescuer.

But on coming back from the Avellinis', Mother was overjoyed. I went back to my homework; she started washing the dishes we had left in the sink, never thinking that we could easily have washed them ourselves.

The incident of the *schiaffo* must have upset my mother more than she knew. She realized that she was now living in a different world and that the standards of Egypt were not applicable or tolerated in Italy. The kindness of so many people in the marketplace buffered her from the hardships she would have faced outside Via Clelia, especially when confronted by administrative matters that she was totally unable to fathom. When it came to the records office in Rome (two buses) for her identity papers, and for mine, or to renewing our passports (two buses), or speaking to a lawyer with ties to Egypt (three buses) or to the foreign office for sending mail to my father's lawyers in Egypt via the diplomatic pouch (three buses plus a very long walk), I spared my mother these administrative errands and chores. When she sometimes came along with me to sign papers of one sort or another, I was always the one doing the talking, thus shielding her from the perverse, ill-tempered, and heartless machinations of petty Italian bureaucrats, many of whom held jobs that hadn't changed since they'd been hired under Mussolini more than two decades earlier. I was the one who would constantly be filling out forms in triplicate, just as it was I who received news of our failed immigration applications for Australia and South Africa. We'd applied *seulement pour voir*, just to see, as my father kept saying. This was one of his many ways of deferring and possibly never deciding to cross any ocean from his home in Paris.

Meanwhile, my mother had grown afraid of meeting anyone who frequented the club, having assumed that Signora Avellini had ratted her out and persuaded everyone that she was a *puttana*. Signor Avellini himself would most likely have taken his wife's side against my mother, though it was hard to imagine how that would not have implicated him as well. The gossip-mongering spread rapidly in that community, as a result of which the Coronaris, too, stopped speaking to my mother, and when my brother and I ran into them in the tiny tram at Via Eurialo in the morning, they acknowledged us with a vague nod of the head before averting their gaze.

The *schiaffo* turned into a yet more difficult moment for my mother, as a result of which she came down with the flu, which developed into bronchitis. Doctor Protospataro, with the beautiful Byzantine honorific name, spoke in the most unfathomable Roman dialect that I had ever heard. He was always rushed but was a good man who put my mother on antibiotics and would come to visit her at our home once, sometimes twice, a day and refuse payment. But the antibiotics he prescribed and that I would get at the local pharmacy disturbed her stomach, so she would not always take them as directed. She lay in bed for several days, and it was Madame Renato who would come to care for her while we were at school.

When we came home, the house smelled different, as Madame Renato always prepared something for supper so that we would not have to cook, and I loved the food she cooked. She swore by her soups and prepared a chicken soup that lasted a whole week. She taught me how to cook it during the second and third weeks of my mother's convalescence. And at night, she said, one or two gulps of brandy with warm water and a bit of honey didn't hurt either. For the rest of my life, whenever I've had or thought I had a touch of fever, her words have always come back to me: buy a chicken, remove the organs if they haven't already been taken out, add a few peeled carrots, a few celery stalks, one or two whole onions, salt, and parsley or whatever herbs you like, because any food without herbs, she said, was a sick man's brew. After which all I need do is lie down and the soup, with the chicken floating inside, will cook itself over a very low flame or high flame, it was fifty-fifty to her so long as the soup didn't boil over. And at night, don't forget, she'd say with a raised forefinger, one or two gulps of warm brandy. If my mother was asleep by the time Madame Renato left in the afternoon, a tiny glass of orange juice was always waiting by her side with a tiny saucer resting on its rim. It was Madame Renato's sign that she'd left while mother was sleeping.

～

On those endless afternoons after school, I would listen to Liszt's Transcendental Études, No. 10 in F minor being my absolute favorite, because it was the only one I owned, and while listening, float out to an anglicized world set in Egypt where my grandmother played Liszt in a setting decked with moments drawn from Virginia Woolf and Katherine Mansfield. I would listen to it while reading and make sure the chicken soup didn't boil over, and when my mother was up, I'd tell her about Kazantzakis's *Zorba the Greek*, which I was reading for class, after buying another copy so as not to ask Signor Avellini to return the one he'd offered to bind. Sometimes I would tell her about some of the boys at school, or about my weird calculus teacher who wore the same shirt for two weeks, and provided there was gossip and comedy in my tales, she'd tell me my stories were better than going to the movies. My brother and I did the shopping, bought her medicine, took our clothes to the laundromat, and studied while the washer and dryer droned on. Because of her deafness, which singled her out, many in the shops nearby knew who she was and all wanted to know *come sta la mamma*, how's your mother doing, and it seemed to me their constant questions showed how much they cared for her, starting with Amina's mother, who'd always stuff a few items of food in my plastic net bag. Their best wishes on those sunlit Saturday mornings when my brother and I would rush to shop for food remind me still of the intense Roman morning light, which we had grown to love, regardless of the perpetual din and chaos of Via Enea.

One day we came back from school and found my mother in her orange plaid dressing gown sitting in a small armchair that she'd moved right by the closed French window leading to our minuscule balcony, enjoying the sun. Madame Renato had come with the doctor and both agreed she looked better and her fever was abating. "It's been gone for a few days already, but I wasn't sure," she said, not budging from her seat as the two of us walked into her bedroom and sat on her bed close to her armchair. "I am still very tired." Then she looked at us with a strange blend of tenderness and fatigue, and said something that unsettled me. "I want to stay sick some more, I like sleeping and doing nothing." It reminded me of Aunt Flora, who had had her appendix removed in Egypt and used to say that she had liked being in the hospital and hadn't wanted to leave. "If you have a moment, do me a huge favor and call my sister in New York," said my mother.

It was five o'clock in Rome, which meant eleven in the morning in New York. Her sister would be at work still.

"No," said my mother, "she'll answer. She's home."

"How do you know?"

"I know. She is sick too. Ask how she is."

Then she turned her face away from me and cast a long, vacant stare through the French window. With the end of her right sleeve, she rubbed a smudge on the glass, then went back to staring. She said she was going to lie down now. "I'm worried for my sister, I want to see her," she said.

I stepped outside her room where the telephone was and dialed the operator to ask her to call a number in New York. She said she would call me back, but I knew that it would take a long time.

While my brother went to brew some chamomile for her, I heard my mother lift the bedcovers, slip under them, then throw the three blankets over her. She didn't like to see light when she slept, and her way of avoiding the slightest ray was to cover her head with the blankets. As I looked at her all wrapped up this way, without even her hair showing, I thought that this was what she'd look like if she died.

I knew I was rehearsing my very worst fear.

Sometimes the only proof we have of our love for someone is the numberless times we catch ourselves preparing for their loss, as if to dilute beforehand the unavoidable grief that is sure to devastate us. We take the loss in small doses every day, the way King Mithridates took venom to immunize himself and blunt the thing he feared most: decline, suffering, and death.

My mother had fallen asleep in less than five minutes. Meanwhile, I dropped in on Gianlorenzo to ask if I could borrow his bicycle again that Saturday in case my mother got better. I told him about her bronchitis, and he responded by saying that his grandmother was also very sick but no longer wanted to stay in the hospital. He looked shaken and finally added, "*Sta morenno, porella,'o sai,*" she is dying, poor woman, you know. After hearing about his grandmother I was embarrassed to ask for something as mundane as a bike, but he quickly added, "*È tua,*" it's yours. He reached out and hugged me. I hugged him back.

When I returned home, the telephone operator yelled at me and reproached me for placing an international call and not being there to receive it. I apologized, she accepted my apology, but warned that the next time there'd be a *multa*, a fine.

When my aunt finally came on the line in New York, she already knew that my mother was doing better and said that she, too, had been sick. It was a sisterly thing, she explained, almost laughing but lacking the strength to laugh aloud. I told her that my mother was in her third week of bronchitis but, with the fever abating, she was doing much better. She had asked me to call and in the interim had fallen asleep. "Let her sleep, let her sleep. Tell her that I think of her all the time. I knew she'd call, because she's had enough of Rome. I need her near me. We are hoping for the visa very, very soon. I think that a year by herself in Rome is what made her sick." I began to agree with her, but didn't say so, in good part because it had never occurred to me how utterly deplorable life was for a solitary, impoverished, and unloved if beautiful deaf person whose only loyal friend, with the exception of Flora, was a loving and devoted charwoman living a few blocks away to whom she had entrusted her life.

A few days later, I realized that Signor Leo had shown up, because I found an uncorked bottle of sweet wine on the kitchen table. My mother was no longer wearing a dressing gown and looked much livelier. I had grown used to finding him at our home when we came back from school, and equally used to watching him leave once he was no longer alone with her.

I thought I was a grown man able to allow my mother her private life, seeing I had allowed my father his. But I was no different from a child who is unable to sit still on his first day in kindergarten. I tolerated her privacy in my head. My heart was elsewhere.

We were going to discuss *Zorba the Greek* in class. To illustrate what a bon vivant Zorba was, the teacher, who fancied himself a bon vivant, read some key passages contrasting Zorba's lust for life with the narrator's timid, indecisive, and clearly withdrawn personality in need of Zorba's bold jostling to unleash both desire and pleasure in his life.

The class of American teenagers who were about to graduate and were already behaving like truculent university students who drank to vomit on Friday evenings at the Piper Club and then danced with whomever they found at Kilt or elsewhere clearly understood Zorba's passionate lifestyle. I was more like the unnamed narrator, whose zest for life was not as unruly, just more guarded and deliberate. Our teacher, who was not a man of the cloth but one who'd come to Rome with his wife and daughter to teach for three years and learn Italian before returning to the U.S., explained that the movie, based on the novel by Kazantzakis and starring Anthony Quinn and Alan Bates, had indeed captured the spirit of the novel and the carefree, pleasure-seeking Zorba. "Take for instance the final dance scene," he said. And to illustrate the point, he had brought to class the same LP of the soundtrack that Cousin Arnaut had given my brother on New Year's Eve in Paris. With the record player already set up in class, he moved the needle to the last cut, which he wanted us to hear.

We heard a few scratches, then a series of slow, introductory pluckings of the bouzouki, which I recognized right away, then after the introduction came the first stirrings of Zorba's dance, eventually erupting at greater and greater speed till it lashed into the vertiginous tune that reminded me that Greek music was in my blood, had always been, and that all you had to do was scratch the surface and you'd find me no less passionate than any Zorba walking our planet, just not as demonstrative. This was my world, tugging at me, calling me back, reminding me of intimate moments in Alexandria, and Paris, and before, of my beguiling Constantinople, which I'd never even seen but where they said my soul was still rooted.

Just then, something totally unexpected happened to me. I stared at the blackboard, at the teacher, at the rest of the silent class, realizing that no one in this classroom could possibly understand the music.

My head, my neck, and my shoulders began to shake, both to the music but also to something like a protest welling up within me, except that as I tried to smother my reaction, my body shook and then tears began to stream down my cheeks, though I wasn't sobbing. These were silent, muffled, bashful tears, whose flow I couldn't hold back, and rather than fool myself into thinking that I was reacting to the strains of the music only, I could tell that something else was taking place, something unremembered and yet so cloistered and faraway that, despite my effort to contain it, my mind flooded with scattered images. I saw my grandmother's archaic penmanship when she wrote from Uruguay urging me never, ever to forget I had a grandmother

I'd never see again. How could I forget the faint, moldy, airless smell of her ancient linen closet after she'd emptied it before sailing for good to Europe, leaving behind only her scent and a stack of yellowed doilies she'd embroidered as a young girl God knows how many decades before in Constantinople. The music remembered her, the way it remembered the sound of her slippers in Egypt when she shuffled from the kitchen to my bedroom with a glass of orange juice she'd just squeezed and, after knocking at my door, mispronounced three words that sounded more German than English: *rise and shine*, she'd say, *rise and shine*. The more I tried not to heed what the music was summoning, the more it wanted me to recall even Aunt Elsa's pots of jam, which she'd brought over by ship because she refused to let go of anything she owned—all, all of these took me back to a world so bygone and lost when confronted with these up-and-coming, latter-day, firmly grounded Americans who were sitting with me in this same classroom, who thought American, lived American, sang American, and whose life course seemed so clearly traced for them, while mine was as uncharted and scrambled as misbegotten scrawls allegedly meant to lead explorers to the source of the Nile. I couldn't tell where I'd be in September, let alone understand whether my eyes were trained on a totally uncertain future or drawn all the way back to a world my parents and grandparents recalled but that I'd barely known. I'd grown alien to both worlds, alien to everyone in Paris, alien to those in my classroom, alien to myself, while the music yammered things I couldn't deny but couldn't probe. I thought of Aunt Elsa at that New Year's gathering in Paris. She'd had more champagne than was good for her and kept rambling on about the day that would surely come when everyone in the family would rummage through her things, which is what happens to Madame Hortense in the film of Zorba—this was how she called it, *the film of Zorba*—as she lies dying while everyone is waiting for her to expire before grabbing anything they can lay their hands on—and if there was one thing she cared for, Aunt Elsa said, it was her things, because something of who she was after being hurled about the globe was tied to her things, because "you don't have a self unless you have your things—yes, I know, your stupid, ugly, insipid things," she repeated, quite a while after my father had yelled at her for being morbidly retentive when it came to her meaningless things. "Things take us back to ourselves, regardless of how life turns. Things hold us inviolate and undamaged. We are nobody without things."

I thought of people who become hoarders to stop the world from changing once it has spun around them too many times. A small, tawdry thing can become a refuge and a wellspring of trust.

Maybe the music was a roundabout call from my Greek past, from the Greeks who spoke to me in Greek and had once made me think I was no less Greek than they were, but whose tongue I was fast forgetting, the way within a few months in Rome I had started to forget Arabic too. As I listened to the music in class, I recalled the Greek grocer who didn't want to go back to a homeland in Greece he'd never seen nor cared to see. "But then is Egypt my home, madame?" he had asked my mother. He shook his head to make her see that the answer could only be no.

— 10 —

Improvising

My mother did not want to travel to Paris late that spring. But my brother and I could go if we wanted to, she said. Flying was out of the question, so we would have to travel by train. My brother, however, changed his mind, saying he wanted to spend time with his friends from school, with whom he'd bonded during basketball practice. After practice on Fridays, he would join them to see English-language films at the American embassy for next to no money. Two other movie theaters, the Fiammetta and the Archimede, also showed films in English, but these were too expensive, and my brother would frequently say he had spent his allowance for the week (we had no allowance).

The weather that spring couldn't have been more temperate, though we knew that soon enough it would bring in a torrid summer. Feeling much better, one Sunday my mother even decided to go to the beach with Aunt Flora. The two were to meet at the *jus de fruits* before heading out to Anzio by train. She had asked me to join her, but I was studying for a chemistry exam the coming Monday for which we were to identify three chemical compounds, the sort of sleuthing I enjoyed. I liked identifying esters by their smell. At the last minute, my brother decided to join the two of them at the beach.

No sooner had my mother and brother taken the bus to Termini that morning than I decided to act on an impulse to call Sabina. I hadn't been speaking to her, but this was a unique moment and I felt no compelling reason not to call. To my surprise, she was extremely pleasant on the phone, repeating that she was happy to hear from me, and when I said I would love to see her again, it was she who suggested we meet in the garden of Villa Lazzaroni. I thought she meant sometime soon, but it became clear she meant right then and there, which surprised and enthralled me. She was just going to put on a pair of shoes and go downstairs. When I saw her coming toward me in the park, I couldn't believe I'd forgotten how beautiful she was. She saw me sitting on a bench and apologized for being late. I told her she wasn't late at all; I had arrived too soon. She sat next to me and within minutes I had put an arm around her shoulder, pressed her to me, and we were kissing passionately, as if we were longtime lovers eager to continue what had been interrupted brusquely the evening before. It wasn't ten o'clock in the morning, yet I was more aroused by her now than I'd been at the movies weeks earlier.

A thought had already crossed my mind but I refused to heed it for fear of raising my hopes and jinxing everything. But it was she who was holding my head, as if I were the dearest thing in her life, she who rubbed it very softly and wasn't going to stop. "Let's leave," I eventually said. "And why not," she responded. Those two words, *perché no*, gave me the boldness I needed, and still cupping both her cheeks, which were so smooth that I couldn't stop wanting to cup them in my palms and kiss her on the mouth, I suggested we go to my home, seeing as my mother and brother had gone to Anzio. "You want me to come to your home?"

I nodded, too scared to ruin the spell by uttering a single word or by dwelling in any way on what I'd just asked. I remembered Uncle Claude's advice about not breaking the silence after posing a question.

"*Ma io non posso,*" but I can't, she replied finally, meaning something like *Surely you'll understand.*

I wasn't the type to argue or attempt to persuade her with the casuistry used by most young men claiming to be champion seducers. My father had taught me that it is women who decide, almost never men, just as it is women who give the green light when men don't always have the courage to ask except when they've intuited a yes.

I did remind her that we'd already done quite a bit at the Trianon, or had she forgotten?

"How could I forget?" she replied, wearing the same lambent look in her eyes that I'd caught when we separated outside the movie theater and I was persuaded that what had happened in the next-to-last row that afternoon was incidental, mechanical, and lacked the slightest hint of feeling. Now *How could I forget?* sounded warm, gentle, and confiding, verging on a long-drawn melancholic caress, as if she implied a degree of intimacy and understanding that I had failed to notice.

I said nothing, sensing that silence might work in my favor.

I can't, she repeated. "*Non posso.*" And, seeing that I still wasn't saying another word, "*Vorrei, ma lo sai che non posso,*" I'd like to, but you know I can't.

A few years later when I heard Zerlina in *Don Giovanni* sing almost the same words, *vorrei e non vorrei,* I understood that maybe Sabina was not giving me a definitive no, and might eventually consent, but not that morning, or not that soon. I, however, lacked the flair and the pluck or the persistence of Don Giovanni and decided not to ask again. Maybe asking was itself wrong.

We bought two ice cream cones instead. "*Almeno questo,*" at least this, she said, referring to the ice cream and giving it the lowly rank it deserved in light of the pleasure we were forfeiting. I liked this about her. Was she perhaps changing her mind and asking me to ask again by letting me see that her *non posso* was as difficult for her as it was for me? I should have asked again but I couldn't bring myself to.

The ice cream was a bit of a pretext. Maybe it was our way of extending an improvised date that had lost its purpose. I didn't know whether the ice cream was her way of claiming she wasn't running away from me, or mine of proving I'd never meant to draw her to an empty apartment. What would we do after the ice cream? I was struggling to come up with something when her sudden words rescued me from giving the matter more thought. "*Mi accompagni a casa?*" Walk me home?

"*Ma certo,*" of course, I said, as if it were the most natural thing in the world.

But then she asked, "*Ti scoccia?*" Are you upset?

For a moment that question spoke our mutual certainty that what sat on both our minds had brought us closer than we'd ever been before.

I shook my head and smiled to prove I wasn't upset at all. The truth is, I wasn't upset. I just knew enough to pretend I was slightly miffed and was, to all appearances, failing to conceal it.

I walked her to her building, and we kissed again, several times, perhaps more emotionally now than we'd done in the park. "I'm not upset," I repeated.

I had planned to ask her about her boyfriend, had planned to tell her that I was going to visit my father in Paris but would be back soon enough. But in trying to come up with a way to delay our goodbyes, I forgot to mention either. What I didn't tell her was that while kissing her goodbye, I had already decided to look up Paola to see if she was home.

Indeed, on leaving Sabina, I rushed to Paola's building, clambered up to her floor, and heard nothing behind her door, even though for some reason I'd expected the light patter of her sewing machine. I rang her bell, not even rehearsing what I'd say. I'd come up with something as soon as she opened the door. She always laughed when I said something remotely funny when we occasionally crossed paths in the courtyard. "*Ti disturbo?*" Once again, I had forgotten to use the formal address to ask if I was bothering her. She must have barely had time to put on her bathrobe. Barefoot and holding the door half open, she stared at me in the doorway as though she'd already guessed why I'd come. She shook her head without uttering a word, but she did it so mildly, as if to mean something between *You've got some nerve* and a forbearing *Just look at you*. She stared me down. "*Dai, entra,*" just come in, she said, with listless reproof and indifferent restraint. But the moment she closed the door behind me, she let her bathrobe drop to the floor to reveal her nightgown and her bare breasts. "*Baciami,*" kiss me, she said, as if she were still sleeping and had found me lying next to her in bed, asleep and naked. I hadn't expected this at all but threw myself into her arms, as famished as she was. But then, reading my mind and sensing I was trying to find a way to ask the question I'd asked the previous time, "*Sono tutta sola,*" I'm all alone, she said. Her sister had gone to Rocca di Papa to see their mother. I asked for a glass of water. I followed her into the kitchen, she turned on the tap and let the water run to cool, then handed me a glass and stared as I gulped it down. Her apartment, when I looked around the kitchen, was still dark, though it was beaming sunlight outside. We smiled at each other, then, without hesitating, she began trying to undress me, and not being able to unbuckle my belt, she finally said, "*Spogliati,*" take your clothes off. We ended up making love not in her bedroom but in the kitchen. Not even half an hour later, we made love again, this time in her bedroom. I went slowly, very slowly. She was beside herself, she didn't want me to stop, and I wasn't going to stop, and quietly, from bestial lovemaking at first hers became a warm and devoted, tender form of intense cuddling, filled with caresses that told me that despite our rhythm we could still say things to each other, that there was nothing wrong even in stopping for a very short moment, that she could stare—and she taught me to stare—*proprio così*, just like this, she said—something still feral but also maternal as she held me in the palm of her hand. It took me a while to realize that I didn't know the first thing about making love to a woman.

She said she was so happy I had knocked at her door. "*Quasi quasi non ti lasciavo entrare,*" I was almost not going to let you in. I replied that I was on the point of running away on seeing that expression on her face. What expression? I mimicked it for her. We laughed.

Her apartment was like ours, except the exact opposite in layout. I liked when she finally pushed open the shutters and let the sun into her bedroom. My room was never bathed in so much light. This was perhaps the best Sunday in my life.

~

When my mother and brother returned that evening, both were red from the sun and looked much healthier. I had prepared something for supper so she wouldn't have to cook. At their home in Anzio, the Anconas had served too much wine, she said. Was she not feeling well? No, she felt fine. She'd have a bite to eat and go to bed.

I had prepared a ragù made with ground meat I'd found in the refrigerator, added a few tomatoes, onions, and had let it simmer very slowly. The pasta took just long enough for my mother to shower and come to the table in the kitchen wearing her bathrobe. I had also prepared the salad. My brother said he'd take a shower later.

Had I studied? she asked.

Yes, I replied, and I wasn't lying.

My mother told me that she had purchased me a round-trip second-class ticket for the train to Paris. Flora had explained at the ticket booth that I needed a seat facing the direction in which the train traveled because, like her, I suffered from seasickness the moment a train, a boat, or a car started to sway and wobble. The person at the ticket booth said there was nothing he could do.

Two days later I ran into Paola just outside our building. "*Quando vieni a trovarmi?*" When will you come?

"*Fra poco,*" very soon. Then I asked: "*Lezione di pianoforte?*"

"*Lezione di pianoforte,*" she replied, which was her way of saying don't take too long, we don't have much time. It became our code.

I returned bottles that Wednesday. Gianlorenzo and I chatted briefly. And then, as I watched him lean a ladder against the wall and attempt to reach all the way up to the ceiling to replace a bulb above the olive oil counter, something hit me in my stomach. Not the patch of skin along his bared waist, nor his outstretched back that betrayed every sinew under his shirt, not even his hand. What hit me came as a question: what if he were me, and I were Paola, staring into his eyes and holding him by the face as she had done when she'd open and then shut her eyes because I wasn't stopping and wasn't going to stop and she kept begging me not to? I put the thought away, but in my bedroom that night, thinking of the layout of her bedroom just a few walls away in the building right next to ours, the vision returned and wouldn't let go.

~

I had brought Kafka's *The Castle*. I found the seat I liked best in the car, put my small suitcase on the overhead rack, and over it a heavy tweed jacket that had once belonged to my father and a scarf that my mother had knitted months earlier, in case the compartment got cold at night. She had also bought me a pocket flask of brandy for the same reason. I still wouldn't allow myself to believe that I was actually headed back to Paris after four long months.

The trip itself was quite an ugly affair and lasted almost eighteen hours. The train originated in Naples and was filled with rowdy furloughed soldiers, mothers visiting their children in the north with lots of boxes tied with string, and middle-aged secretaries who were unfailingly preyed upon by fast-talking, philandering soldiers eager to obtain their addresses and telephone numbers.

On that train ride, however, there was one magic moment. It came about two hours, perhaps a tad more, into the trip, when the train began to elbow the Tuscan and Ligurian coast, racing past large mansions and castles and unending stretches of cypress trees, all of them overlooking what seemed to be the most placid coast in the world. Every other moment, these splendid vistas would be interrupted by a tunnel, or an old wall, or by houses built too close to the tracks, stirring my desire to savor these villas and views long enough to imagine I inhabited them. This is how I learned to worship the Tyrrhenian and Ligurian Seas: in abrupt slices that whipped by you, as if the whole scene were unreal—the way the trip back to Paris had to remain slightly unreal for me to trust it would happen.

I was never able to stare long enough at the names of the stations overlooking the coast, and the sea always came unannounced. Yet this twenty-minute view, interrupted and obstructed as it was, remained one of the most beautiful and most memorable sights I'd seen. What made it so spellbinding might have been leaving Italy, or the joy of going to Paris, or perhaps it was simply the once-familiar, ordinary pleasure—now a luxury—of prolonged vistas, however imperfect, of the sea. It was like meeting a cousin years after a family quarrel: an odd mix of strained familiarity, sudden intimacy, and wistful reminders that, despite embraces, things would never be the same again.

I'd seen the beach in Italy before. But this was different. This had timelessness and, regardless of its fragmentary nature, even plenitude. This was the beach year-round, beach at hand's reach, beach as a way of life, beach as I'd always wanted it. Passing discrete views of the sea was like passing Alexandria the way my mother had done in her dream, waving hello to a house that belongs to others now but still asks after us in the distant hope of reverting to us someday, albeit generations later. It made me remember beach life more keenly, made me long for it and know exactly what I could almost put my mouth to but couldn't because I was on a train, because there'd always be an impediment, because that impediment was always going to be lodged not just in the things around me but in me as well now.

Never in my life had I been served such a huge dish and been left so unsated. I'd felt the same way with *Zorba*'s music in class, with Sabina, even with Paola, as if they were all preambles to something that I did not know how to hold and preferred to think withheld and unfinished, as if the means to hold on to them were not available to me, and might never be. Each promised much joy, yet something in me held them at bay to shield me from disappointment, fatigue, or the near certainty that I might be unworthy of them and should therefore shun them first before being shunned myself.

They always stirred a medley of apprehension and dismay because I desired too much, or not enough, or, as I was starting to believe, never in the right way.

Before entering the countryside away from the coast, I picked up *The Castle*. I had read *The Trial* months before and was determined to finish *The Castle*, if only to say I'd read Kafka.

Two more soldiers walked in and sat in our compartment. They were talking very loudly. It interfered with my reading, or at least I couldn't tell whether it was their loudness or my trying to find the right words to complain that made it difficult to read. I decided to lean a bit back, leave my book open on my lap, and shut my eyes. I thought that this might encourage them to lower their voices, but it didn't. At some point, possibly after I had unintentionally dozed off, their laughter did wake me up. I opened my eyes and asked if they could please talk more softly, I was trying to sleep, I said. "It's not nap time," one of them said. To which the other added, "And how should we speak, *then*?" An elderly man, sitting in the middle seat in front of me, replied, "Speak outside, *then*," mimicking the word *then* to let his own version of it show that theirs was totally inappropriate. One of the two looked at him askance and told his buddy that they'd better step outside because men who might one day have to give up their lives were troubling those doddering away in their sleepy corner. "My best friend in my regiment," retorted the old man, "gave up his life in Abyssinia so you might grow up into two wretched *cafoni*." They stood at the door and were mulling an answer that never came. "And shut the door behind you, there's a draft," added the old man. I liked how he'd spoken, and to show my appreciation without wanting to make too much of his exchange with them, I gave a barely visible half-nod in his direction. He did not respond, which was just as well. He was as loud with them as they'd been with each other.

At some point in the journey, a food server opened our door and asked if we wanted to order anything. Everyone ordered juices and coffees. I ordered a mini panettone—half of which would hold my hunger down until evening, after which I'd eat the other half and hope my father would take me to breakfast when I arrived in Paris.

Ten minutes later the man appeared with coffees, juices, glasses that he filled from one extra-large bottle of mineral water for everyone, and a Motta mini panettone for me. I paid him and couldn't wait to have my first bite of what I knew was a wonderful sweet cake. I picked up *The Castle* again and was immersed in my reading. We were no longer facing the sea now and were racing north.

It might have been the wobbling train, or the mini panettone, or the smell in the compartment, but it was most likely *The Castle* that caused sweat to gather on my forehead and nape and to make me feel slightly sick. I was persuaded it would pass, but within a short while something began to tell me that it wouldn't and that, for safety's sake, perhaps it was time to seek out the bathroom. I excused myself, left the book open upside down on my seat to make sure no one thought it was empty, and headed to the bathroom. Once inside, I locked the door and didn't have time to lean over the bowl because the smell of the room and the sight of its deplorable condition turned my stomach. I was already heaving when I suddenly remembered that a finger in my throat was all I needed. I was dizzy and disoriented and kept making sure to aim into the bowl but what finally crossed my mind were four words: *There goes the panettone.* And I kept repeating it, as if in an incantation, *There goes the panettone, there it goes, there it goes.* I never forgot that it could have been the panettone, but I preferred to believe it was Kafka's fault.

I opened the small bag I had attached to my suitcase, removed a toothbrush, and, hoping no one in our compartment would suspect what had happened to me, went back to the WC and brushed my teeth. When I returned, I cracked a joke about long train rides. The old gentleman said he was getting off at Turin late that night, if all went well. I asked what could possibly go wrong. "Who knows, but something always goes wrong," said the gentleman. "Always does," echoed my neighbor who was clearly eager to engage in talk. So I opened my book and continued reading. But I could read no further, because something about the book was upsetting me, not my stomach this time. The book was quietly revolting. I would eventually finish it the following year in totally different circumstances. I put it aside and began reading a short novel by Stendhal. I'd always loved his sharp, analytic, frequently acerbic pen. And so I drifted into a story set in the 1830s.

Eventually, I sat the book on my lap and dozed off.

When I awoke, it was already night, and the passengers in my compartment had been replaced by a totally different cast. They had seen me sleeping and were kind enough not to make much noise, which I am sure suited them as well. The old man whose baggage I was hoping to help lift from the overhead bin had left with his suitcase. When I looked at my watch, it was already past one in the morning. There was a bit of commotion, which was probably what had awakened me. But I must have fallen asleep again, because by the time I was awakened, we were at the border. I heard what I thought were the first wisps of French. I was overjoyed and then, just as suddenly, disheartened. With everyone sleeping with their shoes off—I might as well have been in a barn.

The passport controller walked into our compartment. We all showed him our documents, he stared at me once or twice, "*Vous avez grandi, jeune homme,*" you've grown older, young man, he said, meaning I had changed since the picture on my passport was taken when I was twelve.

I smiled while shrugging my shoulders to mean *Yes, you are right*. There was no need to utter a sassy remark and get myself hauled off the train. He gave me my passport back and urged me to get a new one. I wasn't a kid any longer, he added. *Ask Paola*, I wanted to retort. But then she would have said I was still a kid. Then why did she invite me upstairs the moment her sister was gone for her piano lesson? But her chocolates declared me still a kid.

A half hour later, the train started to screech, then jostled in place, released a loud bellow of steam that rose up to my window, and started to leave the station. We were in France. I tried to sleep again, to put off the certainty that I had already crossed the border, knowing that there was a side of me that still enjoyed anticipating France. I regretted not being awake to register the precise moment when our train had actually left Italy and crossed into France.

I tried to think of my mother, hoping that thinking of her might draw me back to Via Clelia, where, whether I liked it or not, I belonged now. I wondered if she was asleep, and if she was thinking of me, seeing, as I believed, that mothers are supposed to be thinking of their sons all the time. I thought of why she had decided not to come to Paris. She could have insisted. I wondered what my father had written to her, or she to him. I wasn't always curious to read what they told each other. His letters frequently upset her, though I am sure hers upset or, rather, exasperated him. As a child I would hear them argue at night, then, when I was slightly older, I would watch them argue. Once, he threw something at her; she threw it right back at him. "I'm strong too," she had shouted. Then I'd try to placate them. But to no avail. She always cried. I was asked to comfort her, and this took a long time. Now I could see that it was best for them to stay away from each other. I was happy that my brother had stayed back with her. Maybe when they went to the movies he would interpret for her.

At some point I dozed off again. But not for long. When I awoke, everything was still dark outside, but I could tell that it was almost dawn, though there wasn't a sign of sunlight yet. Still, the view was stunning. Everyone in my compartment was asleep, so I decided to step outside, sliding the door open very cautiously so as not to wake the others, all of whom sat extended in their seats. Outside, I slid the door shut very slowly and leaned my head against the window, wiping away the condensation from my breath on the glass. The train was speeding ever so quietly now, not a rattle, nor a banging of distant doors, no one talking, all of it as though a camera were filming the scene and had turned off the sound while we glided toward Paris. I was alone in the deserted corridor and loving it. All I saw as we sped through the countryside was an endless series of trees studding the plains with a thick, whey-colored fog rising between each one, its pale shade blanketing the wispy, sleepy fields of Chambéry, whose name I saw flitting by three times, pleading with me in its own humble way to remember it and not forget on my way back, *I'll be waiting, remember me*, it said. I promised to look out for this spot of earth, hoping it wouldn't be daylight when I headed back to Rome.

I opened the door again, mindful not to stumble on people's outstretched legs, and eventually found my spot in the corner. Oh, the smell of feet, *vos pieds, messieurs, vos pieds*, even Christ would have slapped a bar of soap on them when washing their feet on Maundy Thursday. There was a horse between the fog and the trees, or was it the fog and the trees between the horse and the barn, or had I thought of Joyce crossing the Alps with Hannibal? Is it here? asks one, "*Non, pas encore*," says the other as they watch good old Wordsworth crossing the Simplon for the nth time and missing the spot where France leads into Italy. Ah, the fog peeking between interminable rows of trees lining the train tracks and behind them the open country fields. I was falling asleep, and what amazed me all the more was knowing that I was actually falling asleep.

～

My father was waiting on the platform wearing new gumshoes. So, we were rich again? Hardly, he snickered, hardly. How was the trip? he asked. Long, very long, I said. I also couldn't resist telling him I'd vomited. What had I eaten on the train? he asked. I told him. But maybe it was Kafka, I added. He looked at me, thinking I meant someone called Kafka, but then realizing I meant the writer, he said, "What made you read such a dreadful writer, surely there are better writers you haven't read yet?" Everyone was reading him, and everyone loved him. "Rubbish," he said. Then he asked if I was starving. Yes. Then a nice *café crème* and a *tartine beurrée* with *confiture*. I was ecstatic. We found a tiny place outside the Gare de Lyon. "I love being here," I said. "Who wouldn't?" he replied.

He told me that he had bought three tickets for the theater that evening, a play by Georges Feydeau. Suddenly I felt anxious. The last person I wanted to meet was his new girlfriend; I'd met several in Egypt, and the experience had never been pleasant. It would force me to side against my mother, and I didn't have the heart for that. Who was the third ticket for? "Aunt Elsa," he replied. "She won't dare go to the theater by herself, and frankly I never take her, because I never go myself, but she loves it."

While we were waiting for our breakfast, I didn't know how to ask him, but eventually I did ask if he had to be at work today.

"No, today I'm with you."

He was happy to see me. I had never seen him this jovial and this young and so thoroughly in his element. When breakfast came and the waiter served the two of us our *tartines* with a jar of jam, everything justified the endless hours by train. This was my city. I wasn't French and I still spoke with a Levantine accent, but I could easily make this my home. Did I want to live here? he asked. Absolutely, I replied.

After breakfast, he hailed a cab and we went to his new home on rue Greuze. The move had been easy. Elsa was looking forward to seeing me and promised to prepare a wonderful lunch.

At home, he said I could take a shower if I wanted to get rid of the odor of the train. Since leaving Egypt, he'd taken many trains in Europe, and when people stretched out and removed their shoes to catch a few hours of sleep, the smell was suffocating. We laughed. I told him about Chambéry, one of the most beautiful spots I'd seen. It was dreamlike. And there were moments I wasn't entirely sure I hadn't dreamed it up, because the fog and the trees and the total silence hovering over the landscape just before sunup had cast a magical spell.

That evening we went to see the play, and we all loved it. Afterward, he said he had heard of a good Greek restaurant in the Latin Quarter. When we arrived, we had to climb up a rather steep staircase, and Aunt Elsa, to prove she wasn't aging, was the first to walk up the high steps at a vigorous pace. My father just behind her, to catch her if she stumbled backward, gave me a look meaning, *Just look at her, she is showing off.* A nod from me got him whispering, "If only I could be in as good a shape at her age."

Our young and stunning waitress was very pleased to speak in Greek, said she came from Rhodes and had learned to speak a variety of languages as a child, most notably French and some Turkish. On hearing that she could speak Turkish, both my father and Aunt Elsa moved from Greek to fluent Turkish. She was so pleased to shuttle between both tongues that she told us she also spoke Spanish. Then my father took a wild guess. "Must be Jewish, then?" "How did you know?" "Because we come from the same stock." At which all of us laughed. She offered us a bottle of retsina on the house. I had never liked retsina before, but on that night, I adored it. Then came the skewered meats, the rice, the aubergines and other fried vegetables, with their succulent sauces and so many *friandises*, as the waitress called them, that by dessert and after finishing the whole bottle of wine, we were all three very happy. The waitress handed my father the check, but she did so with the impish grace of someone who pretends to have almost forgotten.

"The waitress," he said, "was giving me the eye. Clearly, it's her job."

But there was no doubt that he was trying to catch hers. I could see that he was putting on the charm, which I found so awkwardly obvious that I was tempted to remind him that she had given me the eye as well, and had done something of the kind with Aunt Elsa too, who felt particularly rejuvenated by all the attention she was receiving. It would never have occurred to my father that I was as attracted to her as he was, but I was tactful enough not to deflate his bubble. Yes, she'd given him the eye, I said when we walked down the stairs, he in front of Elsa to catch her if she tripped and fell forward. Being the last one, I turned around to give the waitress one last look. She beamed a smile at me. Obviously, it was her job. But even so, such a pleasure.

Afterward, we took a walk along the Left Bank of the Seine, and as we loitered about and observed the magical cityscape by night with all its sites and monuments aglow, I remembered my father driving along the Corniche on the night we'd been to see *Les Parapluies de Cherbourg*. That night, as we'd looked out on the sea and felt so transient and uprooted and yet so tied to Alexandria that it was impossible to imagine being anywhere else, I had dreamed of Paris, and now here I was, not longing to be elsewhere but rooted, here and now. I thought back on the waitress. She had set something afire in me too. Not that I harbored any hopes, because what I felt when she smiled was something like a promise made on the fly and hardly meant to be kept. If it wasn't a promise, it fluttered like a possibility, vague and undefined, to last just a brief while like a votive taper that has a short lifespan but stays aglow long after you've lit it and left the church. I cradled the possibility, but that's all it was, a possibility, and I liked it that way.

We could have walked home and at some point crossed one of the many bridges to the Right Bank but we feared that Aunt Elsa would not be able to endure so long a walk, so we decided to take the first bridge and with good luck hail a taxi. Taxis were out of our budget, except on unusual occasions, and this one merited a taxi.

The next morning, my father woke me up and said he was heading to work. I could meet him for lunch if I wanted to. I told him I had no money, and he gave me a couple of bills. I said I wanted to go with him and see how it felt to go to work, seeing I might have to find a job soon. He gave a little laugh, because, he explained, it had never really dawned on him that I was indeed already old enough to work.

He said I should hurry if I wanted to leave with him. He liked to have a warm *café crème* in the morning, along with a croissant. I dressed in two seconds and was grateful that I'd had the foresight to untie my shoelaces the night before, otherwise I'd have spent forever untying the triple or quadruple knots that kept them from coming undone. "So, these still fit you?" he asked, recognizing his shoes. "They still fit," I replied, with an inflection that almost meant I had no choice in the matter.

What surprised me as we walked out of our building was the total darkness that enveloped the street and neighborhood. It was still night in Paris. He saw my baffled look and asked if I was unused to seeing how dark it still was at seven thirty in the morning. I told him that my brother and I used to leave the apartment in Rome at six thirty, but that by then the sun had already risen. But this wasn't the reason encountering darkness at that hour of the morning had disturbed me. What I saw for the first time was my father going to work at an ungodly hour, as if he were a night porter, and what was missing to complete the image was a uniform and a three-tiered metal lunchbox. What displeased me even more when we reached the métro station was watching him buy me a ticket but presenting his monthly pass to the controller. A monthly métro pass! My father was an employee.

He'd once told me that what had made him successful when he founded his factory was that he hated having to answer to a boss. He'd persuaded a few of his boss's clients to follow him to his new business, asked a friendly family to invest in his plan to build a factory, and become a wealthy man. Now, in Paris, he was back to who he had been thirty years earlier. His oldest nightmare had returned, this time with a vengeance.

We got off at the Havre-Caumartin métro stop and headed to his café, where we each ordered a croissant and a *café crème*. Then I walked him to his building. He asked if I wanted to come upstairs to see his office, but I was reluctant to meet the owner, since I still remembered him as someone we'd known in Alexandria whom my father scorned as a loutish illiterate who couldn't tell a shoelace from a toothpick. "Besides," he added, "he has larceny seeping out of his tiny, cunning, semi-shut eyes. He's a man without honor." "Why?" I asked. "Why? Because everyone knows his wife cheats on him and either he's too stupid to see it or, worse, he doesn't let it bother him. Any other man in his position . . ." He let the subject trail. I'd once been a friend of his boss's son, but I had never liked the parents. My father said I should come back to the building at one o'clock to meet him for lunch. To-night, we were going to see another play, this one by Goldoni, which had been written up very nicely, he said. Now, he added, I was free to *vadrouiller* the streets of Paris. "At your age to wander about freely through Paris, what luck."

It was barely past eight in the morning and I had five hours to myself, and not one obligation. The very prospect of walking, maybe of finding another café a while later, buying a book, visiting a museum, or doing whatever I pleased, thrilled me. I knew that my father was going to raise the subject of my studies during our lunch. He'd been avoiding it the day before, but at some point it would have to be broached, and the prospect worried me. Either I'd have to find a French lycée to accept me, or I'd have to stay in Rome and find work or enter a *liceo classico* before attending university in Italy. I could tell he had no wish to leave Paris—indeed, in the few months he'd been living there he'd settled in very comfortably, and it was up to us to decide whether to move to Paris with him or stay in Rome. *Better they stay in Rome* would have been his thinking, though he'd never say it to me. But living with my mother in Paris would be absolute hell for him and would mean forfeiting his life as a single man in a city where he'd adapted far better than he'd expected. But he added that you find yourself reliving what you thought you'd outlived, and in a matter of hours become the hireling you'd sworn never to be again. Things come back; life repeats itself. Fate isn't very inventive.

What he didn't tell me was that, after becoming Italian citizens in Egypt, we were still considered guests in France and had no permanent status. Every few months, we'd be asked to return to Italy to renew our status as visitors in France.

I mulled some of this as I started walking away from his office, determined to go to the Latin Quarter, where I wished to revisit Shakespeare & Company and hoped to meet the owner of the shop before crowds of English-speaking tourists marched in wanting to talk to him about the one famous author who had published his novel with Shakespeare & Company. The owner had asked me to send him something to print in the magazine he'd started; and out of courtesy, more than interest, I'd purchased a copy of his slim magazine.

That day I didn't go to rue Saint-Denis. After Paola, the urge to seek out the girl on rue Saint-Denis had faded and I didn't want to spend the money. At lunch, my father even asked if I had walked by, *seulement pour voir*, just to see, he added with his usual sense of humor. I told him I didn't want to spend the money. So what did I do, buy books?—again, with irony. I nodded yes. Which is how, past several detours, the long but unavoidable discussion of my future was finally reached, though diffidently, because as I soon saw, neither he nor I had any notion of what my future should look like. What did I want to do? he asked. The answer was so obvious that I was stunned he'd even asked. Make a lot of money, and fast. He didn't try to find out why, but he should have, because I would have told him the truth: to help him live comfortably. But he soon dissuaded me regarding the money scheme. "If you're like me, you're not the type to find much happiness in that. It brings some security, which is always welcome, and it has its pleasures, but before you know it, you'll find yourself literally roped in to a life you can't undo and might grow to resent.

"If you're like me, you'll find consummate joy in what you do if what you do comes from your gut. Nothing is worse than finding yourself trapped in an office where your heart is not welcome and where, before leaving for work, you'll find it safer to leave your heart at home, cautiously tucked in a drawer with your socks and underwear. What a shame to store the very best in you next to what goes on your feet and your pipi. They call this servitude. Vocation is something else. I found mine first in the great authors but then, almost by accident, in my factory. That was my masterpiece, and I rebuilt and reinvented every stone in it, every piece of equipment, every dye. Nobody will ever reproduce my dyes. They might as well spill them on the sidewalk, but the years won't wash away the stain."

I was staring at him. How I loved it when he spoke to me so openly.

"You see, some people call it pride in one's work. It isn't pride at all. It's love. But I had two loves, and it was my other love that drove me, not money and certainly not dyeing cloth," he said. "I loved books. Ironically, I've rediscovered my love of books here in Paris. I've read more great books here in four months than in ten years as a business-man in Egypt. But we were supposed to talk about you, not me."

I didn't want him to stop.

"You'll find soon enough what you love, unless you know already but don't want to say, which would be just like you."

When it came to who I was, I lacked the clarity of thought or the self-possession to confide something I couldn't swear was even true. I told him I didn't know what I wanted to do.

"No life has an itinerary," he said, "life is either improvised or provisional, usually both." He thought for a moment. "Just don't be someone else."

We had coffee at the restaurant, and then he said he had to get back.

I left him and headed to my favorite bookstore near the Opéra.

That evening we met at Aunt Elsa's. She had read Goldoni many years before and adored him. I had never read him. "But you've got all the time in the world!" she said, meaning to comfort me. She offered us a thimbleful of whiskey and English cigarettes, the only ones she smoked, she said. Here—she indicated the sofa in the living room that had been my grandmother's bed when she stayed in Paris—she and my grandmother would sit and drink coffee in the afternoon and sometimes smoke a cigarette. This is what Elsa and her husband had done after lunch every day before being forced to leave Paris once it was clear the Germans had their sights set on the capital. Recently, my grandmother and she had liked to sit and watch television in the evening. They had both lived ninety years without television. Now, after barely two months in the same apartment, they were totally ad-dicted to the news. They liked one anchorman; the other they simply couldn't stand. What brand of cigarettes did they smoke? I asked Elsa. "Craven A, of course." Why *of course* would have remained a mystery had I not suspected that for her, Craven A was a distinguished brand.

We had another twenty minutes before leaving for the theater, and my father asked her to pour more whiskey in both our tiny glasses. She did as asked, but couldn't help adding that whiskey didn't grow on trees, *you know*. Then catching herself, "How are we getting there? The way we did last night?" He gave me a look. We knew that this was her way of asking if we were going by taxi and whether my father was going to pay both ways, as he'd done the night before—which, of course, he did each time the three of us went out together. We both knew she was being shrewd and manipulative, and there was no way for us not to be trapped by her question other than by exposing her inveterate avarice, which would have made her unhappy.

The play was a comedy in the fashion of Molière, but with ill-tempered and passionate Italian lovers instead. We adored it.

Afterward, as we lingered outside the door to the theater and heard the usher lock it from inside, we seemed at a loss for what to do next when of course we'd known all along but pretended it hadn't crossed our minds. "What if we went back to the same restaurant?" my father finally threw in, as though suggesting a thing so outlandish that it would have to be laughed at and summarily rejected. We applauded the idea, and went back to the same narrow streets, then up the stairs, he behind her, I behind him, and sat at the same large table where many people were already sitting. We liked talking to strangers, until the waitress with the luminous glance came and spoke Greek to us and eventually threw in a few words in Ladino, just to show she hadn't forgotten. And as before, there was that look in her eyes.

The following few days saw me continually growing nostalgic for Paris while still very much in Paris, which reminded me of Bashō's haiku, a copy of which I discovered among Aunt Elsa's books while she was preparing a simple lunch *à deux*: "Even in Kyoto, I miss Kyoto." This was pure happenstance; yet Bashō had written me as no other writer ever had.

Aunt Elsa cooked a wonderful spaghetti dish with all sorts of things in it. She had asked me to please, please, please not forget to fill four large bottles with water from the Lamartine fountain. In the afternoons, after coffee and the de rigueur English cigarette, I went out and explored the city, even managed to catch a Humphrey Bogart film before hastening to surprise my father outside the building where he worked. He was elated. We took the métro to Trocadéro, where we sat in a café that he said he liked and stared at the expansive Palais de Chaillot and the Eiffel Tower across the river. We each ordered a long hot dog on a bun, *avec moutarde*, and a beer. My father, I discovered, was a sweet, devoted, and generous person, not the ill-tempered, self-centered, arrogant man I'd always seen at home. Without my mother around, he was patient, youthful, and kind. He suggested we see a film at the Cinémathèque that night, which in those years, before it moved to the douzième arrondissement, was located right under the Palais de Chaillot. I admired my father for knowing so many places and so many arcane and intimate aspects of life in Paris. He had adapted to the city far faster than I had to Rome, and it was obvious, if only by watching his alert, ebullient gait when we walked together, that he was trying to make up for lost time. He was familiar with recent songs and plays; and he had even begun using argot.

We went to the Cinémathèque almost every night during my stay in Paris. We saw a host of classic films: *Rashomon*, *This Land Is Mine*, *Hiroshima Mon Amour*, and several Buster Keaton shorts. After the films, we made it a practice to head to one of the several cafés around the square to order a dessert, usually a small tarte tatin. He also ordered a whiskey. Elsa's bottle of Scotch, he said, probably dated back to Uncle Nessim's cache in Egypt, which he'd hidden under his bed when he was alive so his sisters wouldn't catch him drinking or ask to share a few sips.

On our last evening together my father took me to the same Greek restaurant and then we went to see a late-night showing of *The Leopard*. I had always meant to see the film but never caught it when it played at the Diana, near our home. It told the story of how revolutions can alter long-established cultural and social institutions, and how they can radically change the lifestyle of individuals. The old losers are the new winners, and as for the old winners, they're now drained and debilitated, and in most cases plainly obsolete. My father knew this from personal experience. But the film showed me something I had never fully considered before: that those sunny, rambling mansions built everywhere in Italy were stunning, even when dysfunctional and run-down. Suddenly, and because of the film and the world it portrayed, I found myself worshipping their ocher-colored walls bronzed and blemished by too many summers, their damaged balusters, their chipped marble lintels, their dank, time-ravaged clay roofs whose tiles were so often missing and which couldn't be repaired because they were past repairing but might yet hold up for another few years, a few decades maybe—all of it made me long for Italy. I loved the musty smell of these Baroque buildings when visiting the Ancona home, both in the city and in the countryside, loved the British Institute's terra-cotta alcove where I read *Hamlet*, loved biking down Via Giulia on Gianlorenzo's bicycle, loved how the cobblestones shook me in my seat as I pedaled my way through the crowded Via del Governo Vecchio, loved the early sun-bleached afternoon when I finally sat down by the Barcaccia staring all the way up above to the Trinità dei Monti and still couldn't tell, much less admit, that maybe I didn't dislike Rome as much as I thought. The film—and the paradox did not escape me—was not about Rome at all but about far-flung Sicily. But the transposition of one for the other was easy and it thrilled me.

Correction: I didn't dislike Rome, I grew to like it via Paris, via Sicily, via Egypt itself, and, who knows, via Constantinople, and ultimately, via our allegedly ancestral home in Spain—this was my alignment to so many things, to life, to people, to books, to the earth itself. *Alignment* would become my word. It explained why my way of seeing things was fundamentally gnarled and tortured and possibly flawed but nevertheless tied to my personality, to my experience, and to my way of being perpetually unsettled and refractive, of always finding everywhere an instance of somewhere else; in everything, the features of something else.

I loved Rome's *centro storico* because I knew that it, too, was lay-ered with multiple tiers that kept shifting incessantly from one era to another. I liked the old because the past held deeper sway, spoke to me more, because, just like me, it trusted not things but their long shadow, their passage, not what was living but what had once lived and never died. If I grew to identify with Rome, it was with timeless Rome. Timebound Rome was for others.

Early the next evening, after work, my father met me at the Gare de Lyon. To keep me company before the train was set to leave, he stayed in my compartment, which was totally empty. I was nervous that the train might leave with him on board, but he reassured me that we still had some time. He had given me a wonderful ten days, and I kept thanking him for the best vacation I'd ever had. He said it was a far greater pleasure for him than for me, and hoped that one day, one day, I'd do the same for my son. He also said he hoped that whatever disagreements we'd had in the past, particularly in Egypt—he called them *nuages*, clouds—had been cleared and pushed away. I said there'd never been any *nuages*. Yes, there were, he said, but he appreciated that I was trying to overlook them. He, however, never held a grudge in his life. "How about with Aunt Elsa?" I asked, to lighten things and dispel the darkening farewell mood settling between us. "With Aunt Elsa, peace is easy enough. Explosions always happen in a family, then they go away." I believed him. Meanwhile, I was growing apprehensive about the train. I suggested we should both leave the compartment and stand by the door to the car in case the train moved. He didn't seem anxious at all. In the end, the voice of a stationmaster walking the length of the platform and slamming one door after the other finally persuaded my father it was time for him to leave the train. We kissed and hoped to see each other very soon, in Rome perhaps. "In Rome, then," he said.

When he left the train, I caught him staring at my window from the platform. I wanted to lower the window to tell him something, anything, but it was stuck in place. He was, I was sure, telling me the same thing. I wanted to tell him that I had a strange presentiment that I'd never see Paris again and needed to hear him say I was wrong. But he couldn't hear. And as the train began to move, and he followed a bit, I watched Paris drift away. I wanted to cry. The Cinémathèque, the tarte tatin, the waitress with luminous eyes, the Goldoni play, the thimbles half filled with whiskey. I finally sobbed when I thought of Aunt Elsa, whom I had never even loved. "As for us," she had said, "this may well be the last time."

The train was less crowded and the weak light within the compartment that evening helped soften the mood. There were two other people traveling near me, but neither spoke. A while later, feeling a tiny surge of appetite, I was happy that Aunt Elsa had prepared a few snacks for the trip. A big brioche, a bottle of sparkling water, two sandwiches, one with ham and the other with cheese, and, totally unexpected, three new *bollos*, not hard this time as they'd been when we tried to eat them at Christmas.

She had walked up to me and, with both hands, placed the package in my hands as though she were depositing a priceless jewel at an altar, either as a supplicant or a penitent about to offer the best she had in life to expiate sins she feared were past remission. The humbled smile with which she placed the *bollos* in my hands was meek, hasty, almost self-effacing. It seemed to say *This is for you, just for you. At my age, it's all I have to give.*

I thought of her suppers alone again and of my father eating at his café, most likely by himself as well, beer and a hot dog and a slice of the tarte we liked so much, thinking of me and how going to the Cinémathèque that night would probably not soothe him or allow his mind to drift.

Or maybe he was happy that I'd left. Whoever understands the hearts of others?

I began reading one of the books I'd bought at Gibert and made a point of not forgetting to look out the window for the landscape around Chambéry. I knew it would be just like me to torture myself to stay up to catch that moment only then to doze off or be distracted when we finally reached it.

A third person must have entered the compartment while I dozed and he, like the others, was sleeping. But sure enough, hours later, as though it had woken me up in the nick of time, my foggy landscape reappeared, except that this time I did not have to leave the compartment, but could behold it from my seat as I stared out the window, placing both my palms around my face against the glass to screen the reflection of the light in the compartment. *See, here I am*, it said, *I waited for you.*

~

Via Clelia.

Before opening our door, I rang the bell, and the red lights flashed four times and told my mother I was back. I rang without even thinking, as if I'd been sent on a quick errand to buy milk or grated cheese and had hurried back home within minutes of leaving. I liked sliding back into old habits that belonged to the little world we had built together on Via Clelia—good or bad habits, but ours, and that no one, not anything, not even time itself, could alter or undo. As soon as I rang, I heard my brother yelp a greeting immediately followed by my mother shouting my nickname as she always did with that sharp and strident voice which, even today, I would give anything to hear, the voice of the deaf woman who was my mother.

I was glad that Grazia wasn't there to greet me when I entered the building, glad not to run into anyone.

I had told my mother around when I'd be back, had taken the first bus outside Termini and walked as fast as I could from the bus stop to our home. What I had planned to do after having lunch with her was to change clothes and take a bus back to Piazza Venezia to lose myself in the narrow streets of the *centro storico*, hoping to catch a spellbound Rome still slumbering in glorious, midafternoon languor, which was just how I wanted to imagine it after nursing those lovely images inspired by *The Leopard* in Paris.

But now, in Rome, all I wanted was for the rain to start. I wanted a gloomy, overcast afternoon to remind me of Paris and allow me to believe I was still on rue Greuze and would at any moment now borrow an umbrella to head out to see another film. I had three hours before my father left work. Then the Cinémathèque, then a café, then the walk back on Avenue Georges Mandel, before turning onto rue Greuze. I lay in my bedroom and thought of one thing only: Paola, who lived in the building next to ours. What was she doing? Had she thought of me? Then I thought of Gianlorenzo. Had he passed into oblivion?

Late one night in Paris, after we'd been to the Cinémathèque and were heading back home at a leisurely pace, trying perhaps not to put an end to our walk, my father brought up his life before starting a family. He'd had friends, lovers, but nothing had really gelled for him, as people dropped in and out of his life. On Sunday afternoons in Paris, sometimes before evening set in, he could make out the soft, sinister footsteps of his old phantoms, as he called them, tiptoeing back into his life, spreading their habitual gloom and uncertainty just when he thought that the last few hours of Sunday were going to usher in serene moments before sleep and the start of a new weekday. He hated solitude. He didn't want it again, and he knew it was waiting for him the moment I'd leave Paris. Later, he'd swat away his phantoms with a hasty meal and the Cinémathèque, and who knows, maybe someone. There was always someone if you knew how to want someone badly enough. Phantoms, though, always came back, he said. That was the one constant in his life.

"Sometimes phantoms can be shooed away," I said.

"No, they come back. We call phantoms parts of ourselves we wish weren't there. All we can do is fill their silence with noise so as to drown them out. We give our life an itinerary—there's noise, for you—but there are no itineraries in life. The only way to grasp your itinerary is on your deathbed. And then it's too late. We plan so little. The rest we improvise."

He loved the spontaneous, the uncharted, the unrehearsed—the *improvised*, as he called it when he'd propose doing something whimsical that seemed entirely justified if only because it had sprung unannounced and bore no trace of rigor or slavish adherence to ceremony or planned outcomes. *Improvised*, like going for a second swim at our old beach house when everyone else had already put on their sandals and was getting ready to head home to shower.

Improvised, like taking me to the movies to see *Phaedra*—or was it *Electra*?—on a school night, or inviting people over at the last minute because winter Sundays were terrible without good friends and good desserts. *À l'improviste*, like his wine-tasting parties, which happened almost at the last minute each year and drove my mother to the brink. Like buying himself a necktie while trying to buy her a birthday present, or like buying her a present when he spotted something she'd like, but never on her birthday. Like saying yes to women he'd meet just about anywhere simply because they happened to have sidled up to him in ways he couldn't resist and wasn't going to. *Improvised*, because on those days when love and fortune smiled on him, the one thing he was sure to find—because he knew how to look for it and hold on to it long enough to make sure it wouldn't give him the slip—was not just pleasure, but the romance of pleasure. My math tutor whom he'd drive home in the evening after our lessons, the model who found reasons to call whenever he was home for dinner, the woman behind the counter, the woman sitting on a park bench, the woman enrolled in a Russian evening course for adults that he was taking because he'd always wanted to learn Russian, and if not now, when? The people he met just about anywhere. *Improvised*, because he never believed we decide anything in life—chance does, or others do, or things get thrown your way, and all you have to do is seize what life invariably takes back and then either blames you for dithering or, worse yet, fills you with regret—regret for things lost, regret for what you shouldn't have done and can't undo, regret for the person you almost were but never did become and kept hoping to grow into if only you'd find the cipher, the courage, the key.

The ledger of his life was written in perishable ink.

— 11 —

Elsewhere

On my return from France, my brother told me that he had set aside envelopes that had come for me from America. Hunter College, Queens College, City College. I knew from word of mouth at school that when a very light envelope arrives in answer to a college application, it can only signal rejection. And indeed, all three colleges had rejected me. So much for thinking American, I told myself, remembering the evening with Aunt Flora when the two girls had paid me a short visit in my bedroom. A week or so later, Brooklyn College and Baruch College rejected me. Then Bronx Community College rejected me. By then it became totally clear to me that I would never fit in America and resigned myself to life in Italy or, with any luck, France. I'd do what Toto had done, not attend university and work, say, in a bank.

If I'd nursed the fantasy of studying in the United States, I would have been totally crushed by the news. True, these institutions were not Harvard or Yale, but then my uncle Mischa in New York had not asked me to apply to either of those schools. Instead, he suggested I apply to the City University of New York, as the tuition was almost free and I could get a part-time job. My College Board scores, however, were not good and I knew it.

I had no choice but to read and study on my own while finding employment in Italy as a translator or interpreter, which was what many young men from Alexandria did. Some of my classmates, who lived in Rome and were not going to college in the States, found jobs as tour guides. I could do that too. I bought myself Spanish and German primers. I also decided to learn Ancient Greek and polish the little Latin I had started. Who needed college?

But my mother knew I was more upset than I let on. She suggested that it might help if I called my father and shared the bad news with him. When I did call him, he could tell from my voice that I was thrown off by the rejections but told me that I'd succeed in whatever I put my mind to. It might just take a bit longer. I should learn to trust myself, something he wasn't sure he'd learned, since he, too, these days had once again stopped trusting himself. He could no longer recognize the man who'd built his factory. "You've become a virgin again?" I joked, trying to undercut his somber remarks when we had lunch in Paris that day. "I've become a virgin," he echoed. I shouldn't have said that.

I wasn't qualified to do anything, I said.

"What qualifications do you think I had?" he asked. "Could I dye a throwaway rag? No." He had spent hours in the public library of Alexandria, reading and copying his favorite writers. The rest of the time he was busy working in, of all places, a flour mill. "Your time will come." But here was the other moral to the tale: when the time comes, I should grab the opportunity and never let go, regardless of what others thought or said. "Just be ready and remember that chance knocks twice: the first time she'll tap very softly and you may not even hear her. The second knock, however, is the last. Grab it, and if your fingers aren't strong enough, use your teeth."

After hanging up the phone I tried a bit of humor and pretended to bite fate with my teeth. This was how one did it, wasn't it? I kept asking myself as I extended my lower jaw. What unusual images my father used. I tried biting again and again, as if to practice for the moment that came only twice in life. I practiced until I realized that one of my teeth actually hurt. Clearly psychosomatic. But the next morning I realized that I had real pain in that tooth.

I called Aunt Flora to ask if she knew of a dentist. I hadn't seen one since my early teens. Aunt Flora saw a dentist the way many people see a therapist, once or even twice a week. She recommended hers, but he was exceptionally expensive. He'd given her a good price because one of her cousins owned the building where he had his office. The dentist saw me that very afternoon and, on looking, said I had a cavity. "No need for X-rays," said the short, bald, rather portly man, who in less than thirty minutes had filled the tooth with a temporary filling until a gold filling could be prepared the next week. That gold filling is still lodged in my tooth. His fee was a favor, he said. But his favor ate up almost a quarter of our monthly allotment, which necessitated our asking for an advance from none other than Uncle Claude.

The dentist spoke Italian with a terrible accent and when I told him I had an accent too and attended an American school in Rome, it turned out he spoke much better English than Italian, but still with an accent I couldn't place. So, with a mouth numbed by Novocain, I asked him where he had studied. In New York, he replied, best time he'd ever had, too. Why New York? I asked. He stared out the large window overlooking the Borghese Gardens as if he didn't want to face me and smiled at himself or at me or at the window. It had to do with the war, he said. I had no idea what he meant. In my family, people always referred to wars, but it was never clear which one. He was born in Poland. He'd been studying in New York when the Second World War erupted. He never saw his family again. His name was Doctor Finkel but on the door was a large copper plate stating DOT. FINI. I could have guessed the rest.

Maybe you should become a dentist, Aunt Flora suggested.

Maybe I should study in New York, I replied.

And well you should, she said.

A very thin envelope arrived from the United States. My mother had brought it upstairs after shopping in the market. Again? I thought. She watched me open it, and could already read the signs of rehearsed indifference on my face. The sheet was printed in faded blue mimeograph ink with a printed blank "Dear _____" where my first name was written in by hand. It was an acceptance letter from Hunter College in the Bronx. I was so utterly surprised by the thin letter and its terse, rudimentary language that I decided to ignore it.

My mother was ecstatic, and asked me to call Aunt Flora immediately. I said it could wait. No, it couldn't, she said. Flora was at the office and took the call with a degree of composure that told me others in the office were within earshot. "Oh," she said. Then she added, "Heartfelt congratulations," as if news of an impending wedding justified the interruption at work. I could already tell that she would call us that evening to hear more. Instead, after work she called to say she was jumping on a bus and coming for supper. This was such wonderful news, she kept repeating. Had I told my father? No, I hadn't. "Then we'll call him and I'll speak to him after you."

There was a reason I hadn't told my father. I knew what he'd say. First, he'd congratulate me heartily and with true emotion, but then, especially after I'd told him about the dittoed form with my hastily scribbled first name, he'd start implying that someone might have made a mistake, that it was better to wait and see, to get it confirmed, because it could be a prank. I knew my father well enough to know it wasn't the acceptance that troubled him. He knew, as I knew, as Flora, my brother, and mother knew, that this acceptance was legitimate. What troubled him was that it had obvious ramifications that he was reluctant to confront. "At any rate, congratulations," he said. "It's a feather in your cap, maybe the acceptance letter can be parlayed into admittance to a university either in France or in Italy, if Rome is where you'll want to stay." If anything, I added, I wanted to study in Pisa, which many said had the best university in Italy. "Or in Pisa, then," he added, after hearing my suggestion, as though the matter was resolved. Maybe in a few years, if I had a change of heart, we could renegotiate the admission to Hunter College in the Bronx. Besides, did I really want to go to a school located in the Bronx?

I guess I didn't, I said.

Exactly.

Something had happened to my father when the Egyptian government seized his factory and his assets. He was no longer the same vigorous businessman whom everyone knew. Instead, if improvising had always been his way of easing through a difficult pass in life, postponement had replaced it. Roundtabling was his default setting, as every decision, rather than be made, had to be examined, reexamined, and then deferred.

After hanging up with my father, Aunt Flora said she was very dissatisfied with my father's reaction.

What did I want to do? she asked me.

My mother wanted to help me say what she believed I had in mind.

"No, let him speak," said Flora.

I thought about it and all I could say was: "I'm not sure."

"You're not sure?" she asked, not ironically, not as a question, but in a sort of puzzlement that sounded almost like an admonition followed by muted disappointment. "Why *I'm not sure*? We spent hours writing your statement, and now all you have to say is *I'm not sure*?" Suddenly she reminded me of Paola.

I wanted Italy but I also wanted New York.

Then the solution was simple, said Aunt Flora. "If you stay, you'll forfeit this chance and waste a number of years, possibly the rest of your life. If you go to America, in four years you can always come back and decide what you want your life to be. Chances are you won't want to come back." And then she added the killer: "And I'll be the one to pay for having sent you away."

Leaving Europe was like a second expulsion for me. For my father, who'd left Turkey to move to Egypt, it would be his third. Did one start one's life all over again each time? Dostoyevsky had said that

307

whoever forsakes his country forsakes his God. Did I even have a country or, for that matter, a God to forsake?

What my father feared the most was not just starting life all over again in a country he didn't know the first thing about. He feared leaving France, which was a place whose language and culture he knew perfectly and where life had not seemed terribly unwelcoming. The European Union did not exist then, and he feared that his stay in Paris might come to a sudden end, but for the time being, he had adapted well enough and did not want to give up what he had.

That evening, after Aunt Flora left, my mother told me that we should call her sister in New York and give her the good news. But maybe it was best not to tell my father about the call. I told her that it was only three o'clock in the afternoon in New York. "Then we'll have to wait until midnight. They'll be home by then."

My brother reminded me that it wasn't the first time I was going behind our father's back. That's all he said, but it hurt.

When I finally did call, it was my uncle who picked up and began speaking a garbled sort of pidgin English. He usually spoke French with us, but listening to the way he had answered in English, I realized why Dr. Finkel's English accent had surprised me. Uncle Mischa and Dr. Finkel not only had the same accent, but shared the same mildly choked timbre in their voice when they spoke English. Both were born in Poland, but had spent most of their lives abroad. "But it must be very late where you are!" exclaimed my uncle. I wanted to reply with a darting *You don't say!* My aunt picked up the other phone and was overjoyed by the news of my college admission. Uncle Mischa shouted words of congratulation interspersed with repeated *baruch hashem*s on his phone. They had two telephones. They must be rich, I thought, and mouthed this to my mother, who was equally impressed.

My mother asked me to tell her sister that she'd had enough of Rome and that, if I had to go to New York to study, she and my brother were coming too. It had never occurred to me that if I attended college in New York while my father continued living in

Paris, my mother would want to live with me in New York. Uncle Mischa said that decisions had to be made fast. He reminded me of his friend the legislator. He'd simply ask him to help expedite our visas given my admission to college. "I am not timid like your father. I know how to ask, and even beg if I have to." "And your father, is he coming?" he asked in English. I didn't know about my father. "He's a big boy. Let him decide for himself." My uncle who had risen in the space of a decade from unloading trucks and carrying such heavy crates that he'd almost ruined his organs in the *lower basement*, as he called them, now owned a four-story house off Pelham Bay. His only regret was not coming to the States when he was younger. "Now I have dentures, I can't speak good without them, and God forbid I should receive a call in the middle of the night and can't remember where I put my teeth. Oh, I should have went straight to California, found gold, and come back a rich man, and told my father-in-law, your grandfather, *Allah yerhamu*, may God bless him, where to stick his measly dowry."

Then, without warning, he said he had to hang up because he needed to make urgent calls to various individuals. "But you do want to come to the States, right?" he finally asked, because he could sense that I was starting to recoil, exactly as my father had when I'd broken the news to him. I asked my mother if she wanted to go to America. Her answer was a decisive yes.

A few nights later my aunt and uncle called at two in the morning. *Surprise!* I woke my mother up. "HIAS is preparing your papers," said my uncle, "our legislator put pressure on people in Washington and they put pressure on those in New York. What does your father want to do?" he finally asked. I told him that my father knew nothing about our latest discussions. "Then you must tell him." He didn't say good night; he simply hung up.

I knew that the call to my father was not going to be easy. Things were moving much faster than he might have wished or even anticipated. For him, thoughts of America were little more than far-fetched fantasies to which we could devote hours, if not years, of roundtable conversations riddled with insoluble bureaucratic obstacles.

My father had once suggested a solution that I, too, had found quite appealing. While he was busy consolidating prospects in France—whatever that meant, as I had seen no evidence of any prospects whatsoever during my recent stay in Paris—I might decide to spend an additional year in Italy, not in school but traveling around to its many towns and cities, get inspired, thinking thoughts that no course in any university, even the very best, could stir in someone my age. The best thinkers, the best writers, were invariably autodidacts. My father was not going to preclude studying in a university but why not seize the moment in Italy now, spend a year doing nothing but what I loved, provided I traveled on the cheap and was not extravagant. No one was ever given that chance at my age. I would do nothing but read, study on my own, and maybe join a racket club. "*Mens sana* and so forth," he added.

I loved this alternative. But Flora disagreed. "So you're going to loaf around Italy for a whole year and have what to show for yourself?" I wanted to tell her no one should quantify knowledge and intellectual growth that way. But I lacked the vocabulary to say it and I knew from long experience that she'd have a quick answer to each of my demurs. "After four years of university, you'll have something to show for yourself. Here after a year, you'll have nothing whatsoever."

"What if I wanted to write during that year?"

"And do what? Publish at your age, where, here?"

"I could master Italian in less than a year. James Joyce did."

I immediately caught the snarky glint in her eyes and knew exactly what she could have said but, being Flora, had the grace and forbearance not to say. I might never amount to anything without guidance, without a teacher, without others to tell me what they thought. I knew three languages but none well enough. Plus, my mind was sluggish. I had seen Antonioni's *L'Eclisse* and couldn't understand the ending, whereas my mother, who needed me to tell her what was happening as we watched the film, couldn't see what there was not to understand: the would-be lovers had stood each other up! Any idiot could understand this. I no longer wanted to be in a class with people smarter than I, who wrote better, who got *Ulysses* whereas I had to struggle on every page and was no longer even sure I liked the book because, in my mother's thinking, I was as terrible an interpreter of books as I was of people.

A few days later it was my father who called. He normally preferred to telephone from Aunt Elsa's home, because in his ground-floor apartment he could easily be overheard either by the concièrge or by another nosy tenant with whom he shared the same thin wall, or by people passing by on the sidewalk, who could hear every word when he left his window open. He was calling to see if I'd made up my mind about the year he was offering.

First, I had to reverse his train of thought about my year of travel, and second, I needed to tell him that I had not given up on going to America.

"So, lock yourself up on Via Clelia or in the Bronx, what's the difference?"

But another year on Via Clelia, now that he had put it that way, was the portrait of a failed life every time I watched an elderly man wearing a suit, a tie, and under the jacket a sweater with fraying cuffs as he ambled among the stalls in the market holding a plastic net bag partly filled with lettuce, peppers, and puntarelle that his wife hated slicing. I did not want to be that man in forty, fifty years. Meanwhile, every image of my future felt wobbly, and the more I probed it, the more it appeared as pure fantasy. The money I was going to make to rescue my parents, the people I was going to meet and impress, the clothes I was going to have made so as never to wear my father's, all these crowned by my rapid rise in the world, from bookish upstart to financial wizard, swarmed through my mind to erase the very memory of Via Clelia. And if, as the Greek grocer once told my mother, a grocery was in my future, then I'd own not one but a chain of supermarkets, and end up owning many hotels, exactly as one did in Monopoly, a game I'd mastered just enough to lose every single time.

Fantasies and pipe dreams.

Still, I found comfort in them, because they buffered the shock of what had pounced the moment my father had uttered his cruel, honest, but unsettling words: *Via Clelia or the Bronx, what's the difference?* He could have been right, but even if I were the worst interpreter of literature and, as my brother said, never had a foot planted in reality, I knew that I'd choose a classroom in the Bronx instead of these long, lost, rudderless afternoons in Rome. I loved the *centro storico*, but the *centro storico* was not my day-to-day Rome, and I liked Paola, but I wasn't in love with her. I wasn't in love with anyone. Yet would I be able to live without the life I'd gotten to know in Rome? One thing was certain: after four years of college in New York, I would definitely want to be back in Rome. This was not only my way of not making a definitive break with the city; it also allowed me to be in two places without giving up either. I was booking my passage back before making the journey out, seeking Italy while still in Italy. Bashō's haikus twice over. I wanted to attend university courses, but preferred learning things on my own, promised to make a fortune for my parents but was incurably reclusive and bookish, was Jewish but celebrated Christmas, had a mother tongue I loved but had acquired another I grew to love more but knew far less well. "*Che strano tipo sei,*" you're a weird one, Gianlorenzo said to me after I told him a bit about myself. He was teasing. But he was right. I was weird.

Once back, I might even find a moment to walk down Via Clelia and pay Grazia an impromptu visit, find Paola, even ask Madame Renato to brew me a quick espresso the way she'd turn to me when visiting and beg me, if I had a few seconds, to brew a *petit café fifty-fifty*.

On the phone with my father that day, I couldn't find the courage to confront him with the unavoidable track my admission to Hunter had opened for me. How to persuade him to abandon a lifetime spent nurturing dreams of Paris and trash them for a city he'd never taken seriously? In what selfish well of iniquity would I find the courage to ask this of him?

His words to me that day couldn't have been more direct or more pointed. "For me to go to America means what? To see you grow into someone I'll be lucky to see once a month, if that? What's in it for your mother and me, especially if we're forced to live together? Your mother is deaf and doesn't know a word of English, and the English I know I learned by reading Shakespeare and Byron. How far will that get me, do you think, in a country whose culture is built on baseball, comics, and rock and roll?"

He then added that he knew he was being selfish, and that everyone in the family would hold it against him for being such a difficult father.

Did I want to go to America by myself? "Many people do it these days," he said. "They go away to study and then come back. Or they don't." I recalled watching Dr. Finkel face the window that gave onto Via Porta Pinciana and farther out to the Borghese Gardens, thinking of those he'd left behind and who'd been turned to ash.

What was there to discuss? he seemed to ask. I didn't have an answer.

But something had to give.

Ironically, it was Uncle Claude, the most anti-American person I knew, who, while visiting Aunt Elsa in Paris, convinced my father that France hadn't offered the business prospects he'd expected to find a year earlier. Nor was France or Italy opening any doors for me. My father had become an employee; I would be one as well. There was only one solution left, and it wasn't in Europe.

My father did not disagree, but he couldn't decide.

Another phone call from America, as always at two in the morning, told us we were about to receive the requisite papers but that we needed to put up five thousand dollars to guarantee that Uncle Mischa would not have to defray unforeseen expenses on our account.

This was the excuse my father needed. He didn't trust my mother's brother-in-law in New York. The man would steal our five thousand dollars, he said, and, worse yet, was already in league with Uncle Robert in Paris.

My father was incensed and would have dropped our entire American project but for two things: one, our visas were suddenly available thanks to my uncle's determined efforts to bring my mother to her sister's side in New York; and two, my brother and I were eager to put Italy behind us. My father, however, remained irresolute and the requested five thousand dollars had given him a good reason to demur. "As for your mother's wish to be close to her sister, here's what will happen. On the very day she lands in New York, the two sisters will cry, sit down for tea, and gossip till their mouths run dry, and in a matter of seconds, mark my words, they'll start bickering and then fighting. She fought with her brother when you called him in Paris after she'd not seen him for a whole decade, and it will be no different when she hugs and kisses her beloved sister in New York—I said it first."

But he must have sensed, possibly from very early on, or maybe before even leaving Egypt, that Europe was not a promised land for him. It was a halfway point, not unlike the rest house on the desert road between Cairo and Alexandria, where we'd arrive at the crack of dawn for a so-called lavish breakfast that consisted of nothing more than scrambled eggs and buttered toast but that would hold our hunger till hours later when we reached our hotel by the Pyramids, and realize that, unbeknownst to us, the real thrill of traveling with him lay in the ramshackle old rest house and its scanty eggs. The absolute silence of the desert, the scent of toasted bread rising from the kitchen, and the view of God's good world at sunup were better than Cairo or Alexandria.

We loved in-between points. And maybe, now that I think of it, this is what Rome was to me: the unforeseen and peripheral halfway that suddenly becomes the polestar of life, the interlude that supersedes the before and after. Rome never asked to be loved, and like Flora herself, I wouldn't know that I loved it or wanted to love it until I was about to lose it.

— 12 —

So Now You Tell Me?

After graduation, I decided to spend my days reading and writing. My plan was to read two or three works of literature every week, many in Italian, hoping to complete at least sixty works by September. Maybe I wouldn't mind spending an entire year that way. When I said this to my father during one of our telephone conversations, he approved but also said that I was reading far too fast and might not be seeing the literary merit of each work. I insisted that the literary merit was obvious enough whether I read speedily or labored over every word. Sometimes every word matters, he'd say. A painter is not only a phenomenal draftsman capable of capturing the human face down to its most tenuous inflections; a painter is also a dyer. He invents colors you've never seen before. Giotto, Titian, Goya, van Gogh. Colors, like words, do matter. I argued the point. He had enough experience to let me think I'd persuaded him. Still, what I was doing was wonderful. Go to museums also, and go with Amina, the girl across from your building. I yessed him.

A few days later, after I had emptied my locker at school and bid Notre Dame International School farewell, my mother said she was going to buy a few items in the marketplace, maybe a pair of shoes.

I'd been reading all morning, and when she asked me to join her, my answer was an enthusiastic yes. Then you'll help me carry things. I said I would, of course. She told me she didn't feel like dragging her mini shopping cart, which all women used when they went to market. Walking up two flights carrying her little cart when the elevator was not working wasn't always easy. Maybe she'd buy me a pair of shoes too, I suggested, as I was tired of wearing my father's expensive but not always comfortable shoes. She gave me an uneasy and perplexed smile that I'll never forget. She had enough money to buy one pair, she said, and she needed shoes herself—if I really didn't mind waiting a couple of weeks. There was a note so tentative and apprehensive in her words that I couldn't have felt more inconsiderate and selfish.

After getting what we needed for food that day, we stepped into a small department store nearby, where she tried on a few pairs of simple gumshoes, finally deciding on one that didn't cost much. These were *molto eleganti*, said the salesgirl, who was hardly much older than I. *Molto eleganti*, repeated my mother, who had captured the words from her lips and was making fun of the shoes, which were the furthest thing from *eleganti*. She decided to wear the shoes right then and there, and when the salesgirl asked if she wanted her old shoes in a box, my mother said she could throw them away.

It was one of those gloriously sunny mornings when nothing could go wrong in Rome. My mother said she wanted to look at perfumes in a small cosmetics store. She wasn't going to buy anything, she said, but I shouldn't let the owner know this. She just wanted to smell them again. She walked in tentatively and, not knowing what to say, asked me to tell the store owner that she was eager to buy a perfume, but not cologne. She named them to me, and I communicated them to the owner. It was a perfume by Millot called Crêpe de Chine. When he brought out the Crêpe de Chine and twisted open the cap of the bottle, she took her time breathing in the scent, then asked for a perfume by Houbigant that she had also owned in Egypt. The owner of the store showed it to her. My mother smelled this bottle as well, but moments later, on my telling her the price, she smiled, handed the owner the bottle back, shook her head ever so slowly to mean no, too much, but also to apologize for troubling him, and stood there as though waiting for him to say something, which was her way of apologizing a second time. It was the right gesture from her, and it was clear that the owner of the shop wasn't taking offense. He put the bottle back in the glass case behind him and with both palms on the counter smiled back at her to mean he understood. He must have understood she was deaf by the way I was speaking to her, but I was also sure he could tell she knew her scents, and perhaps because of his courtesy that morning, or of his kindness, I'd like to think that on that day so very long ago now he must have known she was catching the scent of a world forever lost to her.

As we were walking home, I asked her how she liked her shoes. I could see that she was walking faster and with greater ease, but she mocked her purchase and said that within weeks they'd be ruined. Poor workmanship, but for today comfortable enough.

When we got home, she deposited the food on the kitchen table and said she'd make a nice lunch. With my brother still in school, my presence at home on an ordinary weekday was new to her and reminded her of last summer when I stayed home all day, reading. She liked company, and I liked this new chapter in our lives. I said I wanted to help her in the kitchen. She said I could wash the salad and slice the large tomatoes, while she would scale the fish and broil it in the oven. Over the past months she had found a way to tie the handle of the window to a hook nailed to the wall to prevent it from banging shut when we needed to air the kitchen, especially while cooking fish or frying vegetables. We had also found a simple way to protect the glass panel on the kitchen door by placing a heavy chair against it when the window was open.

I liked how the morning light swept through our windows and nestled in the apartment during what still today remains my favorite hour of any day, late midmorning—a movable time that should have a name but doesn't, in good part because it doesn't occur at an established hour throughout the year but is easily recognized, even if the moment slips away before we're able to capture it. Instead of reading in my room, I grabbed the small old shortwave radio I'd inherited from my father with a mind to listen to music in the kitchen. I liked Radio Monte Carlo, and the sound of a particular jingle at that hour of the day used to stir a note of joy. I liked that station because it broadcast classical music that was not entirely given over to military marches, waltzes, and ballet music.

As I was washing the lettuce, I caught an urgent news bulletin. It seemed that President Nasser of Egypt, the man who was responsible for looting our property and for expelling my family from Egypt and ultimately for banishing every sign of the world I'd grown up in, had asked the United Nations Peacekeeping Force to withdraw from the Sinai Peninsula. Since the force had been placed there to ensure that war would not break out between Egypt and Israel, it seemed self-evident that Israel was now in the crosshairs of the Egyptian army. I had grown up with numberless poems at school that glamorized the massacre following the defeat of the Israelis. We had witnessed periodic training blackouts, and for years it was clear that the country was preparing for hostilities to come. The presence of Egyptian air force planes flying at very low altitudes and constantly breaking the sound barrier was a tireless reminder that the modernized Egyptian war machine could annihilate not just the Israeli army but all of Israel itself. Those huge, loud airplanes flying at supersonic speed over our beach umbrellas were always hailed by beachgoers, except by those of us who were Jews and, though not Israelis, had by virtue of our religion been lumped with Israel and treated as an inimical fifth column in Egypt.

My mother and I stood silent, but I continued slicing the tomatoes, adding olive oil and salt, and setting them on the oilcloth covering the kitchen table.

The possibility of the bloodbath to follow was set aside and we didn't think of it again. After lunch she said she was going to lie down. Signor Leo came at around three that afternoon, she made coffee for the two of them and served it in the small living room, and at around four thirty he left. My door was shut, so he wouldn't have to stop to say goodbye to me.

When I listened to Radio Monte Carlo a few days later, the news was worse than I feared. Nasser had not only asked the United Nations peacekeepers to clear the area of the Sinai, but he had blockaded the Gulf of Aqaba and the town of Eilat along its coast. The Egyptians had been training for this moment and banging their war drum for twenty years, since the foundation of Israel. All the anti-Zionist poems I'd had to learn in school and all the antisemitic propaganda I'd lived with and was even told by family and friends to feign endorsing had suddenly emerged in Rome and revealed a scar that had never really healed. I feared the Egyptians and I hated Nasser, and on hearing his voice for half a minute on an Italian news radio broadcast that week, something in me shuddered. I knew that the Egyptians would win and unleash their pent-up fury on the Jewish state.

I was unable to let go of my radio and every few hours would turn it on to hear what was happening in the Middle East on various Italian, French, and English news broadcasts. The worst news, however, the most up-to-date and the most terrifying, came from the English-language broadcast from Israel. It conveyed such a bleak view of Israel's prospects following the blocking of the Straits of Tiran that I would spend a greater part of each day constantly interrupting my reading to catch the latest bulletin.

My mother and I would sit in the kitchen while I read each paper's version of the situation for her. My mother worried for the Pintos and the Levis, who still lived in Egypt. The future of Jews there was certainly going to look far, far worse now than it had in our day only a year earlier. She remembered how Madame Levi would plead with her husband to close his machine shop, abandon everything, and leave on the sly, the way the Chalabi family had done, with their bills stashed in suitcases stuffed with brassieres and women's underwear. Now who knew what would happen to them.

Egypt's Jews were highly vulnerable to Egypt's plenipotentiary leader, who had become the most powerful in the Arab world. My mother remembered that Jews had been murdered in Egypt immediately after the declaration of the Israeli state in the year she married my father. "We'd have been in the Levis' shoes had we stayed. But it's good we left before." It was not our decision to leave, I told her, we were expelled. We were planning to leave anyway, she replied. Yes, but planning might have taken years. That was my way of making light of my father's incapacity to reach a decision. "Yes, we were lucky," she conceded.

The days passed and eventually I got tired of checking the news broadcasts, since they didn't announce anything new, which meant that the Egyptians were not going to attack, and weak, fledgling Israel was going to return to its humble day-to-day affairs with the perpetual threat of annihilation hanging over it.

Grazia gave me the news ten days later. The Israeli air force had obliterated the Egyptian air force while it sat on the ground ready to fly out. She told me thinking I knew already, but broke the story to me with a degree of hesitation, sensing that she might be crossing a delicate line, knowing that we had come from Egypt and might not take kindly to the news. Of course, I did not believe her, but then her brother, coming by while I was speaking to her, told me the same thing. The news was all over Italian television, he said. I kissed Grazia and rushed upstairs to tell my mother and turn on my shortwave radio.

These Italians believe anything, including their own lies, she said. She was not convinced. "Call Flora."

Flora was jubilant as I'd seldom heard her before. "The Italian radio, what did you want," I said, trying to counter her enthusiasm and inject my usual dose of ironic disbelief, hoping her enthusiasm would override my skepticism. I was wrong, she said. Her relatives had been calling since earlier that morning and many had checked various radio programs from all kinds of sources. Toto already said he was heading to the Israeli embassy with his best friend from Egypt to volunteer to fly to Israel. She herself had just heard the news from a German radio station and from France and finally from an American station. At work no one could do anything but sit around the boss's radio. It occurred to me that I was the last to hear the news. Flora called later that very day. I asked about Toto again.

He was leaving for Israel in a few days.

"And the marriage?" my mother asked.

"It will wait."

"*Quelle salade!*" said my mother.

We hung up. That evening my father called.

This was just the beginning, he said, deflating whatever enthusiasm I was nurturing after I'd spoken to various people that day, including Brother John from school, who had telephoned because he knew I was a Jewish refugee from Egypt and suspected I'd be pleased by the news. My father affected cautious optimism the way I had done with Aunt Flora, just in case too much bravado might backfire or turn into a colossal disappointment. "The Japanese destroyed Pearl Harbor," added my father, "but they lost the war. So, no celebrations yet just because the Israelis caught the Egyptian air force with its pants down. The Egyptian army is massive and it has so many more tanks than the Israelis. And besides, the Russians will send them more airplanes; next time they won't be caught unawares."

My mother had a different point of view: "Maybe with an Israeli victory, things could go back to how they once were in Egypt."

My father couldn't help himself: "Tell your mother that she never wanted to stay in Egypt when we were in Egypt. Now she wants to go back? There is no going back, now more than ever. They'll hate Jews more than they already did a month ago."

"He says there is no going back," I repeated to my mother.

She agreed. "Then we should only think of what lies ahead."

"What lies ahead?"

She thought for a moment.

"We don't want to stay here any longer, and we can't go back."

"So, what are you saying?" he asked.

I relayed his question.

"I am saying what both your sons and I are thinking."

"Which is what?"

Clearly, he was playing dumb.

I caught myself in time and also said nothing.

"Exactly," he said, as if silence was our way of conceding the point to him.

I had been generous and silent with him and he had taken advantage of it.

I'd find my moment soon enough.

We said goodbye.

My mother stared at me. "You didn't tell him."

"No, I didn't tell him."

My brother was ready to kill me.

Mother nodded as she used to nod years ago, when, after begging me to find the courage to tell him how hurt we were that he wasn't living with us as a family, she'd come into my room and, noticing that I was shifting my glance away from hers, would intuit that I hadn't spoken to him about his absence. "Why didn't you?" she'd say. "I couldn't," I'd reply. She always forgave me, but I knew I'd failed her because I lacked the courage to speak the truth to him. "Then you tell him," she told my brother. He said he would. And he did.

Over supper that night I turned to all kinds of news broadcasts: France Inter, the BBC, and all the Italian news stations. Everyone agreed that the Israelis had scored a superb victory. I shared everything with my mother.

In the next few days, I sat glued to my radio. My mother would come into my room when we weren't sitting together at the kitchen table and would sit on the corner of my bed to ask what the Italian station said. The Israelis were advancing into the Sinai, into the West Bank, and had taken all of Jerusalem. My mother had been to Jerusalem with her father when she was sixteen and later at the age of twenty-two. He owned land in Jerusalem. Did I want to go there? she asked. I'll think about it, I said.

After just a few days, the Israelis could have gone farther and occupied Egypt. They had also stopped their advance just miles away from Damascus. As for Jerusalem, it was, after two millennia, in the hands of Jews again.

My family might have lost everything in Egypt, but it gave us no small thrill to hear that Egypt had lost everything too.

Soon we began to see in the press pictures of demolished Egyptian planes and airfields, and pictures of the boots that fleeing Egyptian soldiers had removed and left scattered on the sand dunes of the Sinai.

Amina would come and sit next to me by the radio, and together we'd listen to the latest broadcasts. Twice she invited my mother and brother to view the news on her family's television set. Her parents, too, were obsessed with the events in the Middle East and their admiration for the Israelis was boundless. They had always known we were Jewish. But the only one I had told outside school was Gianlorenzo.

More than a month after the Six-Day War, I received a call from my friend Solomon Levi, nicknamed Salon. He had just landed in Italy. His family, like ours, had acquired Italian citizenship in Egypt and, following our expulsion, had hired our Italian tutor, figuring that one way or another they'd eventually land in Italy before moving elsewhere in the world. Salon said he'd just been released from a refugee camp in Naples, the same one we'd known a year earlier.

I saw him the following week in Rome when he stopped with one of his uncles who had come from Belgium to pick him up. He had lost thirty pounds and looked much older, partly because his new crew cut had erased his age, his smile, and his once-ebullient personality. His sunken cheeks gave his nose a protruding quality, and he looked weary, as though he'd been released from a long stay in an intensive care unit. He staggered when he walked, and he knew it, and pointed out his gait before I noticed it. His father was still in a detention camp in the middle of nowhere in the Egyptian desert. All I could think of was my father, imprisoned in some Egyptian camp. Yes, our world had been stolen from us, but we'd been lucky.

"They beat us every day there," he said. Why had he been arrested?

I asked. They rounded up all Jewish males aged sixteen and over. When they picked up his father and him at home, he told me he began to sob like a baby. In the truck that was to take them to jail, his father had whispered to him not to tell anyone he was Jewish and to speak only Arabic. "Be a man now," he spoke ever so softly. Panic-stricken, Salon kept speaking French to him. "Arabic, please!" said his father. Then a guard stood up in the truck, walked over to the father, and, in front of his son, slapped him hard on one cheek. "Don't speak," he ordered. "Not a word," he replied. "I said not a word," yelled the guard, slapping the father equally as hard on the other cheek. Salon, who had just turned sixteen, started crying hysterically. "Do you want one too?" asked the guard, turning to Salon. The father pleaded for his son with supplicating gestures, while Salon whimpered all the way to the prison, where father and son were separated, which caused Salon more tears. "*Parle seulement arabe, et ne dis pas un mot de plus, pas un mot*," speak Arabic only, and don't utter another word, not a word, he whispered to his son.

The reason, as Salon explained, should have been obvious but wasn't clear at the time. They'd been thrown in a cell filled with thieves and outlaws who would have pummeled them to death if they found out that he or his father was Jewish. Salon kept crying, so they didn't touch him, but his father, as I later found out, was put among criminals who asked him his crime. In flawless Egyptian Arabic, he said that he had been driving his car and a fool on a motorcycle trying to impress his girlfriend ran headlong into him. The man was wounded but wasn't taken to a hospital, his girlfriend was safe, but they put him, the driver of the car who'd been minding his own business, in jail. His wife hadn't been told and she'd be so worried and was sure to take out her rage on him. "Worry about yourself, not your wife," said one of the prisoners. He knew by then that they believed him. Eventually, the father and son were reunited when they were taken to a detention camp with other Jews.

In the camp, Salon told me, it was easy to bribe the guards. They liked cigarettes, so when he was able to place a call to his mother, he asked her to bring cigarettes right away. "A cigarette is the currency here," he told her. The Levis' driver delivered two cartons of cigarettes within a few days. With them, Salon managed to buy a new pair of loafers made by a local Bedouin who was related to one of the prison guards. Did he really need new loafers? No. He was also able to obtain a bar of soap, which he shared with everyone in his bunk. Eventually, Salon, who was made in the same sly mold as Toto and Jules, asked one of the guards to procure him a woman. "A woman"—the guard mused a moment—"that would be difficult. But a young man, okay." Salon thought for a moment, then canceled the order. Some guards were willing to trade, but would beat their clients just the same. "Life in the camps. An infested country, Egypt," he said.

Salon was allowed to leave Egypt by mid-July following the Six-Day War and was put aboard the same ship that had carried us to Italy a year earlier.

I couldn't stop thinking that I had narrowly escaped Salon's fate.

I was starting to forget Arabic. I wanted to forget. Any picture of Alexandria stirred a sensation of dread and dismay.

One thing that became self-evident especially after hearing what had happened to the Levis in the wake of the Six-Day War: if we had still nurtured the most elusive hope of returning to Egypt, that fantasy was now permanently expunged. Egypt's Jews were being interned and were all going to be expelled. Egypt was *judenrein*, my father said, which, initially and despite the rabid antisemitism of the Egyptian president, had seemed a capricious, feverish sentiment that was bound to dissipate and that most Jews in Egypt were willing to put up with for however long it took. Now Jews had to leave the country as soon as they could, with or without anything they owned. No thirty-one suitcases for the Levis, who owned a remarkable mansion in the very heart of Alexandria.

Everyone who could was leaving. And no one was ever coming back, Jews and Catholics and Orthodox Christians alike.

I suspect that even in Paris, as he was turning a new page in his life, my father must have nursed the residual hope, absurd as he knew hope was, of waiting out his time until, despite all claims to the contrary, he'd be asked to come back to his beloved Alexandria and resume his old life exactly where he'd left it. But after hearing what had happened to the Levi family, he said that perhaps my mother was right after all. As things stood, France seemed to hold no future for him. "So maybe we'll pay your mother's *Amérique chérie* a little visit," he said. Those were his very words. I knew that he always made life-changing decisions with subdued resignation, topped off with a thick dose of skepticism. Sarcasm was how he accepted the odd and cruel turn events had taken in his life, as if life had toyed too many times with him and all he could do was put up an ironic front to show he wasn't fooled or caught unawares but had seen the catastrophe coming long beforehand, which was why he'd done nothing to avert it, knowing that a wise man always folds before the unavoidable flood. You held your breath while the waves crashed overhead—except that holding his breath had come so easily to my father that it was a sign not of prescience but of paralysis. It was how he lived: provisionally. Whatever caused him to accept moving to America—my mother's sister, my acceptance to college, my brother's persistent hawking— remains undefined, even today. Nor was I ever able to fathom why he'd given up on Paris, especially after dreaming of it since childhood.

His biggest worry, other than moving his wardrobe back to Rome just months after he'd moved a lot of it to Paris, was being blamed by everyone on his side of the family for abandoning France, and on my mother's side for failing to accept New York.

Unable to determine which course to follow, he focused on his wardrobe: he wasn't sure how he'd be able to pack all his things by himself. My mother offered to travel to Paris to help him sort out what he needed and, while there, take the opportunity to bid her brother Robert and his family farewell. But my father demurred. He probably didn't want her in Paris while he took leave of his own relatives, friends, neighbors, and who knows whom else he wouldn't mention and wouldn't want my mother to meet.

HIAS, which was handling all our papers, said we'd have to be

interviewed at the American consulate in Naples. Naples had histori-
cally been the city from which most Italian immigrants sailed to the
United States. One Neapolitan song I'd heard told of the heartbroken
Italian men watching the shoreline of Santa Lucia grow smaller and
smaller the farther out their ship sailed. Then by sunset, Naples was
no more. I had never liked or given Naples a chance from the day that
Uncle Claude had come to meet us at the harbor. How anyone could
miss Naples was beyond me. And yet after hearing the song, I began
to understand the sorrow of emigrants. What startled me was the
ironic possibility that the very person who'd drive us to Naples before
we boarded our ship to the New World would be none other than
Uncle Claude himself. But we were disabused by the kind if impatient
down-to-business woman handling our affairs at the HIAS office.
No one took ships to New York any longer, she said. Immigrants flew
to JFK.

Still, I hesitated to tell the woman at HIAS that our travel plans
were by no means as definite as she was meant to assume. My father
could change his mind at any moment, especially if he refused to send
my uncle the five thousand dollars he'd requested. In which case Uncle Mischa might decide not to host us at all.

What also troubled me when I imagined my first few weeks in
New York was not my initial days in a college classroom, or my first
part-time job, or getting lost in a huge metropolis; what gave me
pause was having to blend into America without that requisite period of transition between the gradual letting go of Rome—with its
rhythms and customs and the people I'd known—and the measured,
diffident acceptance of New York. I needed that long trip by boat,
not to delay arrival but to extend the bridge between both worlds, an
incubation period, as in Plato, between the old life and the new, the
precious hiatus I'd missed when my train was already in France without letting me know that we'd already crossed the border with Italy.

My father's face as we approached the Bronx once we'd left the
airport worried me. What were his thoughts going to be at that moment? He was not only about to face a new life, a new country, a new

language, new hardships, but how was he going to bring himself to show respect and gratitude to a man who had gone to great lengths to facilitate our papers but whom he regarded as no better than a buffoon, a grab bag of goodwill, unshakable loyalty, arrested medieval notions, and incorrigible flashes of larceny, corruption, and greed?

What I myself was reluctant to see happen in Rome was of a completely different order. I wanted at all costs to avoid teary farewells with neighbors and people who had become our friends, and if one way to avoid these cumbersome and emotional leave-takings was to cancel leaving altogether, then I'd accept a life on Via Clelia. A more compelling reason not to leave at all was the thought of people loading all our luggage onto a truck in front of everyone in the surrounding buildings who'd eventually come to their balconies to stare at all our suitcases piled on the sidewalk. Even if we left when night fell, while people dined and listened to their booming televisions as we scampered away to the airport under cover of darkness, I knew that the word would spread, and Amina, Amina's parents, Sabina, Madame Renato, Gianlorenzo, his sister, Paola, Monsieur Renato, Signor Leo, Grazia and her good brothers, and one or two deaf friends would show up to replay their tearful embraces, though we'd have already bid them farewell earlier that same day.

My father had agreed to move to the United States but on the condition that it not be a permanent move. *J'accepte mais pas pour toujours*, but not forever. That had become his mantra. He returned to Rome so we could all leave together in September. He had found a way to have all his clothes and possessions shipped directly to Uncle Mischa's in New York. The cost of shipping his boxes carefully sealed with protective plastic was high, as was the insurance, but he figured he wouldn't need to have any shoes or clothes made for many years. The thought of living the rest of his days in New York, of all places, was such an unthinkable prospect that the only way he could stomach the journey was to anticipate an end to it. Four years (he was copying me), and then he'd ship everything back to Paris. More than that no one could be held to—*I won't immolate my life at your altars*, he used to tell us.

My mother had no idea what he was talking about, though I knew that she had mistaken his *autels* (altars) for *hôtels* and assumed that the first thing he'd do if they weren't getting along in New York was move to a hotel, which he constantly kept threatening to do while we were spending our near-to-last days on Via Clelia. The three of us were so disturbed by his threats that we even begged Flora to move with us to New York for a while, to help diffuse the tension between my parents—a desperate and unthinkable option, which, of course, she refused. Besides, she'd just been promoted to a managerial position in Venice, where the shipping company had its headquarters. The company would pay for her move to suitable lodgings there, and to move the two old pianos given to her by the Anconas, since that had been her condition for taking the new position. Without her pianos, she had told the owners of the firm, she was nothing. Flora was not displeased with her prospects in Venice, and we all envied her. She cared for two things: her income and her pianos. She'd have no difficulty finding students eager to learn from her in her spare hours. She was, as she often liked to say, preparing to age well, *une bonne vieillesse*. She advised both my mother and my father to start thinking about aging well too. It's never too early. "As for you," she said, turning to me and then to my brother, "choose her well."

When she saw the bundle of things that my mother was sorting through to decide what to take and what to leave behind, she caught sight of an unframed picture of me when I was a boy and said that she was taking it. No one could refuse her this, as she'd always been my almost-mother.

I saw that picture two decades later in a silver frame standing on her mantelpiece in Venice. I remembered that day on Via Clelia and how she had knelt to take it, holding it delicately by two corners. Her gesture then was as gracious as everything about her. *Choose her well*, she'd said. What words. I wanted someone exactly like her, just twenty years younger, which was how old she was when she stayed at my great-grandmother's in Egypt after escaping Germany, when all the men in the house, having watched her play the piano in the living room, swore they'd lost their minds over her. My father had loved her, still loved her perhaps, as did my mother when they'd meet at the beach almost every day on those torrid summer days in Alexandria. She loved me and I loved her. *Choose her well.* No one would have said it in just that way, or found words so spare and quick to help dodge the heartrending elegy in her voice.

She was the only person with whom I could discuss ideas—not academically, which is how so many professors pour notions into our heads, but ideas with a completely human dimension, which is what ideas are in the end, not lifeless slugs devoid of human features, but sentient figures of what we live with when we can't even tell a feeling from a thought and can only sketch what is bound to miss the mark. Look for the human, she would say when she wasn't asking me to *think American*—even if there's no proof you're right, look for the human. What a pleasure to spell out my thoughts with her, when she'd ask what did I think such-and-such an author was really, really thinking when he wrote that piece? Then, turning to music, she'd say, This was what Beethoven struggled with when composing this sonata. "Do I know this for sure?" she'd ask. "No. Do I have any proof? No. But am I right? Absolutely."

We saw Aunt Flora not many times after that. She was, now that I think of it years later, trying to protect herself. She would miss us very much, she said, and we would miss her as well, even if my mind was entirely taken with what awaited me across the Atlantic. She came for supper with us three or four times, traveling a whole hour from work to our home, and back, each supper marked by a sort of finality from which the subsequent one was a welcome reprieve, until we couldn't pretend any longer and would be gone indeed. This was not like our farewell in Egypt, when it was clear we'd reconnect in Italy within two to three years at the most. This felt different. It might take years. By then who would I be for her, what would I have done to myself, and how many parts she'd known and loved about me would I forsake in the New World? Flora might not recognize me.

As it turned out, *Look for the human* was what I never forgot. I passed it on to those who listened. It was, however, almost impossible for others to practice, having never met Flora.

~

At the tail end of August, we arrived in Naples to be interviewed. My father had booked rooms at a pension overlooking the sea, and that morning the hostess served a copious breakfast with wonderful pancakes I'd never tasted before. She was German, and she and my father spoke for a while in German. Then, rather than helping us find a taxi or take a bus, she said it would be easier to walk to the American consulate. My father had asked my mother to wear high heels. She complained that the walk to the consulate would kill her. Besides, we were emigrants now, so why wear high heels and look ridiculous? But he insisted, justifying his recommendation by saying that we didn't want to look like run-of-the-mill farmers immigrating to America. She consented. The waiting hall where a functionary summarily told us to sit was already crowded with families looking no different from emigrants captured in sepia photographs waiting to board ocean liners at the beginning of the twentieth century. Everyone was unusually quiet, everyone whispered, waiting nervously to have their papers checked. My father had prepared everything and was wearing a full suit and had told us, too, to dress up for the occasion. You never know with these people, he added, leaving it unclear whether *these people* were American bureaucrats or Italian orderlies who liked bullying people about.

At some point they called my father, he stood up, left the hall, and disappeared. We were on tenterhooks, not knowing why they'd called him, what they were asking him, and why he was gone for so long. About an hour later he appeared, walking down the crowded hall wearing a smile on his face. Everyone caught his smile and the entire hall followed him with their gaze as he headed toward us, all smiling back at him as though silently congratulating him for having passed an arduous formality. They had asked him to sign papers, he said. Had nothing else happened? my mother asked. Nothing. Then why was he smiling? He replied that the panic-stricken expression on our faces had made him want to laugh.

Eventually we were summoned into a room and asked a slew of questions by an American functionary: Had we ever been arrested? Had we belonged to the Communist Party? Had we been prostitutes? He had such a thick American accent in Italian, and his command of Italian was so pitiful, that I interrupted and asked him to please read the questions in English, since my father, my brother, and I knew English perfectly. We chatted for a short while to explain why I knew English, and he asked which schools I'd attended in Egypt and Rome. Then, pausing for a minute or so, he reverted to reading more questions in Italian with his horrible pronunciation. And then I realized why he was reading the questions in Italian. The man was drunk. At some point he asked us to stand and hold our right hands up and to repeat after him words that he spoke in English this time. All four of us raised our right hands, and the three of us started repeating the same words. Seeing us, my mother proceeded to do the same as well, muttering unfathomable sounds so that the drunkard thought she was repeating what he was saying. As far as he was concerned, she, like all of us, had passed the test. He congratulated us and then excused himself, pulling out a large hero sandwich from one of his old wooden desk drawers, which he clearly meant to devour the moment we stepped out of his office.

Forty years later, when my mother, brother, and I were burying my father, the rabbi asked us to repeat after him the Kaddish. My brother and I knew no Aramaic, or Hebrew for that matter, but I found myself muttering sounds that in no way approximated what the rabbi was enunciating with the solemn grandiloquence of a practiced orator. As I listened to the rabbi, suddenly, and despite my sorrow in seeing my father being buried after what he himself claimed had been nothing more than a meager, hardscrabble life filled with empty promises and now consigned to a soil that had never been home to him, I began snickering, especially when I saw my mother pretending to repeat the Kaddish. I remembered how she had raised her right hand and mouthed sounds, the way I was mouthing what was gibberish to me to a rabbi my sons swore was high on cocaine and who was no less indifferent to what we were saying than had been the American functionary eager to seize his sandwich and be done with us.

In Naples, it was time for the four of us to find somewhere to sit for lunch. We wanted a place facing the water, and eventually we found one. We had pasta first, then fish, plenty of wine, and each of us sampled a different dessert. "Not Santa Lucia," said my father, referring to our beloved restaurant in Alexandria, "but decent all the same." I reminded him that we were indeed in the Santa Lucia area of Naples, and that his beloved Santa Lucia in Alexandria was named after this very spot. My brother was about to remind me that I was once again romanticizing, but I knew that my father thought the way I did and a quick look from him was all I needed to know I wasn't exaggerating the elusive meaning of the coincidence. Like him, it is in echoes, not in things themselves, or in places, much less in people, that I find my true alignment to life itself.

When the bill came, my father said, "They rob you, but they rob you with a smile, which makes it tolerable. Of course, they know you know they're robbing you, but you smile all the same and everyone bandies a few jokes back and forth, and in the end, you even tip them for robbing you." My father was not upset. This had been a good day for us. It would also have been a lovely day at the beach, said my mother. "You've had Rome, I had Paris, we've been lucky, and as for New York, who knows how long we'll want to stay there," he said.

None of us was going to the United States hoping to live there forever. We were going to come back, possibly after I and my brother were done with college, and if we finished in fewer than four years, so much the better. We were not resettling; we were visiting.

The next day, rather than head straight back to Rome, we decided to take a ferry to Capri. My mother wanted to window-shop the boutiques in Anacapri, my brother would join my mother and later they would head to the beach, while my father and I wanted to visit San

Michele, where Axel Munthe had built his house by partly restoring an ancient chapel built on a Roman villa. The two of us had read *The Story of San Michele* and adored it. It was at San Michele that I caught my first glimpse of what, with any luck, I wanted for the rest of my life: to hear piano and chamber music played by good friends or emanating from wonderful speakers on a magical spot overlooking the shimmering afternoon sea. And if I couldn't own such a place, then at least I would write about it, because the material was directly before me and I wasn't letting go of it. Even if I couldn't replicate Munthe's home in the years to come, I'd borrow our old house at the beach in Egypt and transpose it, via paper, all the way here, because this spot on earth was already stamped in my heart. As we stood leaning against the balustrade facing the cliff down to the sea from our lofty perch, I knew that I'd made my first rendezvous with the rest of my life. Of course we'd return to Europe, of course New York would never, could never, be our home, of course I'd try my best to give my parents back all that had been taken from them, and of course the house by the beach. Of course so many things.

Early that same evening, on our way back to Rome by train, as my brother and I sat in a crowded compartment and my parents sat in another equally crowded, I put down my book and found myself staring blankly at the westering light. I was trying to think of what I'd miss about Rome, what I'd want to take with me. Winter and the dark evenings after school when I'd roam about the city, going from one bookstore to another, or visiting the glorious churches on Corso Vittorio before turning into the poorly lit Campo de' Fiori, where crowds of young tourists and university students gathered at tables for ice cream, wine, or light fare. Maybe I'd miss Via del Babuino when I was headed to Piazza del Popolo and then down Via del Corso before catching the bus home. The scent of roasted chestnuts in late October when it got dark in the afternoon and my shoes were soaked in the rain and then got very cold, while I kept thinking, *Better here in the library with wet shoes than on Via Clelia*, though, who knows, I might even end up missing coming back to Via Clelia in the evening and stopping to pick up a few *rosette* and mineral water at Gianlorenzo's grocery and hear him speak Roman to me, or miss Amina when she came into my room after her injections and played her ribald songs on my turntable, though I never fully grasped their earthy Roman wit. The evening when my mother walked in with two girls who were helping her carry merchandise from the marketplace and they stepped into my bedroom and asked what in God's heaven a small espresso maker was doing tied to my typewriter's carriage. Who could tell if I'd ever miss this tiny, stifling universe with its dysfunctional *termosifoni*? I'd gotten used to Rome, to Via Clelia, hadn't I? I wanted to stay, admit it; yes, I did want to stay. Would I want to look back at our old kitchen with its shards of shattered glass stuck under our small refrigerator or next to where Amina liked to keep her special shampoo when she came to have my mother wash her hair on Saturdays? How could that weekly ritual come to nothing? Could life on Via Clelia ever end? Or would I forget—or worse yet, never bother to remember—how Madame Renato had shed real tears and couldn't stop crying on hearing that Luigi Tenco had committed suicide? It seemed so implausible that at the next festival of San Remo in January, I would not be there to hear the latest songs. The festival without me? That would be like Via Clelia without me, Rome without me.

I was, as my brother would no doubt have said, romanticizing. Then I thought of the shirtmaker and remembered the three tiny chocolates she'd given me just as she was about to close her door again.

~

A few days after our return from Naples, Gianlorenzo let me borrow his bike. I told my parents that I was going downtown to visit one of my bookstores. By now they knew that I was addicted to these foreign-language bookstores, including the German one with its full collection of bilingual Greek works. But what I had in mind was to repeat my ride around the center of Rome.

I went to Campo de' Fiori, purchased a sweet *cornetto*, then *zeppole*, walked the bike around a bit as I'd done the first time, stopped at Piazza di Spagna but didn't go up the stairs, and finally down Via Giulia, reversing the order of my last ride because what I really wanted, and was impatient to get to, was the Protestant Cemetery, next to the Pyramid, beyond Via Giulia. I wanted to walk through the cemetery, still pretending to be slightly lost, when the one person I wanted to talk with if only for a few minutes was John Keats. I would stand by his grave and tell him what I'd just told Giordano Bruno: who knows when I'll be back, and who knows who I'll be on that day? I remembered that weeks before leaving Egypt, my father had taken me to his father's grave. He must have known this would be the last time he'd be with his father. He wanted me near him because I had barely met my grandfather before he died, though I still remembered him, and it meant a lot to my father that I hadn't forgotten the man after whom I'd been named. So I went along and watched him trying to spend some meaningful moments with him, leaning against the high slab as if trying to touch and be heard by his father. I saw his lips move but couldn't hear what he was saying. I looked at my father and wondered if one day I'd do the same.

What mattered to me now was not just being here with Keats, but also lingering under the serene and tranquil air that hovered over the cemetery once you got inside. I asked the guard to watch my bike. He refused. I begged him and said that I was leaving the country and didn't know when I'd be back and made a point of telling him about John Keats's grave and what it meant to me. I was only going to be there for a few minutes, I said. Keats was my favorite poet. He had no idea who Keats was or why he should matter so much. "All right, then, but only for five minutes, not more. I'll need to pee by then," he said, smiling, adding one word only. "Youth!" he harrumphed, and let me in with the bike. I leaned the bike against his cot and hastened to Keats's grave. What would I say to John Keats? I had no idea. It occurred to me that what really mattered was not being with John Keats, or with anyone else buried in this cemetery. I wanted to be alone but needed the shadow of someone else, as if by having

Keats there, I had found a reason to stay still, stop time, and without knowing it, think about me, just me. I was saying goodbye, but not to Keats, or not to Keats only, but to Rome and, through Rome, to who I'd been in the city. Time changes us, but places change us too. I didn't want to change. I thought of Aunt Elsa and how she'd kept everything she owned so as to stop changing each time the world changed on her.

That afternoon, I bicycled back to Via Clelia to return Gianlorenzo's bicycle. He was busy stacking up the yogurts—raspberry, strawberry, apricot. He was pleased to see me but warned me that the owner was in one of her moods again, so I'd better not talk to him but come later after she left. "Maybe we'll get a juice later," he said. "Maybe," I said.

When I did come by toward evening, I saw he was with his sister. She was reaching to grab something from him, which he teasingly held with his left hand behind his back. "*Dammela, dammela subito!*" Give it to me, give it to me right away! she kept saying, laughing as she said it. "*Nun t' 'o do,*" I won't hand it over, he taunted, laughing too. I liked seeing him in so jovial a mood. When he saw me approach the store, he stopped that game and, turning slightly more serious, but still smiling at her, handed her the zipped purse he must have taken from her. "*Quanto sei noiso, Giannù,*" you're so annoying, Giannù. I liked his nickname. Lucrezia was her name; I'd forgotten it. He hardly had time to add a word when she immediately said my name, either because she remembered it or because they'd spoken about me. I simply nodded, not wishing to intrude, but I could tell he must have said good things about me.

She looked so much like him now that she wasn't wearing work clothes. Her humor, her stylish clothes, her makeup, her mood, caught me totally by surprise. She was going out with her *ragazzo*, she said. "Giannù is so mean," she added, "especially with me."

"He is never mean."

"Nev-er?"

"*Mai, mai,*" I said, remembering Amina's words.

Something did strike me the moment she reached out to kiss me on both cheeks before saying "*A presto*," see you soon. I wanted to know her, I wanted to know their world, their life, their parents and other siblings, their grandmother too. I had never shown much interest—why?

And just by witnessing her instant familiarity, I suddenly grasped what never walking down this street could mean now that I was going away, especially later this fall, when Rome got dark so early and I'd remember that Via Clelia was not so ugly in the evening when I got off the bus and looked forward to a good supper at home.

On impulse, I turned back the clock to those numberless evenings when I'd walk to the grocery store after school to run errands with my brother when my mother was sick. It seemed ages ago now. I wanted to replay those evenings when I hated Via Clelia and couldn't understand how so many people lived there without aching to move elsewhere. But then, a moment later, I moved the clock forward and pictured myself in a college classroom in the Bronx drifting back to those fall evenings and that night when Flora kept telling me to *think American* as we tried to compose a letter that was to change my life.

Gianlorenzo was in a very good mood that evening. The snarky old woman had paid him that day. So, did I want to catch a movie tonight? I shook my head. "My parents," I said. He understood. "Then maybe Wednesday, when you come by the store," he said.

I didn't tell him that I was leaving on Monday. On Tuesday I'd be landing far away.

Feeling awful about my silence, I helped him pull down the rolling shutters and then, while he was bending down and not looking at me and had just slipped in the giant padlock before locking it, I knew that this was my moment and I should tell him now—just say it and let everything out, I thought, for once say what you have to say and want to say—when suddenly just as he wasn't looking and I was still on the point of telling him, I felt something heaving in my chest, and I knew I was not going to tell him, despite my best efforts. He could see that something was troubling me. "*Ma che hai?*" What's wrong?

"*Niente*," nothing, I said. Something still held me back. I was scared, I was sad, I was paralyzed by shame, and could tell by the expression on his face that he was eager for me to say what I was obviously not saying. "*Dai, dimmelo,*" just tell me. Finally I said, "*Parto,*" I am leaving. One word. "*Ma dove?*" Where? He didn't seem to understand, but then I told him. "*E perché nun me l'hai detto prima?*" Why didn't you tell me sooner? "*Perché non lo sapevo,*" because I didn't know, I started to say, but then, catching myself, I told him, "*Perché non sapevo come dirtelo,*" because I didn't know how to tell you. By now I was out of breath. "*E quanno torni allora?*" So when are you coming back? he asked. "*Non lo so ancora,*" I don't know yet.

He, too, was saddened, as if he were losing a close friend who'd just reminded him of his condition in life. I was going away, he was staying behind and would probably remain a hired hand for a long time. I felt terrible for him. "I'm coming back," I finally said. "You swear?" "I swear," I said. I was coming back. I wanted to come back. And I wanted to keep my word.

Then, as if he'd had a sudden revelation and fully comprehended what I had told him, he left me standing, staring at him. "*E m' 'o dici proprio adesso?*" So now you tell me?

I nodded, mortified, as though finally realizing the full impact of what his six last words meant. All these weeks and I'd told him nothing.

"*Che strano tipo sei,*" you're a weird one.

There was no mirth in his voice this time. He looked angry and upset, just as he had the first time I saw him. He held his breath and repeated, "*E m' 'o dici proprio adesso?*"

He was more upset by what I'd told him than by what I might have said instead and had so desperately meant to tell him if only I could have found the courage to spill it. It's the camouflage that gets the soldier killed—not the uniform.

And then he did something I never expected. He pocketed the key to the lock, didn't say goodbye or good night, turned around, and walked away with his bicycle.

I had a mind to call out his nickname, *Giannù!* as if I'd acquired the right to use it, and would have rushed after him, who knows, asked his forgiveness, pleaded, wept, told him everything. I had never felt so lonely as I did that evening. I stood and watched him walk away as if he'd just slapped me hard across the face and didn't have anything more to say. *So now you tell me?* he had said. It was no longer just Gianlorenzo speaking, but through him Rome herself—as had every vendor, every shop owner, down to the barber, Sabina, Paola, and the two whores and the evenings on Via Clelia after the Trianon when something like muted joy coursed through my veins. *So now you tell me?* Everyone seemed to say it, even the scent of bergamot that was the smell of my budding love for Rome on the day he'd lent me his bicycle and had forever changed the city for me, because the bicycle was Rome, and Rome was his bicycle, and he was Rome, and Rome was me. Even the bergamot that I didn't have the heart to throw away and had left on the emptied table where the flowers had once wilted on our return from Paris, even the bergamot should have gone to someone and not been left to linger and die like that. I would have given it to Gianlorenzo and asked him to keep it for me for the day I'd be back. But he was no longer talking to me. There was no one. *So now you tell me?* said the city. I knew the answer and had known it for months. I loved Rome, and Rome loved me, and in saying, *So now you tell me?* Rome was asking me to admit something I'd been so reluctant to say. *Dillo*, just say it, said the city. *Dillo per me*, say it for me.

It would take me years.

— 13 —

Via Clelia

Three summers later a small package arrived. What caught me, even if I couldn't recognize the handwriting, was the sloping bar on the "7": an Italian 7, not a French one. Then I recognized the stamp and, finally, in the smallest script, the sender's address. It contained a cassette recording. In the note, Amina hoped I was doing well, and to help me not forget Rome, she was sending me a song she thought I'd enjoy hearing, because she felt it would remind me of the Rome I knew when the heat was unbearable. Things had changed since I left, she said, but right now with the shutters partly drawn to keep sunlight out, she was studying hard for an exam to become a keypunch operator. In a year's time she would start courses at the university. She was specializing in languages, *your influence*, she added.

That summer I was working in a printer's shop, a machinery warehouse, and one night a week in a department store. I was earning well, and was planning on returning to Europe to visit relatives in France and Italy.

But I didn't want to tell Amina I might be passing by Rome that year. I wasn't sure I wanted to see her. Plus, I had dated other girls and had outgrown my days in Rome when all I did was either read books or wait forever to find a moment to head to Paola's when her sister was out for a piano lesson. I didn't want to run into Paola either. I didn't want to visit Via Clelia.

As soon as I had a moment alone, I put on the song Amina had sent. But before the song there came a taped message from her. "I couldn't find the courage—for a long time I couldn't find the courage. But when I heard this song it instantly reminded me of the afternoons when you were studying for exams at home and I would walk into your room after seeing your mother and together we sat listening to *stornelli*. This is a *stornello* too, though I fear you've most likely forgotten Roman. I know you haven't thought of me, which doesn't surprise me. Grazia, your *portinaia*, used to remind me that you were never going to fall for me. Still, I hoped. Sometimes when crossing the street, I stop by your building and think I'll go upstairs, but of course I never do. [She hesitates a moment.] My parents are happy that I've put on weight. I am happy too. What more do I have to tell you? If you haven't inferred by now, it's no use telling you. But if you do come by, please let me know. A glass of wine or an espresso anywhere would be lovely. I still think of the movies we used to see with your mother. I loved her as much as I loved you. There, I've said it. It's too late to take it back now. Don't forget me. I'll never forget you."

Then I heard the song, a soft, very sweet melody by a singer I had never heard before. It was about heat in hell, which suddenly brought to mind how lonely the city stands on scalding days and how distant was my Roman year now. Four years had passed since I'd taken my American aunt to see the Colosseum and then helped her throw a dime into the Trevi Fountain, to secure her return in not too many years, she said. She'd taken out her purse and given me a dime to throw in as well. The gesture was so predictably touristic that I handed the coin to my brother, who complied, but more out of courtesy. What I never wanted was to go back to Via Clelia and the hapless life we'd lived there, choking bus rides, third-rate films nearby, and empty bottles on Wednesdays. I still loved the other Rome, the one I desperately wanted to get lost in, and belong to, and never did.

I knew I'd have to write back to Amina to thank her for thinking of me and tell her that I hadn't forgotten our scorching afternoons in late June when she'd come downstairs and sit with me near my radio and translate the words of the *stornelli* whose impish, rollicking rhythm I'd recognize right away, although I'd never been particularly fond of their earthy, crude, and shallow tune. But the song she had sent me was a tender Roman love song and lacked the pace of ordinary *stornelli*. Amina's song spoke of a timeless Rome whose shores along the Tiber River hadn't been walled in yet and whose old temples were still built into bric-a-brac homes where the poor had lived for centuries— a Rome where time slowed down and where one spent hours chatting and going over songs on the record player while my mother's tomato sauce simmered over a very low flame and would not be ready until the sun went down. *For you, my handsome*, goes the song, *I burn with love, for you I'll shed all my heart's blood, but you don't want me. My bed is searing hot in this heat wave, but kisses and love are gone from me.*

Gallaccia, what a strange word. My dictionary didn't have a definition. I'd need a better dictionary than my own. A few days later, at my college library, I found the word. *Gallaccia* was the Roman pronunciation of *callaccia*, meaning "heat wave."

I didn't tell Amina that I would ring her door or meet her anywhere for coffee or wine. I waited one week to reply, waited another to make certain my reply sounded authentically pleased that she had written, waited yet another hoping not to sound too warm or not warm enough. Eventually I realized I had no excuse. It was nearing my time to travel and I didn't want to tell her that I was going to visit Rome that summer. So I deferred replying to a time in early September when I knew I'd be back from Europe. Eventually, with the start of my senior year and applications to graduate school, I realized that I couldn't focus on a reply yet. Instead I'd send her a Christmas card. But I never did that either.

A part of me might have wanted to seek her out to reconnect, but it was the thought of reconnecting that made me balk. Did I really want to reconnect? Did I care for Amina and the little world I'd strayed into on Via Clelia or was I hesitant to reconnect because, despite what I believed was my aversion to watching things vanish and lurch into extinction, I feared I still hadn't answered the questions I'd asked of myself when I used to live there, unanswered questions that still left me feeling unstrung, unfinished, and undefined, no different from a piece of thread that never met a needle.

～

I passed by Via Clelia several times over the years. For reasons that had more to do with my reluctance to go back there, these visits either occurred by night, when I couldn't see much, or when I didn't dare ask our cabbie to make a left turn and stop awhile to let me see the old building again. In Rome, when I come back, I seldom venture too far beyond the *centro storico*—except for a brief visit two years ago, when I dared walk down the street and even managed to speak to someone who was about to enter the building. I asked if Grazia the old *portinaia* might still be around, but the man looked at me with an amused and startled smile: there hadn't been a *portinaia* in the building since he'd moved in seventeen years ago.

A decade or so before that I'd walked down the street with my wife and sons. We'd taken the metro. There was no metro in my day; the buses I used to take in the morning have almost all disappeared. We got off at the Furio Camillo stop, two blocks north of Via Clelia, exactly as I'd always envisaged the visit. Two blocks would give me plenty of time to settle into the experience, gather my impressions, and unlock memory's sluice gates, one by one—without effort, restraint, or ceremony. Two blocks would also allow me to put up whatever barriers needed to rise between me and this street, whose grimy, ill-tempered welcome when we came as refugees I've never managed to forget. I can still recall the yelps of boys playing soccer on the street.

I had meant to enter Via Clelia precisely where it ends at Via Appia Nuova and take my time walking the streets around it. I had meant to touch minor signposts along the way: the printer's shop—still there—the makeshift grocer-pizzaiolo, the one or two corner bars, the plumber—gone—the glazier—gone too—the barbershop across the street—also gone—the tobacconist, the wine merchant, Gianlorenzo's store, the tiny brothel where you didn't dare look in when the two old frumps left their rolling shutters up, the spot where a frail street singer would stand every afternoon and bellow gasping, bronchial arias you had to strain to recognize, only to hear, when his dirge was done, a scatter of coins rain upon the sidewalk from people's windows. All gone.

Home had been right above his spot.

As I led my family down Via Clelia, pointing to various aspects of a street I'd known so well decades before, I caught myself hoping that no one I knew back then would be alive today, or, if they were, that none might recognize me. I wanted to give no explanations to anyone, answer no questions, embrace no one. I'd always been ashamed of Via Clelia, ashamed of its good people, ashamed of having lived among them, ashamed of myself for feeling ashamed, ashamed, as I told my sons, of how I'd always misled my private-school classmates into thinking I lived "around" the affluent Via Appia Antica and not in this string of blue-collar buildings off Via Appia Nuova. That shame had never gone away; shame never does, it was there on every corner of the street. Shame, which is the reluctance to own up to who we are, could end up being the deepest thing about us, deeper even than who we are, as though beyond identity are buried reefs and sunken cities teeming with creatures we couldn't begin to name because they've been there since our earliest infancy and never went away. All I really wanted, as we began walking to the other end of Via Clelia, was to put the experience behind me now—*We've done Via Clelia*—knowing, though, that I wouldn't have minded a sudden but muted flare-up of memory to make good the visit.

Torn between wanting the whole thing over and done with and wanting to feel something, even unwelcome, I began to make light of our visit with my sons. Fancy spending a year in this dump. And the stench on hot summer days. On this corner I saw a dead dog once; he'd been run over and was bleeding from both ears. And here, every afternoon, sitting cross-legged on the sidewalk by the tram stop, a young Roma girl used to beg, her bare, dark knee flaunted boldly over her printed skirt—dirty, dauntless, and defiant. On Sunday afternoons Via Clelia was a morgue. In the summer the heat was unbearable. In the fall, having come back after school on the number 85 bus, I'd run errands for my mother, always rushing back out of the apartment before the shops closed, and by early twilight watch the salesgirls head home, and always think of Joyce's "Araby." There was a girl called Sabina, and a shirtmaker in the adjacent building, and a luminous girl I'd speak to with only one word when I'd give her my seat on the tram.

To speak to a stranger, or to the girl at the grocer's or her brother, or to anyone for that matter, I needed to slur my words, plan my words, affect a makeshift Romanaccio to cover up my foreign accent, and, to avoid making any grammatical mistakes in Italian, start undoing every sentence before I'd even finished speaking it and, because of this, end up making worse mistakes. I dissembled with everyone—with those I wanted nothing from, with those of whom I wanted anything they could give if only they could help me ask, dissembled what I thought, what I feared, who I was, which may be why I dissembled in the first place.

Wednesday evenings, I remember, were earmarked for running errands and redeeming bottles at the tiny grocery store at the end of Via Clelia. The girl in charge of stacking the shelves would come to the cash register. I was scared each time I watched her ring up, feeling time was flitting by quicker than I'd hoped. My gaze seemed to upset her, because she always lost her smile when she stared at me. Hers was the dark, ill-tempered stare of someone who was trying not to be rude. With other men, she was all smiles and jokes. With me just the glare.

~

We arrived at the Furio Camillo metro station at ten in the morning. At ten on a late July morning I'd be in my room upstairs, probably reading. On occasion, we'd go to the beach before it grew too hot. But past the third week of the month, the money would run out and we'd stay indoors. I'd listen to the radio, saving up for an occasional movie on Friday evenings, when tickets at the seedy and deserted, next-to-last-run movie theater around the corner were cheaper than on Sundays. There were two movie theaters near our building. One had disappeared, the other, all gussied up now, stands on Via Muzio Scevola. One night, in that theater, a man put his hand on my thigh. I asked him what was the matter with him, and right away he moved to another seat. In those days, I told my sons, you avoided the bathrooms in that theater.

One more block and scarcely ten minutes after arriving, our visit was over. This always happens when I go back somewhere. Either buildings shrink over time, or the time it takes to revisit them shrinks to less than a few minutes. We had walked from one end of the street to the other. There was nothing more to do now but walk back the way we had come. I sensed from the way my wife and sons had paused that they hoped the visit was over. On our way back, I did spend a few more seconds in front of the building, not just to take in the moment, but because I still hoped that an undisclosed something might rush out and tug me, exclaiming, as some people do when they show up at your door after many years, "Remember me?" But nothing happened. I was, as I always am during such moments, numb to the experience.

Writing about it in my journal, as I did later that day, would surely un-numb me. Writing would dust off things that were not there at the time of my visit, or that were there but that I wasn't quite seeing and needed time and paper to sort out, so that, once written about, they'd confer on my visit the retrospective resonance that part of me had hoped to find on the street itself. Writing might even bring me closer to this street than I'd been while I lived here. Writing wouldn't alter much or exaggerate anything; it would simply excavate, re-arrange, lace a narrative, recollect in tranquility where ordinary life is perfectly happy to nod and move on. Writing sees figures where life sees things; things we leave behind, figures we keep. Even the experience of numbness, when traced on paper, acquires a disenchanted grace, a melancholy cadence that seems at once intimate and aroused compared with the original blah. Write about numbness, and numbness turns into something. Upset flat surfaces, dig out their shadows, and you've got dream-making.

Does writing, as I did later that day, seek out words the better to stir and un-numb me to life—or does writing provide surrogate pleasures the better to numb me to experience? Are these polar opposites or is there no difference between the two?

One whole year in Rome and I had never touched this street. It would be just like me to scarcely touch anything, or to have grazed this city all but unintentionally, the way that entire year I saw the Roma girl seated on her corrugated piece of cardboard next to the tram stop and never made a dent in her impenetrable, surly gaze. I called her the dirty girl to hide my arousal and disturbance whenever I spoke of her to schoolmates. But I never mentioned Sabina to my schoolmates and not a word about Paola or Gianlorenzo.

～

Was I disappointed? It seemed a crime not to stumble on at least one quivering leftover from the past. Did numbness mean that even the memory of hating this street had gone away? Or was I relieved? I might as well never have lived here. I felt like someone trying to step on his own shadow, or like a reader who failed to underline a book as a teenager and now, decades later, is totally unable to recover the young reader he'd once been. Maybe I didn't want to recover that person.

For a second, as I stood and looked at our tiny balcony, I felt an urge to call myself to the window, the way my brother's friends used to summon him from the sidewalk. But I wasn't calling myself. I was just trying to picture what I was doing behind that window so many years ago. It's past mid-July, there's no beach, no friends, I'm more or less locked up in my room, reading, and as always shielding myself from the outside world behind drawn shutters, desperately using books to put an imaginary screen between me and Via Clelia. Anything but Via Clelia.

In that room on Via Clelia, I managed to create a world that corresponded to nothing outside. My books, my world, myself. All I had to do then was to let the novels I was reading lend their aura to this street and cast their illusory film over its buildings, and a shimmering spell would drop on this humdrum, here-and-now area of lower-middle-class Rome. On rainy days when the emptied street gleamed in the early evening, I might have been very much alone in my room upstairs, but I was alone in D. H. Lawrence's "faintly humming, glowing town"—better by far. Dying winter light took me straightaway to the solitary embankments of Dostoyevsky's white nights in St. Petersburg. And on sunny mornings when shouts from the marketplace a block down couldn't have sounded more truculent, I was in Baudelaire's splenetic, rain-washed Paris, and because there were echoes of Baudelaire's Paris around me, suddenly the loutish Romanaccio, which I learned to love about the time I left Rome, began to acquire an earthy coarseness that at first made it almost tolerable, then vibrant, and in the end authentic. Earlier in the morning, when I opened the windows, I was suddenly in Wordsworth's England, where "domes, theatres, and temples . . . glitter in the smokeless air" beneath the Beatles' "blue suburban skies." And when I finally put down Lampedusa's *Leopard* after seeing the film in Paris and began to see aging patrician Sicilians everywhere, each more lost than the last in a scowling new world that none of them could fathom, much less belong to, I knew I was not alone. All that remained of these Sicilians was their roughshod arrogance, their ancient, beaten-down palaces with their many, many rooms and rickety balconies that looked over the shoulders of history back to the Norman Conquest. One could step out onto Via Clelia and enter the tiny Villa Lazzaroni park whose scrawny trees and scorched growth told me I'd stepped into the abandoned hunting grounds of Frederick II of Hohenstaufen. That bench of one good Sunday ages ago was still there; I knew that bench. But it wasn't speaking to me.

So why shouldn't Via Clelia feel dead now? It had never been alive to me. I had hated it from my very first day and had almost managed to hate Rome because of it. My Rome was the bookshops and, between them, a network of narrow, cobbled streets lined by ocher walls and refuse. The piazzas with their centered obelisks, the museums, the churches, the glorious remnants, all these were for other people.

I used to like hanging around awhile after the bookstores had closed at night and the streets had begun to empty. I liked ambling about in the *centro storico*, whose streets and spotty lights seemed to know, long before I did, where my footsteps were aching to turn. I began to think that over and above Via Clelia and the books I'd come looking for, something else was keeping me from heading back home, and that if books had given me a good enough alibi, staying in old Rome had a different purpose. I'd grown to love this Rome, a Rome that seemed more in me than it was out in Rome itself, so that I was never sure if my love was genuine or simply a product of my own yearnings.

I wasn't seeing Rome. It was the filter, the veil I'd placed on the old city that finally made me love it, the scrim I went in search of each time I headed out to a bookstore and would come out late in the evening to stroll down my Nevsky Prospect in search of vague smiles and fellowship in a city I wasn't even sure existed outside of the pages I read. It is the scrim I can no longer separate from the books I read back then, the film, the *pelicula*, as Lucretius calls it, that reverberates over time and continues to make Rome mine long after I lost it. Without these fictions, which are both our cover and the archive of our innermost life, we have no way to connect, to touch, or to love anything. What I failed to realize until I was back years later was that I was not only putting books and bookstores between Rome and me; I was putting books between myself and my demons.

I learned to read and to love books much as I learned to know and to love Rome: not only by intuiting undisclosed passageways, but by seeing more of me in books than there probably was, because everything I read seemed more in me than on the pages themselves. I knew my way of reading books might be aberrant, just as I knew that figuring my way around Rome as I did would get me lost each time. I was looking for myself, hoping to run into myself or into me in someone else.

I knew what the authors I was reading desired, what they dissembled; I even knew why. The better the writers, the better they erased their footprints, the more they wanted me to intuit and trace the very footprints they'd covered over. How right was Aunt Flora when she exhorted me always to *look for the human*. With the right hunch, you could read the inflection of an author's soul in a single comma, in one sentence, and from that sentence seize the whole book, an author's entire life's work. What my favorite authors were asking of me was that I read them intimately—not read my own pulse onto their work, but read their pulse as though it were my own, the height of arrogance. By trusting my deepest, most personal insights, I was in fact tapping into, or divining, an author's vision.

⌒

So on my return visit with my family, I looked for the grocery store hoping not to find it, or, rather, to save it for last. When we reached the end of Via Clelia, I realized that the store was gone. Perhaps I'd forgotten where it was. But a second glance told me there was no doubt about it. It had indeed vanished. Gone was the spot where I'd parked his bike once; gone, too, was Kilt. Perhaps I had longed to walk back into that same store and see for myself—my way of closing the circle, settling the score, having the last word, saying, *See, as promised, I did come back*. I'd have walked in, leaned against the glass counter, and just waited awhile, just waited to see who turned up, see if the ritual had changed, see if I'd still be the same person on the same errand on the same street half a century later.

To make light of my disappointment and draw their laughter, I told my sons all that happened: Amina, Sabina, Paola, Gianlorenzo and his sister, the Roma girl, and the girl in the turquoise overcoat. "Were you in love?" one of my sons finally asked. I didn't think so. *He doesn't think so*, they jived, suddenly reminding me of Paola's own words of decades before. "How did you leave?" "I left, almost without saying goodbye." "And you never spoke again?" asked another. "No, we never spoke again."

Had I told them the whole truth? Would they know? Would they dust off the footprints I'd buried in the hope they'd ask the right question, knowing that if they asked, they'd have already guessed the answer?

Writing—as I did later that day—is intended to dig out the fault lines where truth and dissembling shift places. Or is it meant to bury them even deeper?

Before leaving, I took one last look at Via Clelia. All those rides on the bus, the tireless walks through Rome, the books, the faces, the waiting for visas that I had sometimes wished might never come because I, too, preferred abeyance to certitude. I did like this city, the conversations at the kitchen table, the kissing in Villa Lazzaroni, Paola's bedroom, Amina, who'd tiptoe into my room with a timid *Posso?*, and the dream launched like a desperate call on a winter night when I finished reading "The Dead" and thought to myself, I must head west and leave this city to seek a world where snow falls "softly into the dark mutinous Shannon waves"—all, all of it no more than a film, a vision, the aura of my love for Rome, which was perhaps no more than my love for a might-have-been life born from a story Joyce had penned during his hapless stay in Rome, thinking of his half-real, half-remembered Dublin just as I stared now at my half-real, half-remembered Rome. The cold nights I spent staring out my window as rain fell obliquely under the streetlights; the evening I came so close to another body that I knew I could no longer live like this; the sense that life could have started on this improbable three-block stretch—all of it a screen, perhaps the best and most enduring part of me, but a screen all the same.

As we neared the Furio Camillo metro station and could no longer see Via Clelia, something did come to me, distantly at first, then, as we entered the underground station, with a fierceness I'd never expected. Via Clelia was not just littered with the many books I'd read there, but what it harbored unchanged, untouched after so many years, was chilling premonitions of the city across the Atlantic that I hadn't seen and feared I might never learn to fathom, much less love. That city had been dogging me during my entire period in Rome. I'd have to learn to like another city all over again, wouldn't I?—learn to put new books on the face of yet another place, learn to unlove this one, learn to forget, learn not to look back. Who would I be without Rome? Or Rome without me? One might as well ask what happens to life when we're no longer there to live it.

For a moment—and it was a very brief one—I tried to slip into the past: my mother was upstairs preparing supper, my brother had just come back from basketball practice and was about to show me his math homework, Amina was due to arrive any moment for her shot. Soon persimmon and fresh almond season would arrive, then the trip to Paris, then Paola. But this fantasy never lasts. Even when I finally visited our old apartment a few years later with one of my sons, now a grown man, the apartment itself didn't speak to me; I remembered everything, but I felt nothing. I rang four times but this stirred nothing either, and when I asked, the owners said the *termosifoni* always worked and the windows never shattered. But my mother wasn't in the kitchen, my brother wasn't there either, and Grazia, they told me, had thrown herself from the roof of the building many years ago and died right away.

That evening in my diary, though, writing about my mother and Amina in the kitchen, my brother, and the scent of bergamot permeating my room the night I read Durrell into the very late hours, everything and everyone came back to me. On paper, it is 1967, I am a teenager, today is Saturday, I've borrowed a bike, and later I'll return it and lean it against the wall of a street I never meant to love or put behind me. I thought I'd learned to tolerate this city. Instead, it was love.

Now you know, says Via Clelia.

Now I know, I want to say, now I know.